# Beyond
# Declaring Victory
# and Coming Home

# Beyond Declaring Victory and Coming Home

## THE CHALLENGES OF PEACE AND STABILITY OPERATIONS

EDITED BY

## Max G. Manwaring
### AND Anthony James Joes

Foreword by Ambassador William Walker

Westport, Connecticut
London

327.172
B573

**Library of Congress Cataloging-in-Publication Data**

Beyond declaring victory and coming home : the challenges of peace and stability
  operations / edited by Max G. Manwaring and Anthony James Joes ; foreword by
  Ambassador William Walker.
      p.   cm.
    Includes bibliographical references and index.
    ISBN 0–275–96768–9 (alk. paper)
    1. Peacekeeping forces.   2. Security, international.   3. United States—Military policy.
  I. Manwaring, Max G.   II. Joes, Anthony James.
  U270.B48   2000
  327.1'72—dc21        99–055878

British Library Cataloguing in Publication Data is available.

Library of Congress Catalog Card Number: 99–055878
ISBN: 0–275–96768–9

First published in 2000

Praeger Publishers, 88 Post Road West, Westport, CT 06881
An imprint of Greenwood Publishing Group, Inc.
www.praeger.com

Printed in the United States of America

∞

The paper used in this book complies with the
Permanent Paper Standard issued by the National
Information Standards Organization (Z39.48–1984).

10 9 8 7 6 5 4 3 2 1

**Copyright Acknowledgment**

Chapter 7 of this volume is a revision of chapters 1 and 17 of John T. Fishel,
*Civil Military Operations in the New World* (Westport, CT: Praeger, 1997).
Copyright © 1997 by John T. Fishel. Reproduced with permission of Greenwood
Publishing Group, Inc., Westport, CT.

# Contents

# Foreword

Over the past decade I have been involved in four of the international community's costlier and more visible efforts to avoid and/or halt violence and death through direct intervention in a troubled state. As a Deputy Secretary of State, I participated in a failed attempt to talk Manuel Noriega into relinquishing his despotic grip on Panama, a result that led two years later to a U.S. invasion and his forced removal and arrest. While ''Operation Just Cause'' was being planned and executed, I was the American ambassador to the north in El Salvador, having succeeded Ambassador Ed Corr (the author of Chapter 2 of this volume).

Serving during the last three years of that bloody civil war, I was intimately involved in the U.N.-facilitated negotiation process that ended a decade of fighting. I then remained to witness the first months of the government's and the FMLN's compliance with the peace accord dictates. In 1997–1998 I headed the United Nations' Transitional Administration (UNTAES) mission to Eastern Slavonia (Croatia), as such the de facto regional governor in the aftermath of the 1991–1996 Serb-Croat struggle. UNTAES was subsequently acclaimed among the United Nations' most successful peacekeeping operations. And finally, from October 1998 until June 1999, I was in charge of the OSCE's Kosovo Verification Mission, the North Atlantic community's initial effort to resolve Serb-Albanian ethnic conflict through verification of a cease-fire verbally accepted by President Milosevic and the Kosovo Liberation Army.

Between El Salvador and Eastern Slavonia, I conducted a six-month study examining the relationship between a country's commitment to the rule of law and the long-term sustainability of its democratic practices—this in nations emerging from the trauma of conflict and chaos. I looked into Guatemala's inching toward reform in the aftermath of an internal guerrilla struggle; Brazil, several years after decades of military rule; Chile, recovering its democratic bearings after Pinochet; Kenya, decades after its ordeal of colonial rule ended; and Poland, a recent escapee from the trauma of Soviet domination.

I thus have worked for well over a decade at the "pointy end of the peacekeeping spear" (i.e., in field operations among those struggling with political, ethnic, and other deep-seated animosities). For the most part, I implemented policies and strategies designed and mandated by those in the executive offices of prime ministers and presidents; in national foreign and defense ministries; or in the headquarters of international organizations in Brussels, New York, Vienna, and Geneva. Few had the opportunity to visit the object of their interest in the "conflict of the day." While physical distance from a problem has the decided advantage of increased objectivity, less likelihood of contamination brought about by personal involvement and relationships, this is often outweighed by limited knowledge of the conditions that make every conflict unique. Those calling the shots from afar often were applying lessons learned from a past conflict with which they were familiar, either through on-the-ground or intellectual involvement. At times such lessons were applicable; often they were not.

As a peacemaking, peacekeeping veteran, I have attended any number of "lessons learned" conferences and seminars devoted to the issues and concepts discussed in this anthology. A number of the authors are friends and colleagues from the State Department and the National Defense University. Others are among those encountered at meetings convened to discuss the questions asked as each intervention ends and we await the onset of the next—"How should the international community deal with low-intensity conflict and its aftermath?" "What have we collectively learned to avoid errors committed in past involvements?"

Peacekeeping, and the many topics subsumed under that title, has been a growth industry since the end of the Cold War. As Dick Millett points out in his excellent Chapter 1 analysis, notwithstanding the end of the Cold War and the appearance of a number of positive trends, the world remains awash in threat and conflict, and it appears it will remain so as we enter the twenty-first century. The world of the Cold War, while dangerous in the extreme, was nevertheless susceptible to predictable, mutually accepted rules of behavior—those of a bipolar international environment. That is no longer the case. Unfortunately today's conflicts seldom fit neatly into the boxes that those who responded to past challenges are familiar with. Each crisis response generates yet another layer of authoritative voices on the subject. The 50-year history of U.N. peacekeeping operations alone has provided the world with a reservoir of such voices, many with strong opinions and well-meaning suggestions as to how to conduct the next deployment. Much of this advice is of the "how not to do it" variety, since a good number of international community interventions have been less than successful. In Bosnia we did not want to commit the errors of Somalia and Rwanda; in Kosovo, it was the missteps of Bosnia that did not bear repeating.

This volume of essays, the sixth gathered by Dr. Max Manwaring and his collaborators, is an exceedingly insightful contribution in our collective effort to grapple with the similarities and the distinctions among the array of national and international conflicts with the potential to erupt into next month's Kosovo.

The underlying themes of this book are that the international community has a disturbing tendency to "declare victory and go home"; does so without having put in place the fundamental infrastructure that provides either the reality or perception of "justice" or lasting stability; and is then unable to fathom why the problem continues to fester and all too often erupts again. These are all theories that I emphatically subscribe to.

While I preach that every conflict is distinct and must be dealt with as such, I do see patterns and common themes that run through the international peace-keeping community's reaction to virtually every full-blown "hot spot." This framework—at play in each of the four crises I've been involved in—most often evolves through four stages.

The first involves the outside world's "benign neglect" of a lingering, relatively low-intensity struggle, most often between "ins" who feel that the present system is "just fine, thank you, that we and ours have no problem obtaining justice for our families, our businesses, our political friends," versus those on the margins who see few, if any, legal remedies when they become involved in dispute—with their neighbors over property, with criminals involving crime, or in the exercise of their political and civic rights. Without recourse to an honest legal system to settle the disputes that arise in any but the most primitive societies, the "outs" eventually see few options other than to take up arms. Thus the guerrilla armies of the FMLN in El Salvador, and the KLA in Kosovo were born. The international community most often reacts to the appearance of such a force with concern that a "legitimate" regime, albeit corrupt and brutal, could be removed through force of arms. Few sitting governments are comfortable with violent regime changes—and preach negotiation, diplomacy, a political settlement.

International "benign neglect" is also manifested in tolerance of a Noriega or a Milosevic despite irrefutable evidence that they maintain themselves in power, and enrich themselves and their cronies, at the expense of a suffering populace. Such regimes are tolerated with the excuse that they only brutalize, maim, and kill their own. "What is the vital U.S. national interest if General Noriega wishes to treat Panamanians poorly?" "What business is it of the international community if a sovereign state such as the Federal Republic of Yugoslavia has an internal ethnic struggle?" These and similar excuses make it acceptable to maintain one's distance.

The second stage comes when the problem is of a dimension and danger to regional stability level that cannot be further ignored or tolerated. Intervention is necessary, most often backed by the threat and/or use of force. The international players move in and proceed to take complete operational command. This is where the influence, the resources, the arrogance of the international peace-keeping community are most in evidence. The media also swarm around whatever is the latest "intervention," with its heroes and villains, its photo ops of world leaders' dramatic words and actions, its descriptions of personnel and machines being transported to the scene—eye-catching footage on the evening news. It is when the most mistakes can be, and most often are, made. This is when it is decided, either by design or horse-trading, which international players should be, and will be, involved. If the conflict is big enough, or near enough to successful resolution, then a multitude of players want to jump on board. The more players, the more debate over slices of responsibility, titles, and perks.

Next comes the stage when one or more players decide it is time to leave. There is seldom total agreement in selecting this moment, even in a case such as UNTAES wherein an exact end-of-mandate date was specified in the Erdut Agreement. Disagreements over when to depart can be based on substance, lack of a consensus "exit strategy," or evidence that despite international involvement of days, months, years (or in the case of Cyprus and the Middle East, decades), the problem is no nearer solution then at the start and—if the peacekeepers depart—might erupt again. But, thank God, some peacekeeping operations do end. At a point the determination is made that the international presence has done as much as can be expected. It is now up to the belligerents to sink or swim on their own—albeit with commitments by those departing that the international community will continue to monitor and support the long-term objectives of the intervention, often with promises made at a concluding "donors' conference."

The fourth stage involves everything that happens after "victory" is announced. This is where the temptation to "declare victory and withdraw" most often overwhelms many who have solemnly declared they will "stay the course." The reason promises made are seldom promises kept is a simple one. No sooner has today's crisis been thought resolved, than a new one erupts elsewhere. Finite resources must be redistributed. Once yesterday's problem is no longer an imminent threat, attention—and the resources that go with it—tend to be reallocated to deal with today's crisis.

A further reason promises are seldom kept has to do with the effort it takes to get at the underlying causes of so many of today's outbreaks—the absence of a system that provides even a semblance of justice. My study confirmed to my satisfaction that sustained development, sustained democracy, sustained stability are only possible where a nation's population, or any sizable component therein, perceives—for them as individuals, or as members of an ethnic, religious, social or political class—the availability of justice.

Establishing the rule of law is an extremely long and contentious endeavor. Regimes in power, including those which entered office through forceful eviction of a predecessor regime which they decried for corruption of the legal system, seldom welcome judicial reform. A corruptible justice system is too useful for protecting those in office. The temptation to retain such a tool is hard to resist. All parts of a legal system—the judiciary, the prosecutors, the bar, the police, the prison system, the codes—must work properly and in synchronization. If a single component is left unreformed, the system will continue to generate injustice. Decades are required to produce a new police, not to mention a transformed judiciary, composed of officials not schooled in the behavior of the past. Few international donors have the patience, long-term commitment, or resources necessary to assume such a burden.

What lessons have I absorbed in my decade-plus of peacekeeping? Several indeed. But with the proviso that any or all might not fit tomorrow's intervention, here are a few:

- Don't impose solutions designed elsewhere (i.e., in outside capitals) without reference to those unique conditions. Incorporate, to the maximum extent possible, local voices and suggestions, from the outset.

- If you can't stay the course, don't go in. And "the course" will likely include commitment and attention well beyond dealing with the immediate threat, and recognition that the issues at play are more complex, difficult to resolve and resource intensive than previously imagined.

- Some leaders (e.g., a Noriega, a Milosevic) are not amenable to problem solving through negotiation and diplomacy if it means relinquishing even a fraction of their power. Force must eventually be used. It should be applied as early, as heavily as possible. Never let a challenge go unchallenged. That is to look the other way, appear reluctant to respond forcibly, or accept a patently absurd explanation for an offensive act will be misinterpreted as weakness, lack of resolve, and only encourage further challenge.

- Pursuit of an "even-handed," "neutral" approach sounds commendable. It is seldom sustainable. In Kosovo there was not, as some claimed, a moral equivalency between the acts of the Belgrade regime and those of the Kosovar population. Whatever one thought of the KLA and its use of violence to protect Albanians, its violence was distinguishable from Belgrade's use of any and all means to brutalize, terrorize, and eliminate some two million of its citizens based solely on their ethnicity.

Already mentioned, the difficulty of the lessons learned process is that so often a lesson derived from one conflict is diametrically the opposite of wisdom gained in the next. An example from my own experience: in ending the conflict in El Salvador, I concluded that the success of the peace that followed was based on the fact that there was no clear-cut winner, nor loser. Each side could announce that it had achieved its objective (i.e., "won"). The government could, and did, claim that it had prevented the FMLN from shooting its way into power. The FMLN could assert that by taking up arms it had achieved fundamental reforms of the political system. Each also had to recognize that it had not achieved what it had sought with ten years of death and destruction, an outright military victory. As a result, there was neither an arrogant victor, nor a revenge-seeking loser. This was in stark contrast to the conclusive results of the American Civil War, in which the winner's subjugation of the loser created problems that have lasted until today.

The conflict in Kosovo has ended quite differently. One side, the Serbs under

Milosevic, lost. In my mind that was the only outcome standing a chance of long-term success. Thus the lesson I learned in El Salvador about the virtues of a "no-winner" outcome was completely undercut by the outcome in Kosovo.

Enough of my jabbering. The following chapters contain any number of lessons, and cautions, about the application of such lessons, from an array of authors, each well suited to the challenge of analyzing the art of peacekeeping. Among these are eminent practitioners and theorists in the field; several who are both. I highly recommend this collection, which by its breadth and depth presents a picture of enormous complexity, frustration, and—if you agree with Dick Millett's depiction of the problems the world faces today, and most likely tomorrow—importance to us all.

Ambassador William Walker

# Preface

This book is part of a continuing effort to revitalize strategic thinking as it pertains to "uncomfortable" contemporary conflicts. It evolved from General John R. Galvin's December 1986 call for a new paradigm to fight the most prevalent and most likely forms of conflict in the world today.[1]

These conflicts range from acts of terrorism and illegal drug trafficking to warlordism, militant fundamentalism, and ethnic cleansing to intranational conflict, major refugee flows, and other transnational threats and consequences of global instability. They have been called, inter alia, Gray Area Phenomena (GAP). They are not new. What is new is that the ending of the Cold War has allowed GAP issues to emerge as almost chronic complex humanitarian emergencies, peace and stability efforts, and intranational conflict.

We argue that taking responsibility for intervening in the myriad contemporary human emergencies and conflicts requires more than enforcing certain levels of law and order. The requirement is to establish the specific internal conditions that have proven to lead to a mandated peace and stability—with justice.

The political practice of "declaring victory and coming home" has provided a false and dangerous domestic impression of great success for U.S. unilateral and multilateral interventions in failing and failed states. The reality of such irresponsibility is that the root causes and the violent consequences of contemporary global conflict are left to smolder and reignite at a later date with the accompanying human and physical waste. Thus, it is incumbent on the international community and individual powers involved in dealing with the chaos of the post–Cold War world to understand that such action requires a long-term, holistic, and strategic approach.

The intent of such an approach is to create and establish the proven internal "defensive" conditions that can lead to a sustainable peace for a legitimate civil society. The key elements that define those conditions and dictate appropriate response at the high operational and strategic levels include: (1) an appraisal of the contemporary global security environment (Millett); (2) an analysis of the lessons of the "defense" and the "offense" that should have been learned from the "uncomfortable" wars of the past several years (Manwaring and Corr); (3) the physical establishment of order and the rule of law (Adams); (4) the isolation of belligerents (Joes); and (5) the regeneration of the economy (Dewey).

Additionally, we propose salient high operational and strategic means, roles, and responses for moving from the "defense" to the "offense" in peace and stability operations. They include: (6) adjusting to the fact that intelligence will become increasingly important to the civil component in transitioning to a civil society (Dolman) and (7) working to achieve a complete unity of civil-military effort toward a common end state (Fishel). At this point, (8) and (9) fostering and nurturing a legitimate civil society becomes a real possibility (Herrick and Maxwell).

Finally, in (10), (11), and (12), we outline key problems and solutions in coping with chaos in the high operational and strategic security environments (Dziedzic, McBride, and Dorff). All these essential lessons of success and failure in global security and stability comprise a "new" paradigm (13) that will—hopefully—initiate the process of rethinking both problem and response (Corr and Manwaring).

By coming to grips with the lessons of success and failure that we should have learned over the past several years, decision makers, policy makers, and their staffs should be able to develop the conceptual, operational, and organizational instruments necessary to deal more effectively with contemporary GAP issues and conflicts, once a competent decision has been reached to engage U.S. purpose and power.

We wish to thank the contributors whose knowledge, experience, analytical powers, wisdom, and many hours of work made this book possible. We also want to thank Rita Rummel, our professional word processor, who put it all together—in intelligible form. Finally, we want to thank Heather Staines, our editor, for her forbearance and guidance.

We respectfully dedicate the book to General John R. Galvin, USA (Retired), who has been and continues to be an inspiration and a thoughtful strategist on behalf of the United States and the NATO Alliance.

Lastly, neither this book nor the individual chapters in it should be construed as reflecting the official positions of the U.S. government, the Department of Defense, or the Department of State. We, and the various contributors, alone are responsible for any errors of fact or judgment.

## NOTE

1. General John R. Galvin, "Uncomfortable Wars: Toward a New Paradigm," *Parameters* (December 1986), pp. 2–8.

# Part I

# Introduction

The intent of the first part of this book is to analyze the global security environment at the end of the twentieth century (Millett) and to provide the broad guidance for a fundamental paradigm change to deal more effectively with the threats and opportunities for now and the future (Manwaring and Corr).

Albert Camus sets forth the challenge:

> He who dedicates himself to the dignity of mankind, and dedicates himself to the earth, reaps from it the harvest that sows its seed and sustains the world again and again. Finally, it is those who know how to rebel, at the appropriate moment, against history who really advance its interests.
>
> —*The Rebel*

Chapter 1

# A Multiplicity of Threats, a Paucity of Options: The Global Security Environment at the End of the Twentieth Century

## Richard L. Millett

The *1998 Stategic Assessment* produced by National Defense University's Institute for National Strategic Studies opens with the optimistic declaration that "History's most violent century is ending under conditions of general peace, cooperation, and progress."[1] But by the summer of 1999, hopes that a "new world order" would emerge from the end of the Cold War were being undermined by the mounting problems of trying to restore order and curb ethnic hatred in Kosovo and the periodic bombings of Iraq. International peacekeeping efforts in Somalia and Angola had essentially failed, and the head of the U.S. Southern Command was urging the withdrawal of the last American units from Haiti, contending that the threat to their security exceeded any benefits that their presence there provided. Ongoing civil conflicts in Afghanistan, Sudan, Colombia, and Algeria seemed to offer few, if any, opportunities for international peacekeeping missions, and prospects were little brighter for the world community's ability to deal with simmering international conflicts in the Congo, in Sierra Leone, or on the Ethiopian-Eritrean border. Missile tests by North Korea underlined the continuing threats posed by potential "rogue states." At the same time, Russia's increasingly bellicose statements responding to NATO attacks on Yugoslavia, combined with the tensions which accompanied the entry of Russian troops into Kosovo, and the involvement of China in disputes ranging from maritime territorial issues with the Philippines and Indonesia to the future of Taiwan demonstrated that, while the threat of major power conflicts had greatly receded during the 1990s, it had not disappeared.

Perhaps the most promising development in the 1990s was the continuing trend toward the adoption of democratic forms of government. The end of white rule in South Africa, the deterioration of PRI dominance of Mexico's politics, the restoration of elected government in Nigeria, and the end of Suharto's rule in Indonesia were all particularly encouraging examples of this trend. But democratic transitions were proving far from certain or smooth. The inability of many new regimes to provide either economic growth or personal security fed the growth of a variety of forms of religious fundamentalism, virulent populism, and racist nationalism in many nations.[2]

Both emerging democracies and traditional democratic states face increasing threats from a variety of non-state actors. In *A National Security Strategy for a New Century* issued in October 1998, the Clinton administration identified "terrorism, international crime, drug trafficking, illicit arms trafficking, uncontrolled refugee migrations, and environmental damage" as the principal transnational threats to U.S. interests.[3] At its 1998 summit meeting in Birmingham, England, the Group of Eight Industrialized Democracies (G8) devoted considerable attention to international crime, noting that "globalisation has been accompanied by a dramatic increase in transnational crime," and that this poses "a global threat which can undermine the democratic and economic basis of societies through the investment of illegal money by international cartels, corruption, a weakening of institutions, and a loss of confidence in the rule of law."[4]

Responding to such diffuse and at times ambiguous threats poses a growing problem for the United States and its major allies. Adapting to the post–Cold War environment, described by some as "the new world disorder," has proved difficult and frustrating. The reasons for this can perhaps be best understood by comparing the current global security environment with that existing during the height of the Cold War.

During the Cold War, there was at least some degree of consensus as to what constituted vital interests and what could threaten these interests. As debates over U.S. policy in Haiti, Bosnia, Iraq, and Kosovo have demonstrated, such a consensus is much more elusive today. The Clinton administration has divided interests which might require the use of force into three categories: "vital interests," "important national interests," and "humanitarian and other interests."[5] But this does little to make clear what situations require risking lives, which can be approached at least initially by other means, and which can be safely left to their own devices.

Even the concept of sovereignty has become increasingly difficult to define in the post–Cold War context. Transnational threats, combined with the rise of multinational organizations such as the European Union, have both reduced a nation's ability to control developments within its borders and made it more vulnerable to forces which do not respect frontiers. Uncontrolled traffic in arms, narcotics, toxic waste, and migrants increasingly characterizes the modern world. The line between intervention in the internal affairs of another state and exercising the legitimate right of self-defense has become blurred. Conflicts in the Balkans, in Central Africa, and in Colombia all provide graphic examples of this phenomenon.[6]

Since the end of the Cold War, the definition of foes and the delineation of national security goals has been anything but clear cut. There is no single dominant foe, no clearly opposed ideology, to take the place of communism, no unifying national strategy to compare with containment. There is not even consensus on such basic issues as whether a more prosperous China would enhance or threaten U.S. security, whether hostile isolation or active engagement is the best way to promote change in Castro's Cuba, whether Iran is an intractable foe or an evolving counterweight to Iraq in the Middle East, or even whether propping up the Russian economy under its present administration is or is not in our national interest. A disturbing example of these dilemmas is provided by the current situation in Colombia. There a four-sided conflict involving government forces, right-wing paramilitaries, vicious narcotics traffickers, and the hemisphere's most powerful insurgent movement (itself divided between two principal forces) threatens not only the survival of Colombia's democratic institutions, but also the security of surrounding states. While officially providing assistance only for the fight against the narcotics traffickers, the United States has been increasingly vocal in its condemnation of the insurgents' ties to the drug trade. At the same time, Washington has increased pressures on the Colombian government to crack down on the paramilitaries, who are linked to the traffickers and are widely assumed to be responsible for the majority of the escalating toll of human rights violations. But the paramilitaries are also a major foe of the insurgents. To further complicate matters, there is credible evidence that elements of the Colombian military have been corrupted by narcotics traffickers.[7]

In the midst of this, Colombian President Andres Pastrana has launched a major effort to negotiate peace with the insurgents, agreeing as a preliminary step to withdraw all government forces from a vast swath of territory, much of it the source of narcotics production. But his efforts are undermined by guerrilla intransigence, continued paramilitary violence, the weakness and corruption of government institutions, especially in the judicial branch, and the unwillingness of much of Colombia's elite to pay the price necessary to reverse the escalating spiral of violence and social disintegration. Trying to formulate a U.S. policy to deal with these complex realities is immensely difficult, perhaps impossible, absent any national consensus as to the nature and seriousness of the threat posed or even as to who the principal villains are.[8]

Similar problems arise in our dealings with Kurdish nationalists, who may be allies in confrontations with Iraq but are also engaged in a prolonged conflict with our NATO partner, Turkey, or with the Kosovo Liberation Army (KLA), whose actions helped produce the current crisis and whose ultimate aims diverge fundamentally from stated U.S. goals. During the Cold War era, the principal national security debates were over means. Today we frequently cannot even agree on ends.

In the decades of nuclear confrontation with the Soviet Union, the costs of failure were all too clear, but today they are often seen as vague and ambiguous.

Indeed, in cases such as that of Kosovo, an argument can be made that the costs of success could exceed the costs of failure. Success itself has become difficult to define and/or maintain. The 1994 intervention in Haiti illustrates this dilemma. While at the time there was some dissent as to the desirability of American military involvement in that nation, the relatively bloodless nature of our intervention, the obvious enthusiasm of the bulk of the population for the removal of the military dictatorship and the restoration of the elected civilian government, and the curbing of the flow of refugees to the shores of Florida all made the venture appear successful. Nearly five years later, the results are much less clear. Violence is again on the rise in Haiti, politics are in a state of chronic crisis, and the future of U.S. and United Nations (U.N.) involvement in that nation is questionable at best.[9]

While today few would argue that the Haitian intervention has achieved its goals, there is no consensus as to whether this is because it was the wrong thing to do, was done in the wrong way, or was not sustained by subsequent policies. Nor is there agreement as to the risks and costs of failure in this operation. Indeed, the prevailing attitude of both policy makers and the general public seems to be to ignore the situation.

During the Cold War the United States emphasized alliance politics, but beginning with the Gulf War, the emphasis has been more on forming temporary coalitions to deal with specific situations. This was the case in the Haitian intervention, in the attacks on Iraq, and, to an extent, in the ongoing involvement in Bosnia. While NATO is the instrument of choice in the Kosovo crisis, it is by no means clear that only NATO forces would take part in any possible future international presence in that devastated province. Furthermore, the strains which the operation puts on alliance unity and predictions that failure would significantly weaken NATO's credibility and even threaten its future existence do little to encourage additional ventures of this type.

Current U.S. policy makes clear our preference for multilateral rather than unilateral operations. As stated in the Joint Chiefs of Staffs' document *Joint Vision 2010*, "we expect to work in concert with allied and coalition forces in nearly all our future operations."[10] At the same time, the 1998 *National Security Strategy for the New Century* states that "we must always be prepared to act alone when that is our most advantageous course."[11] What is lacking is any criteria for determining when to attempt coalition building and when to act alone. There are no ready answers to such basic questions such as when is a coalition adequate to undertake the tasks at hand, or when does the cost of adding or maintaining a member exceed the benefits of doing so.

During the Cold War, the governments of nation-states were the dominant international actors. Today they compete with a growing number of non-state actors, some multinational, but the majority groups without fixed national loyalties. These include ethnic and/or religious groups, criminal organizations, a host of non-governmental organizations (NGOs), multinational companies, and the increasingly globalized mass media. Governments are losing the power to control the flow of information, goods, and even people across their borders. Nation-states are no longer able to assume that the bulk of the population within their borders give primary allegiance to the nation. Instead, national loyalties increasingly are forced to compete with rampant individualism and revived tribalism, which emphasize identification based on language, race, ethnicity, religion, gender, sexual orientation, etc. As Richard N. Haass has observed, "political movements today are defined more by ethnicity than by ideology or territory."[12]

The erosion of the power of governments contributes to the proliferation of threats which they confront. At times it is difficult or impossible even to determine whether the threat comes from another state (and if so which state) or whether it is generated within one's own borders. Cybercrime provides a graphic example of this dilemma, at times targeted against a government, company, or even an individual; at other times striking indiscriminately around the globe.[13]

Contemporary terrorism exhibits similar behavior. It is less and less common to find clear evidence linking a nation state to terrorist actions. Past terrorist actions were frequently committed by groups hoping to replace an existing government; their purpose was largely to demonstrate their strength and/or the government's weakness. But contemporary ethnic/religious terrorists often want to maximize casualties. Under such conditions diplomacy, sanctions, even the threat of military force is largely ineffective in deterring terrorist acts. While nations are less and less likely to support or condone such actions, these activities still serve to generate friction, suspicion, and even conflict between states. Acts of cyberterrorism are even more difficult to deter or to eliminate. Even if it is possible to determine the nation from which such attacks are launched, locating and dealing with those responsible remains a formidable task. Determining the degree, if any, of government complicity in such actions is also a daunting task as are efforts to have nations prevent future attacks from being launched from their territory.

During the Cold War, military power was concentrated within the two major power blocs. The leaders of these blocs, the United States and the Soviet Union, exercised considerable control over both the weapons which their allies acquired and the ways in which such weapons were utilized. Today, there is a notable diffusion of military power involving both national governments and non-state actors. At the highest level this involves the dangers posed by nuclear proliferation. The potential threats posed by states' possession and use of other weapons of mass destruction (WMD), notably chemical and biological agents, generates at least equal concern.[14] Even more disturbing is the possibility that weak or failing states could lose control over such weapons, permitting them to fall into the hands of terrorist or criminal groups.[15] Throughout history, governments have perceived threats to their security as coming principally from the strength of other states, but today the weakness of states can generate equal if not greater threats. Concerns that a weakened Pakistan possessing nuclear arms could constitute an even greater menace to regional security helped curtail U.S.

sanctions imposed in the wake of its nuclear tests. A dozen years ago an opportunity to disrupt Russia's command and control system would have been viewed as enhancing our national security; today such a possibility is among our worst fears.

The proliferation of weapons is a problem at the micro as well as the macro level. In the wake of the Cold War, there is a frightening dispersal of modern light weapons in areas ranging from Somalia to Central America. All of this is accompanied by a burgeoning international arms trade, much of it in private hands, but often tolerated or even promoted by regimes desperate for money.[16] These weapons, especially when combined with a population experienced in their use and without employment, contribute to the escalation of criminal activity, the spread of ethnic and religious violence, and the inability of governments to provide even minimal security for their citizens. This can complicate or even negate the efforts of international actors to help restore peace and order to troubled states. The ability of Somali clansmen to ambush an elite U.S. combat unit and the American reaction to that event provides a particularly graphic example of this phenomenon. One recent article has gone so far as to assert that ''the adolescent human male equipped with an AK-47 assault rifle'' has become ''the most deadly combat system of the current epoch.''[17]

The end of the Cold War has coincided with what is, in absolute numbers, the greatest migration of peoples in history.[18] In some cases, this is caused by flight from internal conflicts; in others, it is the result of deliberate policies of ''ethnic cleansing,'' but most modern migrants are seeking enhanced economic opportunities. Their search is facilitated by the increasingly porous borders which accompany the globalization of trade, by the growing presence of fellow nationals in nations around the globe, by a network of organized criminal groups engaged in people smuggling, and by the world communications network which makes information on the opportunities for and techniques involved in migrating available to virtually everyone.

These migrations can incite, exacerbate, and/or complicate both intra- and inter-state conflicts. They provide a constant flow of recruits for insurgencies and for organized criminal activities. They motivate, but also hinder and distort international efforts to respond to crisis situations in other nations. Refugee flows from Rwanda helped compel the international community to address that situation but also contributed to the ongoing crisis in the Congo. The desire to curb refugee flows was a motivating factor in the U.S. intervention in Haiti, and the plight of Kurdish refugees in Northern Iraq remains a major issue in our dealings with that nation. The long-term destabilizing impact on the Middle East of Palestinian refugees and the ways in which refugees from conflicts in Bosnia and Kosovo have both motivated and complicated international efforts to respond to those situations are so obvious that they do not need detailed comment.[19] There is every reason to expect that migratory trends, both voluntary and involuntary, will continue at extremely high levels for years to come and that they will remain both a major motivating and constraining factor in our international involvement.

The issues raised by migration also illustrate the intimate nexus between domestic politics and international affairs. Migration has become both a major issue and a domestic factor in the U.S. foreign policy equation. Ethnic groups not only argue for special consideration for particular immigrant groups, they exert influence over policies directed towards their nation of origin. The Cuban, Greek, and Israeli lobbies are the most visible, but numerous others are also active. The Congressional Black Caucus occasionally fits into this pattern as exemplified by its influence on policies towards South Africa and Haiti.

The rise of ethnic politics within the United States is facilitated by a decline in the level of public interest in international affairs. There is also a growing gap between the perceptions of foreign policy leaders and those of the general public. According to a 1999 poll conducted by the Chicago Council on Foreign Relations, 53 percent of the public expect the twenty-first century to experience even more bloodshed and violence than the twentieth, a view shared by only 23 percent of the leaders. Only 54 percent of the public believes globalization has been mostly good, while 87 percent of leaders hold this view. While 82 percent of leaders favor increased contributions to the IMF, only 25 percent of the public shares this view.[20]

The poll also reveals the general public's aversion to the use of U.S. force abroad, with no hypothetical scenario garnering majority support for troop deployment, and only an attack on Saudi Arabia getting a plurality of support. If we must act, most favor doing so only as part of a multilateral force, with 72 percent opposing unilateral military actions. But at the same time, 74 percent favor air strikes against terrorist training camps, and 57 percent even favor the use of ground troops in such circumstances. For the general public, threats come largely from non-state actors, with terrorism topping their list. Other high priority concerns are nuclear proliferation, narcotics trafficking, loss of jobs to other countries, and illegal migration.[21]

The willingness of Americans to pay the price for world leadership, however, is unclear. The Chicago poll, conducted before attacks began in Kosovo, showed support for increased defense spending rising, but it was still only roughly equal to those who favored cuts and less than those who would maintain current levels. Leaders were even less inclined than the general public to favor spending increases. At the same time, 38 percent of leaders favored increased spending on economic assistance to other nations, a position shared by only 13 percent of the general public.[22] Even more controversial is the American will to take casualties. This, in turn, is tied to growing concerns over the extent to which class and race divisions are reflected in the composition of the military, with children of middle- and upper-class families increasingly unlikely to be placed at risk in future conflicts. Samuel Huntington has gone so far as to argue that, in the future, "serious military interventions" must involve no American casualties and virtually no collateral casualties."[23]

The perception of a national unwillingness to tolerate casualties undermines American credibility and raises concerns among our allies. Canadian Lieutenant

General Romeo L. Dallaire, who commanded U.N. forces in Rwanda, asserts that it would be better if the United States abstained from involvement in peace-keeping operations if there is any prospect that taking a few casualties could lead to precipitous withdrawal.[24] The authenticity of such fears and perceptions may well be tested in Kosovo.

Any national lack of will to accept casualties may be related to the difficulty in dealing with complex and ambiguous situations which do not present clear and immediate threats to the United States. As General John R. Galvin has observed, "we search for ways to categorize and then dismiss conflicts which do not fit into our image of war. We relegate those conflicts 'short of war' to theoretical pigeonholes where they can be dealt with—preferably by someone else—while we wait to fight the large, relatively conventional wars."[25]

Unfortunately, most conflicts in the 1990s have been ambiguous, offering no clear threats to vital interests, no neat divisions between evil and virtue. The U.S. military, with reason, has been extremely reluctant to become involved in such conflicts. The prevailing post-Vietnam military doctrine, often associated with the enunciations of former Defense Secretary Caspar Weinberger and for-mer Chairman of the Joint Chiefs Colin Powell, is designed to limit use of force to cases where vital interests are at stake, objectives are clear, and popular support is assured.[26] But most challenges produced by the "new world disorder" offer no such options. Reluctance to use force is a desirable, even necessary, quality, but only if it does not extend to the point where the credibility of the potential use of force is seriously degraded.

The inadequacies of past strategies, such as those contained in the Weinberger-Powell Doctrine, underscores a basic dilemma confronting national security strategy at the end of the twentieth century; when should we resort to the use of force? I've characterized this as the vultures' dilemma, as illustrated by an old cartoon of two vultures in a tree. One turns to the other and says "Patience my ass, I'm going to kill something." Today's conflicts rarely provide a clear-cut moment when the use of force becomes the only viable option. There are no tank columns rolling across the 38th parallel in Korea or overwhelming a small nation like Kuwait. Challenges as direct to our security as the installation of nuclear missiles in Cuba are unlikely to reoccur. Instead, situations will likely resemble those we confronted in recent years in Haiti or Bosnia, or that we currently face in Kosovo. There are not, and probably cannot be, clear guidelines as to when patience should be exhausted. We can never be completely sure when diplomatic efforts, peacekeeping or peace monitoring projects, or even sanctions can no longer control, much less resolve, an issue and force becomes the least undesirable option. Like the vultures, we will never know whether further patience would have made the use of force unnecessary, nor can we expect that decisions we make today will provide clear guidance for those we must make tomorrow.

Determining the goals and limits of any involvement provides another set of dilemmas. The failed mission in Somalia underscored and magnified military fears of "mission creep." What was initially advertised as strictly a humanitarian relief mission turned into an exercise in nation building, then into an active combat mission which ultimately cost the lives of 44 American servicemen and thousands of Somalis. This seemed to provide a textbook example of mission creep, of the unplanned and ultimately disastrous expansion of a mission's goals beyond those originally envisioned.[27]

An obsession with the dangers of mission creep, however, can produce mission paralysis. Whenever military forces are deployed inside the boundaries of a foreign state, the very act of exercising force creates new dynamics and new problems. Peacekeeping can be transformed into peacemaking if agreements break down. Effective humanitarian aid may prove impossible without some involvement in nation building. Preoccupation with avoiding mission creep, like an obsessive aversion to taking casualties, produces a focus on short-term goals to the detriment of dealing with the underlying realities which created the problem in the first place. A daunting task confronting contemporary leaders is to remain flexible enough to adapt to changing circumstances without making open-ended commitments that may entail costs far beyond the value of the situation. As David Callahan has observed in his study *Unwinnable Wars: American Power and Ethnic Conflict*, policy makers "cannot allow themselves to be paralyzed by the fact that U.S. involvement in ethnic conflict, including military action, carries no guarantee of success. . . . Rogue state leaders and paramilitary extremists are more likely to fear a United States that uses its military power liberally, and at times unsuccessfully, than a United States that never uses its military power at all."[28]

A related dilemma is what one study has labeled "triage for failing states."[29] This is the problem of determining where and to what extent to become involved in the political and humanitarian disasters which occur with increasing frequency around the globe. In the words of one perceptive analyst, we must "reject the reasoning that, if the United States responds to one humanitarian crisis, it must react to all. The United States must exercise judgement, recognize its limits, and decline to intervene without apology."[30]

Neither past experiences nor any domestic or international consensus provide clear guidelines for making these decisions. As Thomas Carothers has noted, "International norms regarding intervention have evolved in recent years, but only to a state of confusion."[31] Academic analysts and policy makers argue endlessly about the need, the right, and the world's reactions to the role of the United States in peacekeeping, peacemaking, and humanitarian interventions. Some contend that a more active American engagement is the only way to stop the slide into global chaos, while others see an expanded role as likely to provoke resentment and perhaps even support for our worst enemies.[32] The only point of general agreement is that we can no longer afford to ignore civil conflicts in distant regions.[33]

In Washington, much of the discussion is subsumed in domestic issues such as the relative powers of the congressional and executive branches, budget debates, concerns over the impact of peacekeeping missions on troop readiness, and the endless search for partisan political advantage.[34] Public debate is usually conducted on a case-by-case basis, with little strategic framework except for repeated, generally inaccurate, analogies to Munich or Vietnam. A lingering Cold War heritage ensures that those advocating American involvement in any crisis frame the issue as a confrontation between global forces of good and evil, while those opposing further involvement often portray a limitless commitment as the only alternative to refraining from action. Neither side seems willing or able to put issues in the context of a dangerous and frequently ambiguous world in which pretensions to leadership will always come with a hefty price tag.

The ambiguity of the decision-making process is further complicated by a number of factors. Any decision to intervene in another state's internal affairs depends not only on the assessment of the existing situation, but on calculations as to how such a situation is likely to evolve and impact neighboring states absent external intervention. Such calculations are, ipso facto, impossible to prove. Enhancing, restoring, or even creating the legitimacy of a central government has been a benchmark objective of most previous American involvement in these situations. The experiences of the Reagan administration in Lebanon and the Bush and Clinton administrations in Somalia have thrown this concept into question. When religious or ethnic disputes or the activities of powerful criminal organizations are a central cause for state failure, seeking to establish a regime which all major actors will accept as legitimate may become an exercise in futility. At times, the question can even arise as to whether external actors must accept the territorial unity and integrity of a nation as a given in any peace or humanitarian operation. To do so may be to doom to failure any effort to form a consensus on the legitimacy of future government. On the other hand, failure to do so could open a proverbial Pandora's Box of similar issues in neighboring states, making this yet another arena where there are no good, safe options.

Even the goal of negotiating an end to civil conflict may prove impossible in some situations. Ties between insurgents and criminal groups significantly reduce incentives to negotiate. The same is true for governments which have made practices such as ethnic cleansing a central element of their policies. In such cases, the risks of peace may exceed the costs of continued war for one or all sides to a conflict. As David Keen has noted, ''Winning may not be desirable; the point of war may be precisely the legitimacy which it confers on actions that in peacetime would be punishable as crimes.''[35]

Building coalitions to respond to such situations poses its own dilemmas. Public efforts at coalition formation impose limitations on future actions. The failure of such efforts makes the alternative of unilateral or even bilateral action more difficult to justify either domestically or internationally. Coalition building also generates its own costs, both in restricting the goals and scope of possible actions and in the subsequent payments which nations may expect or extract as the price of their participation.

Once they are created, maintaining coalitions becomes a priority in and of itself. This can even become the dominant priority, overshadowing the original goals of the mission. Efforts to maintain or disrupt the coalition become a major feature of subsequent conflict. Actual and potential foes are likely to craft public statements and negotiating positions in a manner designed to produce the maximum strain on alliance ties. In today's world the struggle to influence and shape the global media has become almost as important as actual combat operations.[36] Steps taken to enhance capabilities and counter hostile actions in either of these areas may actually degrade capabilities in the other.

Efforts at peacekeeping or peacemaking can be further complicated by the trend towards privatization of security within states and/or the use of private armies in civil conflicts.[37] As violence from social unrest, ethnic conflicts, or rampant criminality increases, powerful actors within a state turn to private security forces to defend their interests and eliminate their foes. The rise of the paramilitaries in conflict arenas such as those in Colombia or the former Yugoslavia is an illustration of this. At the same time marginalized sectors of society turn increasingly to lynching and other forms of mob violence to make up for a near total lack of state-provided security. All this tremendously complicates the task confronting external efforts to resolve a situation. At the least, it requires a commitment to an extended active involvement with the attendant costs and risks of casualties.

There is a constant temptation to turn to technology for answers to the array of challenges confronting us. Improvements in information-based technologies, in the ability to locate and target enemy forces, and to precisely deliver lethal firepower swiftly and accurately receive increasing attention. Often labeled "the Revolution in Military Affairs," this technology gives the United States and its allies potentially decisive advantages in any conventional war situation.[38] Furthermore, it offers the prospect of significantly reduced casualties. But it also presents the problem of increasing vulnerabilities to information warfare and offers only limited help in confronting the non-conventional small-scale contingencies which increasingly challenge us.[39]

Perhaps the most perplexing aspect of confronting the "new world disorder" is that of defining and measuring success. As Ambassador David Miller has observed, "The American public expects major U.S. involvement overseas, especially if it involves military force, to leave the world a better place."[40] This task is made even more daunting by the tendency to demonize opponents, when forcing their removal is not an integral part of American strategy. Thus any operation which leaves in place a Saddam Hussein, a Slobodan Milosevic, or some similar tyrant is likely to be viewed as a failure by much of the public, especially if, as usually occurs, we face future difficulties with this same leader.

An area where it is particularly difficult, and at times dangerous, to define success is in dealings with international criminal elements. Efforts to break up the major Colombian drug cartels have met with some success, but the result has been to spawn a plethora of smaller cartels, to increase the importance of ties between narcotics traffickers and insurgent groups, and to transfer many operations to other areas, notably Mexico, whose strategic importance to the United States clearly exceeds that of Colombia. The growth of organized criminal activity in Mexico and its corrupting and debilitating influence on that nation's government and society is among the most serious security challenges facing the United States today. Crime and narcotics trafficking are rampant, the corrupting influence on institutions on both sides of the border is pervasive, and the corrosive effects of the situation on prospects for democracy and the rule of law in Mexico can hardly be exaggerated.[41]

Our current *International Crime Control Strategy* recognizes that "Safeguarding our nation's borders is one of the federal government's most basic responsibilities. It is also one of our most daunting challenges."[42] When efforts to deal with problems in one area of the world magnify the problems of control along our borders, how do we measure overall success? Similar problems arise when our use of one nation's territory to conduct operations against another threatens the security and/or political stability of the host nation, when policies designed to promote economic liberalization and free trade exacerbate existing social inequalities and increase corruption, or when pressures to gain allied support for specific actions threaten to undermine the basis of support which sustains the alliance. Today it is impossible to insulate actions in one sphere from impacting on a much broader array of threats and interests. An obsession with achieving success in one case may ultimately generate disproportionate costs in others.

Failure to deal with root causes rather than just the symptoms of violent disorder occurs all to frequently. If there is any clear lesson in post–Cold War peacemaking efforts, it is that ending, at least temporarily, internal conflicts is often the easy part of the task. Providing jobs for combatants, constructing credible institutions of government, especially in the areas of security and justice, providing for the victims of the conflict, and promoting national reconciliation are all daunting long-range tasks. Failure to provide the resources needed for such tasks and failure to ensure that they are undertaken in a climate of security for all factions can produce a revived conflict more intransigent than the original one. This threatens to become the case in Angola, Somalia, and Afghanistan and has the potential to develop in several other areas. Simply proclaiming victory and going home is not a definition of success; indeed, it may be a recipe for failure.

The daunting array of challenges posed by the current global environment is unlikely to diminish as we enter the new millennium. The *1999 Annual Defense Review* predicts that "the variety of actors that can affect U.S. security and the stability of the broader international community will continue to grow in number and capability," and "more nation states will fail between now and 2015, creating internal conflict, humanitarian crisis, and the potential for regional instability."[43] The power and influence of organized criminal elements are also likely to increase, taking advantage of "clashes of values between economic profit and political security, and between individual freedom and collective order," and contributing to a world where governments "find themselves experiencing declining capacities to govern and possessing declining legitimacy."[44]

Domestic political interests and concerns will continue to provide major obstacles to the formulation of consistent and effective responses to future challenges. President Clinton's admission in an interview with Garry Wills that he had "not yet convinced the core majority of the country that there is no longer an easy distinction between domestic policy and foreign policy" is likely to remain true for his successor.[45]

Predictions that "instability and conflict will characterize the post–Cold War world" have proven all too true."[46] Responding to the challenges posed by such a world requires developing strategies which provide a framework for determining where, when, and under what circumstances the United States will engage. Costs of action must be weighed against the risks of inaction, commitments must be sustainable in both military and political spheres, and determinations must be made as to whether the goal is simply to contain the impact and limit the costs of conflicts or to attempt to deal with the root causes of violence and instability.

In his April 15, 1999, speech to the American Society of Newspaper Editors, President Clinton declared "at the end of the 20th century, we face a great battle between the forces of integration and the forces of disintegration; the forces of globalism vs. tribalism; of oppression against empowerment. And the phenomenal explosion of technology, including that of advanced weaponry, might be the servant of either side or both."[47] Avoiding this battle is not an option, defeat would entail unimaginable costs. Achieving success will entail major risks and high costs, necessitate abandoning outdated strategies for the uncertainty of new approaches, and require acceptance of decades of continued insecurity. Unpleasant as such prospects may be, there are no better alternatives.

## NOTES

1. Institute for National Strategic Studies, National Defense University, *1998 Strategic Assessment: Engaging Power for Peace* (Washington, DC: National Defense University, 1998), p. 1.

2. For a discussion of some of these problems, see Fareed Zakaria, "The Rise of Illiberal Democracy," *Foreign Affairs*, Vol. 76, No. 6 (November/December 1997), pp. 22–43; and the responses to his article by John Shattuck and J. Brian Attwood, "Defending Democracy," and by Marc Plattner, "Liberalism and Democracy," *Foreign Affairs*, Vol. 77, No. 2 (March/April 1998), pp. 167–180.

3. The White House, *A National Security Strategy for a New Century* (October 1998), p. 6.

4. Group of Eight Industrialized Democracies, *The Birmingham Summit: Final Communique*, May 17, 1998, p. 7.

5. The White House, *A National Security Strategy*, pp. 5–6.

6. For a discussion of these issues, see Richard N. Haass, *The Reluctant Sheriff: The United States After the Cold War* (New York: Council on Foreign Relations, 1997),

pp. 38–39. For a fuller discussion, see Dennis F. Caffrey, "Confronting the 'Hard De-cisions' of Redefined Sovereignty and the Tools of Intervention in the New Security Environment," in *Managing Contemporary Conflict: Pillars of Success*, Max G. Man-waring and William J. Olson, eds. (Boulder, CO: Westview Press, 1996), pp. 104–106.

7. Tim Johnson, "Colombia's Air Force Under Suspicion," *Miami Herald*, Novem-ber 13, 1998, Internet edition.

8. For a recent assessment of the problems confronting U.S. policy makers, see Ga-briel Marcella and Donald Schulz, *Colombia's Three Wars: U.S. Strategy at the Cross-roads* (Carlisle Barracks, PA: Strategic Studies Institute, U.S. Army War College, 1999).

9. For a description of Haiti's problems, see Richard L. Millett, "Haitian Democracy: Oxymoron or Emerging Reality," in *Assessing Democracy in Latin America*, Philip Kelly, ed. (Boulder, CO: Westview Press, 1998), pp. 173–184.

10. Joint Chiefs of Staff, Department of Defense, *Joint Vision 2010* (Washington, DC, 1996).

11. White House, *A National Security Strategy for the New Century*, p. 2.

12. Haass, *The Reluctant Sheriff*, p. 37.

13. Computer viruses such as "Melissa" or "Chernobyl" provide graphic examples of such indiscriminate targeting.

14. Official U.S. concerns in this area are summarized in *United States Strategic Plan for International Affairs*, p. 11. For a fuller discussion of the issue, see Haass, *The Re-luctant Sheriff*, pp. 31–33.

15. Colonel Michael J. Dziedzic, "Troubled States, How Troubling, How Managea-ble?" manuscript version for publication in *Strategic Assessment*, 1999, p. 596.

16. For a description and critique of this problem, see Robert Mandel, "Deadly Trans-fers, National Hypocrisy, and Global Chaos," *Armed Forces and Society*, Vol. 25, No. 2 (Winter 1999), pp. 308–310.

17. Michael Klare, "The Kalashnikov Age," *The Bulletin of the Atomic Scientists* (January/February, 1999), p. 18.

18. In terms of percentage of populations on the move, the mass migrations accom-panying the collapse of the Roman Empire may have been equal or greater, but obviously accurate figures are lacking.

19. For a detailed analysis of the interplay between refugees and current policy, see Kathleen Newland, "The Impact of US Refugee Policies on US Foreign Policy: A Case of the Tail Wagging the Dog?" in *Threatened Peoples, Threatened Borders: World Migration and U.S. Policy*, Michael S. Teitelbaum and Myron Weiner, eds. (New York: The American Assembly, 1995).

20. Chicago Council on Foreign Relations, *American Public Opinion and U.S. For-eign Policy 1999* (Chicago: Chicago Council on Foreign Relations, 1999). For a summary and analysis of the report, see John E. Reilly, "Americans and the World: A Survey at Century's End," *Foreign Policy*, No. 114 (Spring 1999), pp. 97–114.

21. Chicago Council on Foreign Relations, *American Public Opinion and U.S. For-eign Policy 1999*.

22. Reilly, "Americans and the World," pp. 102 and 106–107.

23. Samuel P. Huntington, "The Lonely Superpower," *Foreign Affairs*, Vol. 78, No. 2 (March/April 1999), p. 39.

24. Discussion with then Major General Romeo L. Dallaire, Quantico, VA, September 1997. For additional information on this issue, see Eric V. Larson, *Casualties and Con-*

*sensus: The Historical Role of Casualties in Domestic Support of U.S. Military Operations* (Santa Monica, CA: Rand Corporation, 1998).

25. Max G. Manwaring, "An Interview with General John R. Galvin, US Army (Ret.), Dean of the Fletcher School of Law and Diplomacy, 6 August, 1997," *Small Wars and Insurgencies*, Vol. 9, No. 1 (Spring 1998), p. 9.

26. Kenneth J. Campbell, "Once Burned, Twice Cautious: Explaining the Weinberger-Powell Doctrine," *Armed Forces and Society*, Vol. 24, No. 3 (Spring 1998), pp. 364–367.

27. For a discussion of this issue, see Karl L. Holmes, "Post-Mogadishu Syndrome, Mission Creep, and Expansive Doctrine Syndrome: Learning Theory and the Lessons of the Somalia Debacle," paper presented at the April 1996 Annual Meeting of the International Studies Association, San Diego, CA.

28. David Callahan, *Unwinnable Wars: American Power and Ethnic Conflict* (New York: Hill and Wang, 1997), pp. 235–236.

29. Edward Marks and William Lewis, *Triage for Failing States*, McNair Paper 26 (Washington, DC: Institute for National Strategic Studies, National Defense University, 1994).

30. Matthew S. Klimow, *Moral versus Practical: The Future of US Armed Humanitarian Intervention*, Martello Papers No. 14 (Kingston, ON: Centre for International Relations, Queens University, 1996), p. 41.

31. Thomas Carothers, "Lesson for Policymakers," in *Haitian Frustrations: Dilemmas for U.S. Policy*, Georges A. Fauriol, ed. (Washington, DC: Center for Strategic and International Studies, 1995), p. 117.

32. For examples, see Haass, *The Reluctant Sheriff*, pp. 93–100; and Huntington, "The Lonely Superpower," pp. 39–49.

33. Steven R. David, "Saving America from the Coming Civil Wars," *Foreign Affairs*, Vol. 78, No. 1 (January/February 1999), p. 103; Richard L. Kugler, *Toward a Dangerous World: U.S. National Security Strategy for the Coming Turbulence* (Santa Monica, CA: Rand Corporation, 1995), p. xix.

34. For a discussion of many of these issues, see Nina M. Serafino, *Peacekeeping: Issues of U.S. Military Involvement: CRS Issue Brief* (Washington, DC: Congressional Research Service, January 22, 1999). For an analysis of domestic political issues as viewed from abroad, see Joel J. Sokolsky, *The Americanization of Peacekeeping Implications for Canada*, Martello Papers No. 17 (Kingston, ON: Centre for International Relations, Queens University, 1996), pp. 8–18.

35. David Keen, *The Economic Functions of Violence in Civil Wars: Adelphi Paper No. 320* (Oxford: Oxford University Press, 1998), p. 12.

36. The conflict in Kosovo has provided mounting evidence of this trend.

37. David Shearer, "Outsourcing War," *Foreign Policy*, No. 112 (Fall 1998), pp. 68–81.

38. For a summary of current Defense Department views on the Revolution in Military Affairs, see Department of Defense, *1999 Annual Defense Review*, Chapter 10, Internet version at http://www.dtic.mil/execsec/adr1999/cha10.html.

39. For a critical examination of this topic, see Michael O'Hanlon, "Can High Technology Bring U.S. Troops Home?" *Foreign Policy*, No. 113 (Winter 1998–1999), pp. 72–86.

40. Ambassador David Miller, "Structuring Foreign Policy in a Post–Cold War

World,'' in *Managing Contemporary Conflict: Pillars of Success*, Max G. Manwaring and William J. Olson, eds. (Boulder, CO: Westview Press, 1996), p. 25.

41. For a graphic description of the chaos on the border, see Sebastian Rotella, *Twilight on the Line: Underworlds and Politics at the U.S.-Mexican Border* (New York: W. W. Norton & Co., 1998).

42. The White House, *International Crime Control Strategy*, May 12, 1998, Chapter IV, p. 1.

43. Department of Defense, *1999 Annual Defense Review*, Chapter 1, p. 2.

44. Mandel, ''Deadly Transfers, National Hypocrisy, and Global Chaos,'' p. 323.

45. Garry Wills, ''Bully of the Free World,'' *Foreign Affairs*, Vol. 78, No. 2 (March/April 1999), p. 56.

46. Steven R. David, ''The Necessity for American Military Intervention,'' in *The United States and the Use of Force in the Post–Cold War Era: Aspen Strategy Group Report* (Queenstown, MD: The Aspen Institute, 1995), p. 40. See also Kugler, *Toward a Dangerous World*, pp. xiv–xvii.

47. The Associated Press, ''Text of Remarks of President Clinton to ASNE-2,'' April 15, 1999.

Chapter 2

# Defense and Offense in Peace and Stability Operations

## Max G. Manwaring AND Edwin G. Corr

In the mid-1980s it was deemed important to begin to face the so-called Vietnam syndrome and try to understand the variables that make the difference between winning and losing "uncomfortable" wars. The intent was to improve prospects for success in contemporary conflict situations and to do a better job of protecting and advancing U.S. national interests in the developing global instability. As a result, practitioners and academics have examined and reexamined the Vietnam experience and other unconventional internal conflicts that have taken place in Asia, Africa, and Latin America in the post–World War II period. The lessons distilled from these experiences have been analyzed through the application of several models, notably the so-called Small Wars Operations Research Directorate (SWORD) Model, and are repeatedly validated in the various conflicts of the post–Cold War era.[1]

Nevertheless, lessons regarding contemporary *intranational* conflict remain unlearned. This is primarily because of a mind-set or expectation among many officials in the U.S. national security establishment that some equivalent of Soviet Combined Arms Armies crashing through the Fulda Gap or Iraqi armies again maneuvering in the open desert can still provide a "real" war for real soldiering. What many "first world" military leaders and their slow-learning political masters have not grasped is that the purposes and the uses of power have changed in much of the world and that "Wise competitors . . . will seek to shift the playing field away from conventional military confrontations toward unconventional forms of assault. . . . Only the foolish will fight fair."[2]

An account of a conversation that took place as long ago as April 1975 in Hanoi makes the point:

"You know you never defeated us on the battlefield," said the American colonel. The North Vietnamese colonel pondered this remark a moment. "That may be so," he replied, "but it is also irrelevant."[3]

Thus, this chapter will briefly discuss: (1) the fundamental lessons that should have been learned from the SWORD Model; (2) five additional lessons; (3) the basic elements that define the threat and dictate response; (4) the essential elements that can steer an *intranational** conflict intervention toward a "durable peace"; and (5) the main challenges and tasks associated with the vast majority of conflicts the world has experienced since the end of World War II—and is likely to encounter in the future.

By coming to grips with the most salient issues that dominate the contemporary security environment and dictate response, political and military leaders should be able to do what "wise competitors" already do. That is, develop a strategic vision that people can understand and support—and that *can* show the way to what may be perceived to be a relatively better intranational, national, regional, international, and transnational stability and peace than that now experienced. B. H. Liddell Hart reminds us that for now and into the twenty-first century, still, "The object in war is to attain a better peace—even if only from your own point of view. Hence it is essential to conduct war with constant regard to the peace you desire."[4]

## THE SWORD MODEL

In 1984, the Vice Chief of Staff of the U.S. Army, General Maxwell Thurman, understood that in order to get out of the intellectual vice-lock imposed by one's own experience, it is necessary to examine the general process by which a government in power either resists or defeats or succumbs to an organized violent internal foe. As a result, he mandated the empirical examination of a large sample of intranational wars that would: (1) allow the testing of competing theoretical approaches (i.e., paradigms) to internal conflicts; (2) determine the extent to which the outcome of such conflicts is predictable; and (3) generate a new paradigm (i.e., the SWORD Model) to improve prospects for success in future similar conflict situations.

The results of part of the mandated research were published in 1992.[5] There is nothing really startling or radical about them. The results suggest basic security strategy and national and international asset management. What is new is, first, the SWORD Model was not conceived a priori—it was developed empirically and warrants confidence that the findings are universal and explain much of the reality of intranational political-military chaos. Second, the specific combination of dependent variables (i.e., dimensions) that define the paradigm is new. Third, the stress on the fact that those dimensions are highly interde-

*The terms intranational and internal conflict are used synonymously.

pendent is new. Finally, the statistical indicators of "Goodness of Fit" are considerably higher than competing models—that is, the adjusted $R^2$ is .90, the paradigm is statistically significant at the .001 level, and the percent of cases correctly predicted is an unprecedented 88.37.[6]

The theoretical construct of the SWORD Model, thus, suggests that seven dimensions (i.e., dependent variables), each composed of multiple independent variables, determine the success or failure of an intranational conflict. The resultant theory links these dimensions in a concept of dynamic interaction. It recognizes four major types of actors—the host government, the violent internal foe(s), the external power(s) supporting the host government, and the external actor(s) supporting the internal player(s). These political actors interact in several arenas. This is the idea of a multiorganizational and multilateral conflict.

It would appear, also, that in fighting or intervening in an intranational conflict, one or a coalition of powers is not simply attempting to destroy an "enemy" military force in the classical sense. In addition to the relatively traditional shooting "war," there may be as many as five or six other non-traditional "wars" being conducted at the same time that correspond roughly to the various dimensions of the paradigm. This is the idea of a multifront and multidimensional conflict.

These wars within the greater war are not exhaustive, but they relate to the major military—and other—strategic dimensions that determine the outcome of an externally supported intra-state conflict. These additional controlling dimensions take into account what Michael Howard calls the forgotten social-moral aspect of war and stress that "if this part of a conflict is not conducted with skill, no amount of operational military or police expertise, technical advantage, or outside support can possibly help."[7]

These "wars" would include: (1) a legitimacy "war" to attack or defend the moral right of the incumbent regime to exist; (2) the more traditional shooting or police-military "war" between belligerents; (3) and (4) "wars" to isolate belligerents from their internal and external support; (5) the closely related "war" to stay the course; that is, the effort to provide consistent and long-term support to a supported host government—or supported illegal (i.e., violent) internal group; (6) intelligence and information "wars"; and (7) "wars" to unify multidimensional, multilateral, and multiorganizational elements into a single effective effort.

### The Dimensions

Even though each conflict is situation specific, it is not completely unique. Throughout the universe, there are analytical commonalities in all types of struggle. The seven highly interrelated dimensions—or "wars" listed above—were identified as a result of an examination of the general process by which 69 post–World War II governments either resisted or succumbed to an organized and externally supported internal foe.[8]

In that connection, it should be emphasized that the resultant paradigm has power and virtue in part because of the symmetry of its application—both for a besieged government and its supporters, and for a violent internal challenger and its supporters. That is to say, no successful intranational strategy—on either side of the conflict spectrum—has been formulated over the past 50 years that has not explicitly or implicitly taken into account all the following wars within the general war.

*The Legitimacy "War."* Experience demonstrates that legitimacy is the most important single dimension in an internal conflict. The thrust of a program to subvert and depose an incumbent regime relies on grievances such as political, economic, and social discrimination as the primary means of attack. This is the essential nature of the threat from a violent internal foe, and it is here that any response must begin. A campaign that fails to understand this lack of legitimate governance and responds only to "enemy" military forces is likely to fail.

As an example, it was recognized early in the conflict in El Salvador that this dimension would be key to success or failure for the insurgents or the government. Speaking for the insurgents, Guillermo M. Ungo identified the legitimacy of the regime as the primary center of gravity in that situation.[9] President Jose Napoleon Duarte understood the problem and countered with a program designed to preempt the efforts of the insurgent organization. His argument was simple: "If the Christian Democrats demonstrate in El Salvador that a democratic system can bring about structured changes peacefully, then the polarized choice between domination by the righest oligarchy and violent revolution by the Left will no longer be valid."[10]

*The Shooting "War," or Paramilitary "War."* Experience affirms that the strength of an asymmetrical program to subvert and depose a governing regime is nourished by the alienation of the governed from the government.[11] Thus, great care must be taken to be sensitive and accommodating to the general population while in the process of finding and dealing with a violent internal foe within a divided society. A successful war against organized violent internal foes must be conducted by a highly professional, disciplined, and motivated security force that is capable of discrete, quiet, rapid, and decisive surgical action anywhere in a country—anytime. Moreover, the use of "soft" power must be designed to achieve political and psychological as well as police-military objectives. The bottom line is that success is most likely to go to the competing security organization that has the mentality and ability to engage its enemy within the polity without alienating the general citizenry.

At the height of the terrorist threat in Italy during the late 1970s and the early 1980s, Red Brigades and other terrorist groups were indiscriminate in their violence and contributed inadvertently to an alienation program that led to their ultimate destruction. On the other hand, Italian counterterrorism planners understood that legitimacy considerations implied that the blunt force of military formations supported by heavy weapons and tanks in the streets would be counterproductive and that the role of the regular armed forces should be limited to supporting the major police organizations. They also understood that a good example of an appropriate counterterrorism force is the ever-present but relatively unobtrusive paramilitary carabinieri. As a result, the regular military took over generally routine, inconspicuous, and unobtrusive police functions to allow the state police and the national carabinieri freedom to concentrate more subtle types of power on the counterterrorism mission.[12]

*The "Wars" to Isolate Opponents.* The objective here is for a belligerent to isolate politically, psychologically, and militarily his opponent from his primary sources of support and sanctuaries—whoever and wherever they may be. To ignore this dimension of internal conflict as too difficult and too dangerous in its internal and external political-military ramifications is simply to deny the possibility of "winning."[13]

This dimension is clearly demonstrated in virtually all the 69 cases examined, but the classic example of this type of war is Greece, 1946–1949. In this case, the Greek insurgent forces received logistical and other support from Greece's Communist neighbors—Albania, Bulgaria, and Yugoslavia. This support included food, clothing, arms, ammunition, training camps, transit areas, replacement centers, field hospitals, and supply depots. Countermeasures undertaken to control those borders by the Greek government and the army failed to have any significant effect on reducing the offensive activities of the insurgents. The Greek National Army was only capable of pushing their foes from one area to another. In the north, the "guerrillas" would simply move into adjacent Communist territory and subsequently reappear in another part of Greece. However, in the spring of 1949, the Yugoslavian and other frontiers were closed to the insurgents as a result of political decisions made in London, Moscow, and Belgrade. Denial of the various external supporting facilities to the insurgents made it only a matter of a relatively short period of time before the "war" was brought under control.[14]

*The "War" to Stay the Course of the "War" and to Maintain the Supporting Actions of an Intervening Power.* All support to a besieged government or, conversely, to a supported violent internal challenger, must be consistent to be effective. Examination of the post–World War II conflict spectrum clearly indicates that when military, economic, or political aid to a client was withdrawn by an "intervening" power or coalition of powers during a conflict, or when any of this support was provided inconsistently, the possibilities for "winning" the general war were minimal. When aid was provided consistently over the long-term, chances for success in an internal war were considerably enhanced.[15]

As a consequence, appropriate political, economic, and military aid provided consistently, over the duration of a "prolonged" conflict is vital to a supported government, or to any other political actor. In this situation, for example, the center of gravity lies in the "community of interest" of the supporting power(s) and the supported organization.[16] Destroying or disrupting this crucial objective can be as decisive as the destruction of any "enemy" military force; thus, a "War" to Stay the Course. In these terms, what happens politically and psychologically in capitals of the world thousands of miles from a "war zone" may be more decisive than any series of military engagements. A host of cases from the Algerian war, 1954–1962; the Vietnamese reunification, 1954–1973; the El Salvadoran War, 1980–1989; the U.S. intervention in Haiti, 1994–1995; to the current Bosnian situation provide examples of this phenomenon.[17]

*The Intelligence and Information "Wars" against Subversion.* It is individual men and women who lead, plan, execute, and support a given conflict. As a result, a major concern in intra-state war must be individuals. The intelligence apparatus must be in place, or created, that can locate, isolate, and neutralize a violent internal foe's—or a government's—organizational and leadership structure. The data show clearly that the best police or paramilitary forces are of little consequence without knowing exactly who the foe is and precisely where it may be located. Likewise, willing support to the state on the part of a majority of the populace, motivated by legal, democratic, and honest informational actions on the part of the government are directly related to the synergism and effectiveness of the "War" against Subversion. In the final analysis, legitimate long-term military and political power depend on the proverbial "hearts and minds" of a people.[18]

The key role of effective—or ineffective—intelligence is clearly demonstrated in the Cuban and Nicaraguan cases of 1956–1959 and 1979, respectively. In these cases, the intelligence organizations of the Batista and Samoza regimes continued a "business as usual" attitude during the insurgencies. That is, priority targets tended to be the personal enemies and legitimate internal political opposition of the two dictators. Because of the misdirected effort and lack of concern for any kind of human rights for detainees—innocent or not—the real motives of the Cuban and Nicaraguan dictators came into focus. Consequently, the sacrifices necessary to press a fight against insurgents who promised reform were not readily forthcoming from either citizen or soldier, and the key element of legitimacy was totally subverted.[19]

A more positive example of intelligence is found in the Italian case. The state had a large and increasingly unified and effective intelligence net at its disposal. Ironically, however, it was probably the role of the Italian Communist Party (PCI) that was decisive in this matter. The PCI's capillary structure—strengthened by a large number of efficient ancillary organizations—was able to identify and locate specific terrorist organizations, leaders, and members. The PCI furnished a great deal of this kind of information to the Italian security organizations and made them appear to be much more effective than they really were. In any case, timely and accurate human intelligence provided by the PCI considerably enhanced government efforts to find, discredit, and neutralize terrorist organizations and leadership.[20]

Finally, again, a good example of an Information "War" against Subversion is found in the Italian case. In that situation, the state and the media embarked on a strong counterterrorist public diplomacy campaign. The objective was to expose and exploit the fact that the various left-wing, right-wing, separatist, pacifist, and other terrorist groups operating in Italy during the late 1970s and the 1980s were not organizations of the masses. Rather, they were self-appointed elites whose goals were not what the people in general wanted or needed; those goals were what the terrorist leaderships wanted or needed.

The antiterrorist information "war" demonstrated that, for the terrorists, those Italians who were not fellow ideological "true believers" were not really people. As an example, the 2,384 victims killed, maimed, or abducted by terrorists in 1979 were not considered by them to be human beings made of flesh and blood, and deserving of some personal dignity. They were considered "tools of the system," "pigs," and "watch dogs." Moreover, the government and media exposed the fact that Red Brigadists considered everyone else—even other comrades on the Left—to be mere "shit."[21]

It is not appropriate, however, to give the Italian government all the credit in this "war." It is important to understand that the government's success in information warfare was based on a certain level of failure on the part of the terrorists. An information war is supposed to generate at least tacit support for a cause. Terrorist propaganda, information, and public diplomacy were communicated to target audiences in a virtually unintelligible jargon without any serious attempt to educate the public regarding terms and dogma. It was assumed that everyone in Italy thought and talked in the terrorist's own terms. The terrorists' assumption was erroneous and only indicated the level of psychological and physical isolation of the terrorists from the rest of the population. Terrorist legitimacy was greatly eroded, supporters were obviously alienated, and counterterrorist intelligence was willingly provided.[22]

*The "War" for Unity of Effort.* This dimension of conflict involves overcoming parochial bureaucratic interests, fighting "turf" battles, overcoming cultural obstacles, and ensuring that all efforts are focused on the ultimate goal—survival. That is to say, the necessary organization at the highest level to coordinate and implement an effective unity of political-diplomatic, socioeconomic, psychological-moral, and security-stability efforts against those who would violently depose a government. Again, this applies equally to an organization that threatens an incumbent regime. In any case, the ability to accomplish these things in a manner acceptable to the populace is key. And that equates back to legitimacy. Without an organization that can establish, enforce, and continually refine a holistic plan and generate consistent national and international support, authority is fragmented and ineffective in resolving the myriad problems endemic to survival in contemporary conflict—thus, failure.[23]

Ambassador Robert Komer has pointed out that unity of effort was a major deficiency in the Vietnam War.[24] This was also the case at the Bay of Pigs (Cuba) in 1961; Aden, 1968; and the Spanish experience in the Western Sahara, 1975–1976.[25] Others have observed that the "strategic ambiguity" of the past United Nations (U.N.) and current NATO efforts in the former Yugoslavia is also a result of lack of national and international unity of effort.[26]

On the positive side of the unity of effort dimension—with the exception of the fiasco in Aden—the unilateral British experience seems to dominate as a good example. For instance, an overall coordinator of all military and civil activities has usually been appointed by the prime minister. A committee of the cabinet provides periodic general direction and support for this individual. The coordinator may hold other appointments and has been known to be the flag officer commanding the armed forces involved in the conflict—as was the case in the Falklands War in 1982. He may even be the appointed head of government, as was the case when General Templer in Malaysia and Field Marshall Lord Harding in Cyprus carried out this task.

But regardless of other positions, the purpose of the "director of operations" or "coordinator" is to act as the executive officer of the supreme national body (i.e., Parliament). In this context, it is assumed that he or she has the authority to deal with relevant people in the British government and with responsible individuals in the supported country. Together, long-term and short-term mutually supportive objectives are determined and pursued.[27]

In sum, post–World War II internal conflict has been highly political and psychological, as well as military. By transforming the emphasis of war from the level of military violence to the level of a multidimensional struggle for legitimacy, a violent internal foe can strive for the complete overthrow of an incumbent regime, instead of simply attempting to obtain leverage and influence for limited, economic, social, or political concessions in the more conventional sense. Thus, it appears that intranational war is the result of careful political calculation and political-psychological-violent action. In ironic philosophical rhetoric, modern conflict turns Clausewitz upside down. War is not an extension of politics; politics is an extension of war.*

## FIVE ADDITIONAL LESSONS REGARDING THE NEW GLOBAL SECURITY ENVIRONMENT

"When we think about the possibilities of conflict, we tend to invent for ourselves a comfortable vision of war"—a situation with the kind of battlefields that are well understood, with an enemy who looks and acts more or less as we do, and a situation in which war is fought by the military.[28] We must recognize, however, that in fighting a foe today and in the future, the situation has changed. We can see that change in several ways.

### Ambiguity

First, the definition of "enemy" and "victory" is elusive, and the use of "power" against that foe to achieve some form of success is diffuse. Underlying

*Because the scope of this chapter is oriented toward attacks against the state by violent political opponents, we do not address a different kind of assault on the state by organized criminal or illegal drug trafficking organizations. Suffice it to say here that "narcos" and other organized criminals do not normally seek to destroy and replace a government. Rather, they tend to seek to maintain a weak government and a chaotic environment in which to conduct more easily their activities. At the same time, the seven dimensions of the paradigm are still applicable.

these ambiguities is the fact that contemporary conflict is more often than not an intra-state affair that international law and convention is only beginning to address. It is part of one society against another. In these wars there is normally no formal declaration or termination of conflict, no easily identifiable enemy military formations to attack and destroy, no specific territory to take and hold, no single credible government or political actor with which to deal, no legal niceties such as mutually recognized national borders and Geneva Conventions to help control the situation, no guarantee that any agreement between or among contending authorities will be honored, and thus, no specific rules to guide the leadership of a given intervening "peace," "stability," or small-scale contingency mission.

## The Need to Redefine "Enemy," "Power," and "Victory"

Second, the ambiguous political-psychological-moral nature of contemporary conflict thus forces the redefinition of "enemy," "power," and "victory." The enemy is no longer a recognizable military entity or an industrial capability to make war. The enemy now becomes "violence" and the causes of violence. Power is not simply combat fire-power directed at a traditional enemy military formation or industrial complex. Power is multilevel and combined political, psychological, moral, informational, economic, social, military, police, and civil bureaucratic activity that can be brought to bear appropriately on the causes and the perpetrators of violence. And victory is no longer the obvious and acknowledged destruction of military capability. Victory, or success, is now—more and more, and perhaps with a bit of "spin control"—defined as the achievement of a "sustainable peace."

## A "New" Center of Gravity

These ambiguities intrude on the "comfortable" vision of war in which the assumed center of gravity has been enemy military formations and his physical capability to conduct war. Clausewitz reminds us, however, that "In countries subject to domestic strife . . . and popular uprisings the [center of gravity] is the personalities of the leaders and public opinion. It is against these that our energies should be directed."[29] Thus, in contemporary intranational conflict the primary center of gravity changes from a familiar military concept to an ambiguous and uncomfortable political-economic-psychological-security paradigm.

## Conflict Has Become Multidimensional, Multilateral, and Multiorganizational

Fourth, conflict is no longer a military to military confrontation. Conflict now involves entire populations. Conflict now involves a large number of national civilian agencies, other national civilian organizations, international organizations, non-governmental organizations, private voluntary organizations, and subnational indigenous actors involved in dealing in one way or another with complex threats to international security and well-being. As a consequence, an almost unheard-of unity of effort is required to coordinate the multilateral, multidimensional, and multiorganizational paradigm necessary for success in contemporary conflict. That ideal has never really been achieved in the past. Nevertheless, in this new and infinitely more complex situation, governments and organizations involved in such endeavors must find ways and means to work toward a more effective unity.

### Contemporary "War" Is Not Limited; It Is Total

Finally, contemporary non-traditional war is not a kind of appendage—a lesser or limited thing—to the comfortable vision of conflict. It is a great deal more. As long as opposition exists that is willing to risk all to violently take down a government and establish its own, there is war. This is a zero-sum game in which there is only one winner. It is, thus, total.

In *The Centurions*, Jean Larteguy vividly captures the difference between traditional warfare designed to achieve limited political, economic, or territorial concessions and the totality of the type of conflict we confront today. He contrasts the French (i.e., traditional) and the Vietminh (i.e., total) methods of waging war:

It is difficult to explain exactly, but it is rather like [the card game] bridge as compared to belote. When we [the French] make war, we play belote with 32 cards in the pack. But the Viet Minh's game is bridge and they have 52 cards: 20 more than we do. Those 20 cards short will always prevent us from getting the better of them. They've got nothing to do with traditional [military] warfare, they're marked with the sign of politics, propaganda, faith, agrarian reform. . . . What's biting [the French officer]? I think he is beginning to realize that we've got to play with 52 cards and he doesn't like it at all. . . . Those 20 extra cards aren't at all to his liking.[30]

These are the realities for now and into the next century, "Everything else is illusion."[31]

### BASIC ELEMENTS THAT DEFINE THREAT AND DICTATE RESPONSE

Our analysis of the problem of contemporary conflict resolution indicates that if powers or coalitions of powers decide to intervene in an intranational conflict situation, they should take the full responsibility of that action. That is, they normally should go beyond the "defensive" idea of simply "winning" temporarily in some conventional sense to the "offensive" idea of achieving a "sustainable peace." One can envision situations in which U.S. interests might dictate acceptance of a less than ideal solution to a problem. However, long-term interests as well as logic would "normally" dictate a durable peace rather than a crisis management solution.

In this context, the problem of preparing specifically for "peace" or "stability" operations, or a so-called small-scale contingency operation to resist some form of aggression, is mute. An enforced "peace" can only provide the beginning environment from which to establish, protect, and sustain a legitimate civil government that can and will deal with the root causes that brought on the conflict in the first place. Otherwise, the intervening power(s) face the unhappy prospects of either declaring victory, going home, and waiting for the inevitable relapse into the status quo ante; or risking taking part in little more than a static and limited military occupation.

The first step in developing the strategic vision to conduct a responsible intervention is to recognize the elements that define the basic threat and dictate response. The second step is to examine the question of appropriate short-, medium-, and long-term responses to a complex and multidimensional threat.

### The Complex and Multidimensional Threat Situation

The threats in contemporary conflict come in many forms, both direct and indirect. A very visible form of a direct challenge to the state comes as public violence against officials and institutions that are somehow defined by the challengers as "bad." An indirect threat usually comes in some form of progressive political and psychological discrediting of public institutions. The intent is to psychologically erode the basic public support that must underlie the legitimate functioning of the state. Moreover, a specific challenge to the state may be both direct and indirect. To further complicate the matter, a given challenge may reflect both the causes and consequences of instability and the eventual destruction of the state.

Thus, the threat situation can be circular. Terrorism, for example, can be both the consequence and the cause of intranational, national, and international instability. As an example, the direct consequence of a terrorist attack on a national Supreme Court and the "assassination" of several of its justices could "indirectly" cause that key institution to function even more slowly and less efficiently than usual. This inefficiency could lead to a further discrediting of the court and the substantial weakening of the state. This weakening could lead to the possible destruction of the state. In turn, the destruction of a given state could affect its neighbors—and, thus, create regional and international instability. Interestingly, the real or perceived cause of the terrorist attack on that Supreme Court could likely be the corruption and indolence of the justices.

In this connection, it is helpful to think of instability as a third-level threat to national or regional security. Root causes that generate political, economic, and social injustices may be considered a second-level threat to security and stability. The unwillingness or inability of a regime to develop long-term, multidimensional, and morally acceptable reforms to alleviate societal injustice and—sooner rather than later—to enhance national well-being should be understood to be the most fundamental first-level threat.

At the same time, another threat emerges at a fourth level that is both a cause and an effect of instability and violence. That is, once a violent internal foe— such as Red Brigades, Mafia families, archaeo-Trotskyite groupescules, Sendero Luminoso Maoists, Somalian or Southeast Asian warlords, Serbian ''ethnic cleansers,'' militant Muslim fundamentalists, or militant environmentalists—becomes firmly established, first-level reform and development efforts aimed at second-level root causes would be insufficient to control or neutralize a third-level (e.g., terrorist) threat. That third-level violent internal foe—regardless of whether or not it is sincerely trying to achieve specific political-economic-social-moral reforms, or only trying to gain some visceral satisfaction—can only be finally defeated by a superior organization, a holistic and unified strategy designed to promulgate deeper and more fundamental reforms—and deadly force.

### Response to the Threat(s)

The sum of the parts of an effective response equals (1) the recognition at the highest levels of a destabilizing problem; (2) a sure capability to coordinate political, economic, social, and security objectives on the first and second levels; but also (3) to exert effective force at the third and fourth levels. This, in turn, requires: (1) political competence based on a foundation of legitimacy; (2) national capability building designed to eradicate the root causes of instability and its resultant violence; and (3) a security apparatus designed to control, neutralize, and/or eliminate a violent and entrenched third- or fourth-level internal foe (see Figure 2.1).

Thus, one must consider the logic of defining response in terms of the explicit and implicit ''defensive'' and ''offensive'' actions indicated by the SWORD Model. Defensive action is relatively short term. It is primarily military/police and focuses on stopping parties to a conflict from shooting or moving against each other. Limited defensive (i.e., remedial) action can also be taken against causes as well as consequences of instability and violence.

Offensive action is generally medium to long term. It is primarily civilian and political, but is likely to have to be coordinated with police and military action. It focuses on following up the defensive action by attempting to diminish and remove the social, economic, and political causes of the instability and resultant violence. Additionally, this kind of offensive political-military-moral action can initiate the steps necessary to develop institutions, procedures, and attitudes necessary to create a legitimate civil society—and a durable peace.[32]

Unfortunately, a vulnerable, failing, or failed government is not likely to have the multilevel and multidimensional capabilities that are required for survival in the contemporary global security environment. If it had the implied capabilities, it probably would not be threatened and there would be no need for any kind

**Figure 2.1**
**Threat Dimensions**

| Level of Threat | Type of Threat | Forms of Response |
|---|---|---|
| 3rd (Third) | Instability (e.g., personal violence, increased strikes, kidnappings, bank robberies, violent takeovers, death squads, bombings, murders/assassinations, criminal anarchy) and the beginnings of insurgency, ethnic cleansing, and refugee flows. | Short-term political, economic, and social reform; minimum force to guarantee personal security. |
| 2nd (Second) | Widespread social violence (e.g., increases in third-level instability). | Medium to long-term deep reforms to deal with poverty and other root causes of instability, and the careful application of force to enforce reforms and law and order. |
| 1st (First) | Regime unwillingness or inability to promulgate and enforce second- and third-level reforms and to provide personal and national security. | Long-term deeper reforms to create changes in mind-set, and development of political, military/police competence under an umbrella of legitimacy. |
| 4th (Fourth) | Completely entrenched, violent "revolutionaries." | Continuation of reforms and development of deep regime legitimacy, plus development of superior organization, unity of effort, and ability to exert deadly force against a violent internal foe. |

of intervention. In the short term, then, a vulnerable state will likely require outside support. Nevertheless, no group or force can legislate or decree these qualities for itself or anyone else. The legitimacy and stability qualities required derive from popular and institutional perceptions that authority is genuine and effective, and uses morally correct means for reasonable and fair purposes. These qualities are developed, sustained, and enhanced by responsible actions and behavior over time.

Probably the best an outside power or group of powers can do is to "defensively" help establish a level of security that will allow the "offensive" *guided* development of the essential elements necessary for the promulgation of a legitimate civil society and a sustainable peace. The general rule would be that decision makers and policy makers must carefully calculate possible gains and losses, and when the case warrants, intervene earlier rather than later. If done earlier, this implies the initial and intense use of low-cost diplomatic and civilian resources and military support units to ensure legitimacy and stability. If done later, this normally implies the initial and intense use of high-cost military combat units to respond to a losing situation. Ultimately, however, the only viable test for intervention is national self-interest.

Separately and together, the complex and multidimensional threats resulting from a lack of legitimate and strong governmental institutions generate a vicious downward spiral that manifests itself in disparate activities in which the lowest common denominator is instability and violence. Thus, intranational, national, and international security will depend on a combination of internal and external political, economic, social, and security activities that provide for defensive and offensive actions to achieve political reform, economic opportunity, social justice, and national and personal security.

## THE ESSENTIAL "OFFENSIVE" ELEMENTS THAT CAN LEAD TO A SUSTAINABLE PEACE

In any case of intervention, the final step in developing an appropriate response to the instability and violence "that threaten the security and well-being of the international community" is to revisit the seven dimensions of the SWORD Model. The logical generally "offensive" extension of those dimensions generates the foundational elements required to address the central strategic objective—that of a legitimate civil society and a durable peace.

These essential foundational elements are postulated as clusters of related political, economic, informational, and security activities that must be performed at the strategic/macro level to transform a "war-torn" state to a point where peace is sustainable without the presence of a unilateral or multilateral force to enforce that peace. Essential functions, then, are those considered necessary and sufficient to provide a foundation for a mandated peace and to preclude a return to the instability and violence that had originally provoked a unilateral or multilateral intervention.

In cases where "peace," "stability," or small-scale contingency operations are undertaken, the extent to which these "essential elements" are applied will vary—depending on the situation. Yet when all the "essential elements" are strong and dynamic, one can see greater chances of success. When some of the elements are weak or applied in an ad hoc, piecemeal, or unbalanced manner, one can see greater chances of failure.

The dimensions of the SWORD Model and their "offensive" extensions are as follows.

### Legitimacy

First, the Legitimacy "War" continues and is expanded to "Foster Peaceful Processes of Conflict Resolution," and "Nurture and Sustain a Civil Society."

Tasks associated with the first "Peaceful Processes" component include (1) overseeing the implementation of the political framework called for in a peace agreement, including the monitoring of elections; (2) assisting in the formation of culturally acceptable processes and institutions for decision making and leadership selection; and (3) promoting governmental accountability by helping to develop a free press, institutional guarantees of minority rights, and fundamental political freedoms (e.g., expression, assembly, petition, and competent and honest government).

Tasks associated with the second "Civil Society" component of the Legitimacy "War" include (1) developing societal mechanisms to protect the political and human rights of minorities and political opposition; (2) promoting reconciliation among former adversaries; and (3) fostering the development of civic attitudes and values supportive of the rule of law, peaceful resolution of disputes, toleration of minorities and political opponents, and working together to reform or create and sustain viable national social, economic, and political institutions that are honest and efficient.

### The Shooting "War"

The Shooting "War" or Paramilitary "War" and the "Wars" to Physically Isolate Belligerents from Sources of Support may perhaps continue, but would be increasingly directed at "Establishing Order and Promoting the Rule of Law" and at "Protecting and Sustaining Life, and Relieving Suffering." Tasks associated with the first "Establishing Order" function would include (1) overseeing the process of separating belligerent armed groups, confining them to designated areas, and disarming and demobilizing ex-combatants and lawless elements; (2) establishing and conducting a reintegration program for ex-combatants; (3) training, mentoring, and monitoring the police force, constabulary, judicial system, and prisons; and (4) addressing transnational criminal activity.

Tasks related to the second "Protection of Life" functions include (1) combining efforts with indigenous forces and with the humanitarian relief community to provide protection for and satisfy the basic security and physical needs of the general population, refugees, and internally displaced persons; (2) facilitating the resettlement of refugees and displaced persons; (3) organizing and overseeing a mine removal campaign; and (4) assisting in the expeditious transition of the responsibility for essential social functions and for eventual autonomous governance to appropriate civilian organizations.

### Staying the Course

The "War" to Stay the Course involves all the various elements, but is primarily directed at "Assisting in the Regeneration of Economic Activity." Basic tasks in this long-term situation include (1) assisting in the repair of infrastructure; (2) generating meaningful jobs; (3) providing financial and technical assistance necessary to regenerate and expand the domestic economy; and (4) helping to get in place appropriate reforms, models, strategies, and relationships for economic growth and economic justice.

### Information and Intelligence "Wars"

The Information and Intelligence "Wars" against Subversion involve "Shaping Political Consent and Support to Negotiate and Implement a Durable Peace." That also involves "Informing and Supporting Broad Efforts to Help Build Trust and De-escalate Tensions." Tasks associated with the "Shaping Consent" element include (1) mobilizing and applying international diplomatic, informational, economic, and military instruments in support of a negotiated, mutually acceptable, and sustainable peace accord; and (2) orchestrating the application of "offensive" multilateral force and diplomacy to ensure compliance with the peace accord and to help isolate possible "spoilers."

Overlapping tasks associated with the "Informing and Supporting Broad Efforts" include (1) helping build trust and de-escalating tensions between peoples and between peoples and their governing bodies; and (2) informing and supporting broad political, economic, social, informational, public diplomacy, and security efforts designed to diminish and eliminate root causes of instability and violence.

### Unity of Effort

The "War" for Unity of Effort continues. The legal, bureaucratic, and cultural obstacles to unity and strategic clarity must be overcome. The sooner, the better. What may have begun as a problem of unity of command, control, and communications must evolve to a matter of cooperation, coordination, and consensus among and between the disparate array of actors involved in fostering a durable peace.

### Final Statement

There is very little glamour or excitement in much of the work outlined above, but it does have the potential for directing progress toward a relatively less chaotic and more peaceful world.[33]

## IMPLICATIONS: THE MAIN CHALLENGE, THREAT, AND TASK

Over the past several years, it seems that many decision makers and policy makers have been constantly surprised at the chaos and violence emerging out of deeply divided societies. They have also been confused and unable to decide what to do or how to do it beyond the usual "crisis management" and "spin control.'' Rwanda and Burundi provide good examples. Warning signals regarding the potential for major violence between Hutus and Tutsi between and within those two countries have been relatively consistent since the two countries gained their independence in 1962. Rwanda exploded in 1963. Massacres took place in Burundi in 1965, 1966, and 1969. In 1972 and 1973, over 100,000 Hutu reportedly were killed. In 1988, about 20,000 more Hutu were considered victims of genocide. A new wave of violence erupted again in 1993 and 1994—reportedly leaving more than 500,000 dead. Once again, officials expressed surprise and debated what—if anything—could or should be done.[34]

This kind of crisis management approach to contemporary conflict reminds one of Alice's conversation with the Cheshire Cat:

"Would you tell me, please, which way I ought to walk from here?" "That depends a good deal on where you want to get to," said the Cat. "I don't much care where," said Alice. "Then it doesn't matter which way you walk," said the Cat. "—so long as I get *somewhere*," Alice added as an explanation. "Oh, you're sure to do that," said the Cat, "if you only walk long enough!"[35]

## The Challenge

The challenge, then, is to come to terms with the fact that contemporary security—at whatever level—is at its base a "governance" issue. In this connection, it is postulated that legitimacy rather than military power constitutes the central strategic problem that is the hub of all power and movement on which virtually everything in the international security environment depends. The corollary is to change from a singular military to a multidimensional political-economic-psychological-security paradigm.

## The Threat

The ultimate threat is that unless and until leaders at the highest levels recognize what is happening strategically, reorient thinking and actions appropriately, and are able to educate and lead their domestic publics into the realities of the post–Cold War world, it is only a matter of time before the destabilizing problems associated with illegitimate governance will mortally consume one vitally important political actor or another. By then, it will probably be too late to exert decisive influence on the situation—and political-military chaos and criminal anarchy will continue to spread.

## The Main Task

The main task in the search for security now and for the future is to construct stability and sustainable peace on the foundation of a carefully thought-out, holistic, long-term, phased planning and implementation process that focuses on the "essential elements" derived from the seven dimensions of the SWORD Model. They take into account the major unifying and legitimizing dimensions of contemporary security requirements. Hopefully, they will reinitiate the process of rethinking both problem and response.

## NOTES

1. This research is based on more that 300 interviews conducted by Dr. Max G. Manwaring and Colonel Alfred W. Baker, USA. The individuals interviewed were civilian and military experts directly involved in 69 post–World War II intranational conflicts. The interviews were conducted in the United States, Europe, the Middle East, and Latin America over the period 1984–1992. Since 1992, more than 80 additional interviews were conducted by Manwaring with government ministers, former government ministers, military officers, businessmen, journalists, and former "guerrillas." The resultant paradigm, originally called SSI-1 and SSI-2, is called the SWORD Model. The SWORD Papers, although long out of print, are archived in their entirety by a private research organization, the National Security Archives, in Washington, DC. The first publication of the paradigm dealt specifically with "insurgencies"—in Max G. Manwaring and John T. Fishel, "Insurgency and Counterinsurgency: Towards a New Analytical Approach," *Small Wars and Insurgencies* (Winter 1992), pp. 272–305. That work and the original SWORD effort has been validated in Edwin G. Corr and Stephen Sloan, eds., *Low-Intensity Conflict: Old Threats in a New World* (Boulder, CO: Westview Press, 1992); and John T. Fishel, ed., *The Savage Wars of Peace: Toward a New Paradigm of Peace Operations* (Boulder, CO: Westview Press, 1998). Finally, the SWORD Model has generated and informed a slowly growing literature dealing with contemporary conflict.

The SWORD model is statistically significant at the .001 level, and the adjusted $R^2$ = .900. Six models were tested: the SWORD model, two U.S. Southern Command (USSOUTHCOM) models proposed by General Paul Gorman at different times, a Central Intelligence Agency (CIA) model, and General Sir Robert Thompson's model. General Gorman's USSOUTHCOM correlary tested closest to the SWORD model at $R^2$ = .727. Other models with similar variables include those of General Vo Nguyen Giap ("Factors of Success"), John Norton Moore ("Radical Regime Syndrome"), Barry M. Blechman ("Force Without War"), and Bard E. O'Neill ("Insurgency in the Modern World").

2. Ralph Peters, "Constant Conflict," *Parameters* (Summer 1997), p. 10. See also Ralph Peters, "The Culture of Future Conflict," *Parameters* (Winter 1995–1996), pp. 18–27.

3. Harry G. Summers, Jr., *On Strategy: The Vietnam War in Context* (Carlisle Barracks, PA: Strategic Studies Institute, U.S. Army War College, 1983), p. 1.

4. B. H. Liddell Hart, *Strategy* (New York: Signet, 1967), p. 353.

5. Manwaring and Fishel, "Insurgency and Counterinsurgency."

6. Ibid.

7. Michael Howard, "The Forgotten Dimensions of Strategy," in *The Causes of War* (London: Temple-Smith, 1981), p. 109.

8. See SWORD Papers; and Manwaring and Fishel, "Insurgency and Counterinsurgency."

9. Guillermo M. Ungo, "The People's Struggle," *Foreign Policy* (Fall 1983), pp. 51–63; and author interviews.

10. Jose Napoleon Duarte, *Duarte: My Story* (New York: G. P. Putnam's Sons, 1986), p. 279; and author interviews.

11. A classic example may be found in Jeffrey Race, *War Comes to Long An: Revolutionary Conflict in a Vietnamese Province* (Berkeley: University of California Press, 1973).

12. This and subsequent assertions made in this chapter are consensus statements based on interviews with senior officials. In this particular case, the author is indebted to General Carlo Alfiero for his guiding remarks. However, the intent is to allow anonymity for those who wish to remain anonymous. Thus, in subsequent notes of this type, these assertions are cited as author interviews.

13. General Vo Nguyen Giap, "The Factors of Success," in *People's War, People's Army* (New York: Frederick A. Praeger, 1962), pp. 36–37.

14. Author interviews.

15. See as examples, Julian Paget, *Last Post in Aden* (London: Faber and Faber, 1967), p. 159; Frank Kitson, *Low Intensity Operations* (Harrisburg, PA: Stackpole Books, 1971), p. 50; and Frank Kitson, *Warfare as a Whole* (London: Faber and Faber, 1987).

16. Carl von Clausewitz, *On War*, ed. and trans. by Michael Howard and Peter Paret (Princeton, NJ: Princeton University Press, 1976), p. 596.

17. Author interviews.

18. Ibid.

19. Ibid.

20. Ibid.

21. Quoted in Enrico Fenzi, *Armi e bagagli: un diario dalle Brigate Rosse* (Genoa: Costa & Nolan, 1987), p. 76; and author interviews.

22. Donatella della Porta, "Left-wing Terrorism in Italy," in *Terrorism in Context*, Martha Crenshaw, ed. (University Park: Pennsylvania State University Press, 1995), pp. 129–132, 157–159, and author interviews.

23. Giap, "The Factors of Success," pp. 34–37; see also "The Role of Unity in Revolutionary War: An Interview with Juan Chacon," in *Revolution and Intervention in Central America*, Marlene Dixon and Suzanne Jonas, eds. (San Francisco, CA: Synthesis Publications, 1983), pp. 41, 43; Juaquin Villalobos, "El Estado Actual de la Guerra y Sus Perspectivas," *ECA Estudios Centroamericanos* (March 1986), pp. 169–204; and author interviews.

24. Ambassador Robert Komer, *Bureaucracy Does Its Thing: Institutional Constraints on US-GVN Performance in Vietnam* (Santa Monica, CA: Rand Corporation, August 1972), pp. ix, 75–84.

25. Author interviews.

26. Ibid.; and "An Interview with General John R. Galvin, USA (Ret.), Dean of the Fletcher School of Law and Diplomacy, 6 August 1997," in *Toward Responsibility in the New World Disorder*, Max G. Manwaring and John T. Fishel, eds. (London: Frank Cass Publishers, 1998), pp. 1–11.

27. Author interviews.

28. General John R. Galvin, "Uncomfortable Wars: Toward a New Paradigm," *Parameters* (December 1986), pp. 2–8.

29. Clausewitz, *On War*, p. 596.

30. Jean Larteguy, *The Centurions* (New York: E. P. Dutton, 1961), pp. 181–182.

31. This quote attributed to Abimael Guzman, in "El Documento Official de Sendero," in *Los Partidos Politicos en el Peru*, Rogger Mercado U., ed. (Lima: Ediciones Latinamericanos, 1985), p. 110.

32. See as an opening discussion of this approach, David M. Last, "Winning the Savage Wars of Peace: What the Manwaring Paradigm Tells Us," in *The Savage Wars of Peace*, John T. Fishel, ed. (Boulder, CO: Westview Press, 1998), pp. 211–239.

33. The author is indebted to Colonel Michael J. Dziedzic, USAF, of the U.S. National Defense University for his conceptualization of the "essential elements" necessary to generate a just civil society and sustainable peace.

34. For a more detailed account of this situation, see David Callahan, *Unwinnable Wars: American Power and Ethnic Conflict* (New York: Twentieth Century Fund, 1997), pp. 3–6.

35. Lewis Carroll, *Alice in Wonderland and Through the Looking Glass* (New York: Grosset & Dunlap, 1982), pp. 66–67.

# Part II

# The Essential Internal "Defensive" Conditions that Lead to Mandated Peace and Stability with Justice

In this part of the book—with the discussions of the need to establish an appropriate rule of law (Adams), to isolate the belligerents (Joes), and to sustain life and regenerate the economy in a failed or failing state (Dewey)—we are reminded that some form of cosmetic military victory over some form of evil is not enough to establish sustainable peace with justice. That is only the short-term ''defensive'' phase of a peace or stability operation.

In accepting the responsibility for intervening in situations determined to be threats to the stability and well-being of the international community, a power or concert of powers must go beyond declaring victory, going home, and leaving the problems that brought on the intervention in the first place to smolder and reignite at another time. Thus, there is a transition phase and an ''offensive'' phase to conflict that leads to the mandated peace.

B. H. Liddell Hart reminds us that:

> The object of war is to attain a better peace. . . . Hence it is essential to conduct war with constant regard to the peace you desire. . . . If you concentrate exclusively on military victory, with no thought for the after-effect, it is almost certain that the peace will be a bad one, containing the germs of another war.
>
> —*Strategy*

Chapter 3

# The Establishment of Order and the Rule of Law: Legitimacy in the Tradition of Non-Traditional Operations (NTOs)

Thomas K. Adams

## THE PROBLEMATIC BUSINESS OF LEGITIMACY

The first chapter to this volume identifies legitimacy as one of the key elements that define the initial internal conditions of a healthy or failing state. The fundamental problem of legitimacy is that it exists only in context as the product of the norms and values of a specific society. In the conduct of non-traditional operations (NTOs), especially large-scale interventions, what we often find is not legitimacy in any deep sense, just a sort of de jure legitimacy, a sense that we are following our own rules.

International interventions have now been conducted in failed states in Somalia, Haiti, Cambodia, and the former Yugoslavia with uniformly dubious results. The focus of legitimacy in these interventions is on the legality of the intervention and the conduct of intervening forces. This sort of legalist positivism ensures the de jure legitimacy of the intervention. Unfortunately, de jure seldom equals de facto. Legality is not sufficient; what we need is legitimacy.

### Legitimacy

The study of international interventions during the later part of the twentieth century suggests that legitimacy is the critical dimension, determining the success or failure of such interventions.[1] This should not be surprising. Legitimacy is about power, and if there is a fundamental question in political science, it is the question of power and how it is exercised. In turn, power, along with right, is the central concept within the idea of legitimacy. Power (the ability to carry out one's will despite resistance) can be effective, but it is not in itself legitimate.[2] Legitimacy is not an intrinsic product of power or political rule. Instead, it is the sum of the moral or normative aspects of power relationships within a particular culture. The relationships most relevant to the present discussion are those involving states in their exercise of presumed authority. Legitimacy underlies obedience to law and is necessary to the physical establishment of order and stability.

Any discussion of legitimacy is handicapped from the start by the lack of an accepted theory of legitimacy. The most widely accepted is probably the formulation of Max Weber who stated that political orders are not de facto legitimate; expediency or outright coercion may sustain some. Legitimacy arises from voluntary obedience to a leader, a tradition, or a legal code.[3] This idea has become central to modern conceptions of legitimacy—legitimacy proceeds from the subjective beliefs of the ruled. As phrased by Paul Rosen, "this conception of legitimacy as the product of collective belief is a primary working assumption of modern political science."[4]

Legitimacy limits a governing authority's right to coerce its citizens, thereby helping to create faith and long-term support. Because a major function of governance is to enforce cooperative rules and prohibit wrongful self-interested conduct, governance necessarily involves an exercise of coercive authority. In modern theory, it is because groups and individuals fail to abide by agreed-upon rules that governance is needed in the first place. To limit the coercive power and prevent oppression, the principle of consent is invoked. Those governed must have some genuine influence (directly or through representation) in determining the nature and substance of the laws.

The most important aspect of the modern concept of legitimacy is the idea that legitimacy carries with it the strong idea of duty. We have an obligation to obey based on three presumptions—that we have endorsed the rules (consent), that they are for our benefit (obeying the rules), and they are correctly executed (expertise). This duty to obey makes legitimacy extraordinarily desirable to any ruler since social control is far simpler and easier if obedience is voluntary, consensual, and self-enforcing. This also helps identify illegitimate systems as those in which the ruled feel no such obligation. If, for example, the people of a polity have a rooted belief that legitimacy can only be conferred by popular sovereignty expressed through a democratic election, they will accept no other form of rule. The same is equally true if they believe God confers legitimacy on a hereditary leader.

Legitimacy also functions as social shorthand. As social systems become more complex, it is impossible to examine each order or demand for obedience for its validity (legal conformity, etc). Instead, belief in legitimacy engenders trust and loyalty, meaning simply that followers have faith in their leaders' correctness (rectitude) rather than basing their obedience on continual skeptical evaluation.

A lesser form of legitimacy, but still important, is that stemming from expertise, ability, or effectiveness. Individuals, organizations, or institutions may

**Figure 3.1**
**Dimensions of Legitimacy**

| Form of Legitimacy | Criteria of Legitimacy | Form of Non-Legitimate Power |
| --- | --- | --- |
| De facto | Expertise (effectiveness, utility) | Ineffectiveness (inept, unproductive) |
| De jure | Legal (conformity to rules) | Illegitimacy (breach of rules) |
| De facto | Justifiability of rules in terms of shared beliefs | Deficit of legitimacy (absence or violation of shared beliefs) |
| De facto | Historical precedent | Violates historic precedents |
| De facto | Consent (expressed/demonstrated consent) | Deligitimation (withdrawal of consent) |

*Source*: David Beetham, *The Legitimation of Power* (Atlantic Highlands, NJ: Humanities Press International, 1991), p. 20.

be seen as legitimate when they perform a task, role, or function for which they possess particular expertise. Likewise, armed forces, like any other social institution, are an instrumentality—they perform a specialized and exclusive function. They derive legitimacy from the general belief that their function is useful and necessary and requires special expertise. The primary expert legitimacy of the military derives from their ability to provide physical security. But it also derives from their ability to secure objectives generally considered valuable or important—preventing aggression or fighting totalitarianism, for example.

The preceding discussion suggests that legitimacy is not a single quality that systems of power may or may not possess. It is a multidimensional phenomenon that provides moral grounds for compliance or cooperation. David Beetham offers a useful table displaying the dimensions of legitimacy, here edited, revised, and expanded by the present author.

Figure 3.1 illustrates the two forms of legitimacy, de jure and de facto. Of the two, de facto is arguably the more effective and is what is meant by "deep legitimacy." But the de jure form receives the greatest amount of official attention.[5] It should also be noted that, as principles of rule, it is possible for these forms to be in conflict or outright contradiction.

The issue is further compounded by the fact that there are at least four levels of legitimacy to be satisfied and that those levels may have more than one significant actor. As an example, legitimacy issues become very complex in a case like Bosnia-Herzegovina (BH). Here a military alliance, the North Atlantic Treaty Organization (NATO), is acting with the consent of an overseeing body

**Figure 3.2**
**Levels of Legitimacy (effective simultaneously)**

| Level | Example |
| --- | --- |
| National (dispatching nation) | United States |
| International | United Nations /NATO |
| Participating forces | U.S./British/French forces |
| Receivivng entity(ies) | Bosnia-Herzegovina |

(the U.N. Security Council) to monitor a peace accord among two political entities (the BH Federation and the Republika Srpska) composed of three factions (Croat, Muslim, and Serb). Other players including the Organization for Security Cooperation in Europe (OSCE), interested foreign nations, and various non-governmental organizations. Another complication is that organizations such as NATO (a military alliance) maintain that, although they value U.N. consent, they do not require it in order to act. This makes it difficult to identify the United Nations as the definitive legitimating body for such actions. Unfortunately, this kind of complexity is not uncommon. To satisfy all these actors at any level of legitimacy beyond de jure is probably impossible. Fortunately, deep legitimacy does not have high salience for all the actors. The critical ones are the intervention forces and the entities that are actually contending (or cooperating). This is the level where willing cooperation is required, the others are generally satisfied with de jure legitimacy.

Figure 3.2 could obviously be subdivided indefinitely, identifying all the subcomponents of national and international influence and decision making at all levels (press, decision-making elites, international organizations, military members, etc.). But, for present purposes, it is probably permissible to treat them as unitary actors.

*De Jure Legitimacy versus "Deep" Legitimacy.* "Deep" legitimacy may or may not be legal at any level, but it is justifiable according to shared beliefs, effective in execution, and confirmed through actions affirming consent. It involves the willing consent of those upon whom the intervention is practiced. Apathetic acceptance is not sufficient. This is much more difficult but much more important. The problems experienced with the interventions in Somalia, Haiti, and the Balkans do not stem from lack of legalistic rationale/legitimacy. What they lack is the willing compliance and active support of those intervened upon. The two forms of legitimacy most easily produced are legalistic legitimacy and legitimacy through effectiveness. Because of this, they receive great emphasis in planning and execution of interventions. They provide legitimacy in the shallow sense of satisfying some body of rules or in the sense of effective performance. They are also the least important because they are shallow, or fragile, in the sense of being easily lost or shattered.

This issue is encountered in most forms of non-traditional operations, especially large scale rescues (Rwanda and Somalia) or the attempt to restore non-functional states (''collapsed states'') as in Haiti, Bosnia-Herzegovina, and Cambodia. The formula for international intervention in these situations has been cynically described as ''hold an election and leave.'' Indeed the professed world-wide faith in electoral democracy does tend to make it seem obvious that if a government is elected (i.e., a product of consensus), it will have automatic legitimacy. However, elections, especially where there is no tradition of free and open elections, do not necessarily equate to consensus. Furthermore, this misconceives the nature of legitimacy as wholly a positivist legal matter. The basis of legitimacy is not in electoral majorities, nor is it guaranteed by some percentage result in favor of a decision. Legitimacy is a matter of general acceptance and support for particular institutions and the absence of explicit, successful resistance to these institutions. ''It has to be measured against the existence of a belief in a common political culture and that government will function in accord with this culture.''[6]

## Legitimacy of States

> The State is the coldest of all cold monsters. It tells cold lies, too, and a lie
> creeps out of its mouth when it says, ''I, the state, am the people.''
> —Friedrich Nietzsche, *Thus Spake Zarathustra*

As implied in the previous section, the state is the modern locus of authority and legitimacy, even if that legitimacy originally springs from popular sovereignty and the consent of the governed. As Nietzsche suggests, the state's claim to legitimacy is the claim that it is the collective embodiment of its people. For this reason, the question of legitimacy has become bound up in the idea of statism, by which we mean the vesting of power in a state.

Thomas Hobbes gave rise to the liberal democratic state with his idea of the social contract: humans create a metaphorical contract in which they subjugate themselves to a ruler in return for peace, protection, and a share of ''commodious living.'' Receiving these benefits, collective self-interest makes it our duty, our obligation, to obey legitimate rule. Hobbes, and later John Locke, like those who have followed them, argued that the state is necessary to secure social order. Without it, the society would degenerate into a condition of perpetual conflict and insecurity. This is the standard liberal justification for the state—without the restrictions of government and law, we would give vent to our basest impulses; without restraint there would be no society. In Weber, the legitimate state employs its internal power of coercion and violence only in exceptional circumstances, normal politics being carried out in a much less repressive manner.[7] It is only as the state loses legitimacy that those in power must resort to progressively more repressive means to retain power.

For most modern societies, the state is necessary to the health and well-being of its citizens. Complex societies cannot function without it. This makes the question of state collapse very important indeed.

### The Roots of Military Legitimacy

Closely related to state legitimacy is that of the military, the state's sole authorized agent of deadly violence. Because states are the highest level of sovereignty, they cannot depend on some higher authority to come to their defense, nor can they appeal to higher authority to legitimate and enforce their internal authority. If the state and obedience to its dictates were all matters of universal consensus, this would be of little importance. But because they are not, coercion in the form of military forces and their lineal descendents, police forces, is employed to enforce state decisions.

Just as the individual is entitled to defend himself or herself, so is the collective entity that we refer to as the state, and military legitimacy arises from its role as the defender of the state. As agents of states, military forces have two essential functions—external defense and the maintenance of internal order. American soldiers, for example, take an oath to defend the country ''against all enemies, foreign and domestic.'' Stable states with little internal dissension and large, efficient police forces tend to ignore the military internal order function or view it as an aberration. But conditions of state failure reduce police forces to ineffectiveness unless, as in Bosnia, they become military organizations. When the state must defend itself against internal threats, another of the conundrums of legitimacy arises. In modern theory, internal threats only arise because the state has lost some measure of legitimacy and, in principle, ought to alter its internal arrangements to restore that rather than simply forcing compliance.[8] For example, the ethnic minority Tamil rebels in Sri Lanka claim that, although they live in a functioning democracy, the majority population systematically persecutes them. However, as in the Tamil case, such threats often arise from marginal elements, and because the disputed arrangements themselves often benefit from multiple forms of legitimacy, they are often difficult or impossible to change. The remaining response is coercion directed against the dissenting elements. This, in turn, leads some to claim that such coercion is ipso facto illegitimate.

This underlines the fact that military legitimacy is a social and psychological phenomenon more than a legal one. Gwyn Harries-Jenkins and Jacques van Doorn suggest that the intra-societal legitimacy of armed forces is initially maintained through an emotionally determined public loyalty which arises from a combination of public opinion and military self-image that creates a special relationship.[9] Although the state claims to be the embodiment of its people, for many of its citizens, it is the military that is the collective embodiment of the nation. The practical reason for this is that the military is usually quite large relative to the number of legislators, judges, or even police officers—it is the only governmental institution with direct, immediate participation by a large number of members of the society. This also gives it a special connection with the values of mass society. The military is thus perceived as legitimate, either for its own sake or as an expression of shared values: security, self-reliance, and, most importantly, the need to maintain order and stability.

When the armed forces are used to maintain internal order and stability, their legitimacy in so doing is derived from the principle of self-defense and their legal position as an authorized arm of the state. When the rules and the methods of enforcement are based on shared values and traditions, this builds consent, the most valuable form of legitimacy. On the other hand, a force that employs draconian methods in enforcing internal order, even to secure reasonable and popular goals, can lose legitimacy. Unfortunately, societies are seldom unitary, and there are often those who do not agree with or support the legal order. For these elements, the law is not always seen as a cohesive force that reflects a value consensus. It can also be seen as an instrument that maintains and confirms the exploitation or alienation of some part of society. Likewise, the military that enforces that law can be viewed as a legitimate force promoting social cohesion or as an illegitimate force perpetuating exploitation and injustice.

Legitimacy in military operations is always a dicey business since, as discussed, the entire notion of legitimacy revolves around the ideal of willing compliance. The problematic part is that "legitimacy" means that those who accord legitimacy to some authority will, at least within limits, abide by the dictates of that authority. The core concept of military operations, however, is that of compulsion, not compliance. In most military operations, the object of those operations does not accord legitimacy to the opposing military force. If they did, there would be no need for the use of military force.

## LEGITIMACY OF NON-TRADITIONAL MILITARY OPERATIONS

Unlike conventional military operations, where force or the threat of force is the decisive factor, legitimacy is the decisive element in many forms of nontraditional operation (NTO). Traditional military methods seek victory through combat, and the opinions of the opposing force are largely immaterial. On the other hand, the forms of NTO we are concerned with here seek to create conditions of order and stability in which the affected state can resume control of its own affairs, and the intervening military force can depart. This may enable a failed state to exert its de jure legitimacy for a time but is only a very preliminary step in restoring deep legitimacy. It is not too strong to say that, in the worst cases, the basic object of the intervention should be to restore lost legitimacy on a much deeper level.

The most prevalent forms of international military intervention are complex humanitarian assistance and various forms of peacekeeping or peace enforcement. Unfortunately, these cases are also the most desperate and the most difficult. The use or the threat of military force is a significant component of these operations, ideally as one component of a comprehensive humanitarian and political solution. Most of these missions occur in cases of state collapse or near failure accompanied by humanitarian emergencies or disaster, political unraveling, and armed conflict. There are usually thousands of refugees or displaced persons. In too many instances there are widespread atrocities along ethnic or religious lines. The problem, however, is not the atrocities or the refugees—the problem is societal failure. Any intervention force must include substantial political and diplomatic components to facilitate the return to civil order. But order is not legitimacy.

### The Legitimacy of Intervention

Legitimacy is crucial to any intervention. It is the difference between assistance and an invasion. At the international level there are really only two forms of legitimation for an intervention—invitation by the distressed sovereign and the so-called "international mandate." There is a great desire for de jure legitimacy at this level, however superficial. If there is even the remnant of a government left in an affected nation, it may come under great pressure to request U.N. intervention. Lacking a government, any facsimile will do. In December 1992, the Security Council mandated the U.S. intervention at the request of a Somali diplomat who clearly represented no lawful authority, thereby justifying subsequent actions under Security Council resolutions.[10] The authority for these resolutions is usually Chapter VII, Article 42, of the United Nations Charter (legal authority to use military force to maintain or restore international peace and security). But U.N. "permission" in the form of a mandate is at best an enabling condition. It is not a guarantee of strong legitimacy, even at the international level it purports to represent.

Those inclined to overemphasize the juridical place great stock in these mandates, but de jure seldom equals de facto. Even as an enabler, U.N. mandates can have fairly severe limits. An example is the ill-fated mission of the U.N. Operation in the Congo (ONUC) to halt intra-state fighting in the Congo during July of 1960. The mission had unarguable de jure legitimacy, operating with both Security Council Resolution authorization (UNSCR 143) and an invitation from the Congolese government. In theory this mandate represented the will of the "international community" and certainly the will of the Security Council. Despite this, it was opposed by several nations—notably three Security Council members, the Soviet Union, France, and Britain. None was willing to exercise its veto in this case, but all took active measures to thwart the mission. France, for example, banned the use of its territory by U.N. forces and overflight by U.N. aircraft. Paris also used its influence to see that Brazzaville and the Central

African Republic did the same. Britain and the colonial government of Rhodesia cooperated to provide sanctuary for the rebels and slowed the transit of U.N. supplies. The Soviet Union supplied the Congo central government with mobility assistance (trucks and airlift), which enabled the resumption of fighting despite the presence of ONUC.[11] In this case, all three were acting on national interest, which had much more salience for them than the legalistic legitimacy conferred by the UNSCR.

## Internal Order and Stability

In order to proceed with state restoration, the first necessary condition is public order. The restoration of internal order and stability is a profoundly political process, sometimes deeply affected by the intervention force, despite the extreme reluctance of those intervention forces to recognize their role in it. The idea that a substantial military force can occupy portions of a country in anarchy without becoming part of the local political situation is unsupportable. Even the most minimalist ''intervention undertaken for purely humanitarian reasons leads inevitably to two quintessentially political tasks: guaranteeing the borders of countries under challenge, and constructing an apparatus of government in places where it is absent.''[12] Nevertheless, the mandates drafted for international military interventions generally avoid issues of internal order and never engage them on any substantive level. For example, despite obvious anarchy in Somalia, the U.S.-led United Task Force provided for no such activities by the American-led task force. Although it was immersed in Somali politics from the outset of the operation, UNITAF carefully disassociated itself from difficult political decisions, leaving them for the United Nations follow-on force.[13] Nor is the United Nations more eager for such involvement. In 1993, the United Nations disgraced itself when that body rejected the pleas of its commander in Rwanda and refused to allow its peacekeeping troops to intervene in the genocide occurring there.

Even at the level of de jure legitimacy, military elements involved in peace operations are truly the victims of a dilemma in attempting to exert control over territory or populations or to deal with armed resistance beyond immediate self-defense. As Michael Hoffman points out, military interventions have only two sources of de jure legitimacy for their activities on the scene following the actual intervention—the law of war and the law of peace, neither of which applies. Further, the law of internal armed conflict applies only to warring factions within a state, not to foreign military forces.

Operation Restore Hope and the follow-on U.N. operation were bedeviled by the absence of a legal framework for action. Captured Somalis could not be held under the law of war and there was no authority to hold them under the law of peace. Civilian communities were not regulated under the law of war, but there was no authority to intervene in any aspects of civilian life under the law of peace. Crimes of rape, murder and pillage went unpunished in Somalia because there was neither an effective police force nor a functional judiciary in the country—and the military commander lacked the legal authority to intervene in civil matters.[14]

If operations in Bosnia and Somalia are any guide, the peace force commander has:

1. No power to detain or try members of opposing forces, other individuals that pose a security risk to the nation or the intervention force, or even common criminals.
2. No authority to regulate any aspect of civil life for the good of the local population.
3. No status as a privileged combatant to protect members of the intervention force that may be captured or wounded.[15]

## Too Much Legitimacy

Local political involvement, while inevitable, is not an unalloyed good thing. As described by Lieutenant Colonel Murray Swan, the Canadian contingent commander, the Cyprus case offers an example of too much legitimacy accorded an international force at the expense of the local government. Under its mandate the U.N. Force in Cyprus (UNFICYP) was to be an impartial body, deriving its legitimacy solely from its U.N. mandate (legal legitimacy) and taking no role whatsoever in determining or even influencing political solutions to Greek-Turkish conflicts on the island. Because of the fractious relations between the two communities on the island, UNFICYP soon found itself defusing military issues and then, because of its effectiveness in that arena (effectiveness yields legitimacy), dragged into local politics as a referee by the parties. Meanwhile, local politicians found the U.N. mission a convenient foil that allowed them to take credit for any successes, while shifting blame for failures to the United Nations. As time passed, the perceptions of both the public and the political leadership on the island "actually transferred a large part of the responsibility for resolution of both security and political issues" from local authorities to the United Nations.[16] This, in turn, created a need to prolong the U.N. presence on the disputed island and help the inhabitants avoid hard solutions that might have ended the decades-long conflict. Note also that local politicians were a major force in this development, as they sought to use the United Nations to their particular advantage.

The legitimacy gained by adherence to objectives agreed to by the international community may result in legitimacy at the international level but does little to restore the legitimacy of the failed state. Likewise, the intervening force may gain legitimacy for its presence and its actions by restraint in the use of force, careful selection of the type of forces employed, and by disciplined conduct. This is legitimacy derived from expertise and, like international legitimacy, does nothing in itself to restore civil cooperation with the failed state. The perception of legitimacy by the U.S. public is strengthened if there are obvious national or humanitarian interests at stake. This is legitimacy derived from "rightness" (rectitude) or moral purpose.

In the case of the rural Vietnamese, in the author's experience, much more legitimacy was accorded to rule by influence (rather than direct authority) exercised by elders according to tradition. Elections were seen as the product of foreign influence (therefore bad) and corrupt as well. The rebellious National Liberation Front, understanding this, made it a point to de-emphasize the revolutionary aspects of their program and gain legitimacy by portraying themselves as ethnic defenders fighting to preserve a traditional way of life. This kind of situation (if they even understand it exists) creates enormous problems for a military force (however well intentioned) bent on promoting individualist liberal democracy.

### Is Deep Legitimacy Possible?

The larger lesson that comes of all this is that legitimacy cannot be imposed by democratic elections, clever manipulation, or international fiat. It is a bottom-up process as well as a top-down one, and the exact nature of that process is heavily culturally determined. This raises profound and perhaps intractable questions.

In the case of the Haitian intervention of 1994, the U.S.-led task force took deliberate steps to deal with legitimacy issues. These measures, however, too often ran directly counter to the nature of Haitian society. Dr. Donald Schulz of the Strategic Studies Institute is a student of Haitian politics. He points out that following the 1994 intervention both American and Haitian politicians believed that Haiti's condition was the result of a "predatory state" that had long dominated the nation. For the United States, this meant the existence of an embedded system of behavior and values that crippled the development of a stable democratic polity and prevented economic growth beneficial to the average impoverished Haitian. But Haitian leaders rejected the idea that Haiti's problems were a fundamental part of their political culture. Instead, they believed a small class of corrupt leaders and their paid supporters perpetuated the "predatory state." Their preferred solution was not fundamental democratic reform, but rather the selection of good leaders which, supported by generous international aid, would save the impoverished nation.[17]

This raises obvious questions about the larger, moral legitimacy of interventions. On whose behalf is the intervention conducted? Given the liberal, individualist philosophies of the major intervening powers, it is presumably on behalf of the individuals affected. Does this mean intervening powers should be willing to make a pre-intervention decision as to the moral qualities of the suspect state? This was done in Haiti, but on purely de jure grounds—that an elected president had been illegally disposed.

Aggressive information management on the international level has proven successful in influencing world political opinion and legitimizing U.S. efforts in

NATO. But they cannot produce legitimacy where it is needed, at the grass roots level. In theory, the prudent use of psychological operations (PSYOP) and humanitarian and civic assistance (HCA) programs can assist in developing a sense of legitimacy for the supported government but have been much more successful at legitimizing the intervention force in its tasks. Haiti is a case in point where the U.S. Psychological Operations unit did an excellent job of selling the intervention force, but unfortunately, very little of that transferred to the Haitian government. Similarly, the Joint Psychological Operations Task Force had great success in legitimizing the military effort in northern Iraq through information management among the international media but, not surprisingly, had little success among the Iraqis.

The Uphold Democracy Task Force psychological operations personnel set out to help the restored Aristide government and promote public cooperation. Because the majority of Haitians are illiterate, information dissemination concentrated on loudspeaker teams, pictograph handbills, and radio broadcasts. This was especially important in support, not only of national legitimacy objectives such as reconciliation and the return of democracy, but also of more mundane issues such as relying on local authorities to settle petty grievances, rather than mob justice. The U.S. Army's 4th Psychological Operations Group's "coherent information strategy" attempted to "recast a Haitian police system long known for its brutality and corruption."[18] Police reform was the business of the U.S. Department of Justice and the Haitian ministries, which together organized an Interim Public Security Force (IPSF) while a new National Police Force was being trained. The Aristide government, wise in the ways of Haitian politics, however, placed its emphasis on appointing police and "supervisors" who were politically loyal but often corrupt and incompetent.[19] Working with the Ministry of Information, military information specialists tried to promote acceptance of the new police by the public and attitudes of public service on the part of the IPSF and later the Haitian National Police (HNP).[20] The problem with the campaign was that it could not be divorced from reality. While skillful information dissemination can correct an erroneous perception, the perception was not erroneous. The fact was that most of Haiti's governmental institutions, including the police, really were not worthy of respect, and legitimacy was (and is) largely withheld because most Haitians knew it.

If a state and society are truly dysfunctional, and for this reason have lost deep legitimacy, it is remarkable to believe that a temporary, indeed short-term, international intervention can restore it. The 1994 military intervention never set out to reform Haitian society. But that was what was really needed. However, the fact that it is needed does not make it feasible or even possible. Perhaps William Lind had a bit of the truth when he observed, "It is not possible to go into another country and change its culture to conform with our ideas of human rights, good government, military efficiency, or anything else. Culture is the basis for everything, some cultures work better than others, and all are remarkably impervious to change, especially change promoted by outsiders."[21] The key here, I suggest, lies in the last part of Lind's observation—"especially change promoted by outsiders."

## Back to the Problematic Business of Legitimacy

All of the previously listed interventions have two serious flaws. They were severely time constrained and largely imposed from without. These two flaws are strongly interrelated. If legitimacy is, as this article suggests, the subjective product of the perceptions of the members of some polity, then that is where the change must occur. Clearly, this is not a short-range proposition. However, international and great power interventions in the post-colonialist era have been directed for the most part at the quick-fix, imposed from without, followed by a speedy disengagement. Furthermore, because the desire is for a rapid "solution" to a very serious problem (mass killing, starvation, refugee exodus, etc.), it is extremely difficult to involve the receiving polity in any substantial way. This leads back to the problem of imposed solutions.

Responsible intervention then becomes vastly more complex and possibly more expensive. After the initial "rescue," there is a need for social reform, a reform that may be bitterly resisted by the local leadership, which has often brought about the original catastrophe and sometimes benefited enormously from both the disaster and the subsequent relief efforts (e.g., Somalia). This logic then leads to the uncomfortable position that successful intervention would probably require something like a long-term military occupation. However, it is difficult to point to a successful example of this type of intervention, with the possible exception of the post–World War II occupation of Japan. In this case, a constitution and governmental forms were imposed on the Japanese, who then proceeded to adapt them to their national culture. The problem with this example is that Japanese culture was essentially healthy and had suffered defeat in war, not collapse from within.

What this discussion leaves us with is not very comforting. Responsible intervention may not, in principle, be impossible. But it may require a length and degree of involvement and a commitment to reform that the international community has yet to either approve or support on a large scale. Until that happens, deep legitimacy remains out of reach and the ultimate success of international interventions remains problematic.

## NOTES

1. John T. Fishel, "The Normative Implications of the Savage Wars of Peace," in *Toward Responsibility in the New World Order*, Max G. Manwaring and John T. Fishel, eds. (London: Frank Cass, 1998), pp. 102–113.

2. Max Weber defines power as "the probability that one actor within a social relationship will be in a position to carry out his own will despite resistance, regardless of

the basis on which this probability rests." *Economy and Society*, Guenther Roth and Claus Wiitich, eds. (Berkley: University of California Press, 1968), p. 53.

3. Max Weber, *Law in Economy and Society* (Princeton, NJ: Harvard University Press, 1954), p. 31.

4. Paul Rosen, "Legitimacy, Domination and Ego Displacement," in *Conflict and Control*, Arthur J. Vidich and Ronald M. Glassman, eds. (London: Sage Publications, 1979), p. 76.

5. It is also important to note that legitimacy does not guarantee moral correctness in any universal sense. Prior to the mid-nineteenth century, human slavery was widely considered legitimate with law, tradition, and established practice to support it.

6. Gwyn Harries-Jenkins and Jacques van Doorn, *Introduction, The Military and the Problem of Legitimacy* (Beverly Hills, CA: Sage, 1976), pp. 23–24.

7. Paul Q. Hirst, *Social Evolution and Sociological Categories* (London: Allen & Unwin, 1976), p. 85.

8. Even the existence of large-scale criminal enterprises indicates some loss of legitimacy since they can flourish only where the state is corrupt or grossly inept.

9. Harries-Jenkins and van Doorn, *Introduction, The Military and the Problem of Legitimacy*, p. 4.

10. Walter Clarke and Robert Gosende, "The Political Component: The Missing Vital Element in US Intervention Planning," *Parameters* (Autumn 1996), pp. 35–51, especially p. 49.

11. J. Matthew Vaccaro, "U.N. Peace Operations in the Congo," in *The Savage Wars of Peace*, John T. Fishel, ed. (Boulder, CO: Westview Press, 1998), pp. 73–90, especially p. 77.

12. Michael Mandelbaum, "The Reluctance to Intervene," *Foreign Policy* (Summer 1994), pp. 3–18, especially p. 4.

13. Clarke and Gosende, "The Political Component," pp. 36–37.

14. Michael H. Hoffman, "War, Peace and Interventional Armed Conflict," *Parameters* (Winter 1995–1996), pp. 41–52, especially p. 49.

15. Ibid.

16. Murray J. M. Swan, "Peacekeeping in Cyprus," in Fishel, *The Savage Wars of Peace*, pp. 21–40, especially pp. 26–27.

17. Donald E. Schultz, *Whither Haiti?* (Carlisle Barracks, PA: Strategic Studies Institute, U.S. Army War College, 1996), pp. 2–4, 20.

18. Stephen D. Brown, "Psyop in Operation Uphold Democracy," *Military Review* (September/October 1996), pp. 57–64, especially p. 57.

19. Colonel Mark Boyatt, U.S. Army Special Forces, personal correspondence with the author, January 25, 1997.

20. Brown, "Psyop in Operation Uphold Democracy."

21. William S. Lind, "An Operational Doctrine for Intervention," *Parameters* (Summer 1995), pp. 128–133.

Chapter 4

# Isolating the Belligerents: A Key to Success in the Post-Counterinsurgency Era

## Anthony James Joes

> No major proposal required for war can be worked out in ignorance of the political factors.
>
> —Carl von Clausewitz, *On War*

It is close to a certainty that governments friendly to or of concern to the United States will find themselves challenged by guerrilla insurgency. The ideal choice for U.S. policy makers in such circumstances would be to assist the affected government through economic aid, intelligence, equipment, and transport, rather than by sending ground combat troops. If the need for outside help in the form of ground combat troops is undeniable, U.S. policy makers should encourage friendly or available regional powers to provide them.

What should the United States seek when it intervenes, to whatever degree, in a guerrilla conflict? Clearly, the circumstances of each intervention will vary. In all foreseeable cases, nevertheless, the United States ought not to aim at military victory through killing guerrillas. Such a victory would be a very rare thing indeed. Besides, while lasting military victory over guerrilla insurgents is often impossible, and often unnecessary, its pursuit is always costly financially, politically, and morally.

Instead of victory, the primary U.S. objective in waging or assisting counterinsurgency ought to be to *establish peace*. Peace does not mean that the guerrillas have been wiped out; there are exceedingly few examples of this ever happening. Nor does peace mean that the guerillas have gone to ground; this is a lull, not a peace. *Peace means reconciliation.* Reconciliation occurs through integrating the majority of the guerrillas, or at least the majority of their supporters and sympathizers, into normal political processes that do not, per se, threaten the regime. Reconciliation depends to a vital degree on how the government fights the war. *The time for winning the peace is during the fighting.* In this chapter we will review some experience-based methods for waging counterinsurgency that do not jeopardize the possibility of reconciliation. One may experiment with some of these approaches, mutatis mutandis, to circumstances of "urban guerrilla war." But, in general, professional police operations will continue to be the best antidote to that phenomenon.

## THE BASIC APPROACH

To prevent the insurgents from seizing power and simultaneously lay the groundwork for eventual reconciliation, the basic concept is the progressive isolation of the insurgents. This isolation needs to be both physical and moral. We will consider these aspects separately, although they are closely related.

## PHYSICAL ISOLATION OF THE INSURGENTS

Physical isolation of the insurgents means separating them from the civilian population from which for whatever reasons and by whatever methods they derive recruits, intelligence, and supplies. The counterinsurgency needs to drive the guerrillas away from populated and otherwise desirable areas with the least loss of life and destruction of property. This aim can be accomplished by interrelated means, including (1) clearing and holding territory, as in Malaya; (2) erecting fortified lines, as in South Africa and China; and (3) constructing impassable barriers, as in Algeria.

### Clearing and Holding Operations

Clearing and holding is a classic method for separating guerrillas from civilians.[1] The first objective of this method is to chase the guerrillas out of a specific area, which is not very hard to do. The second objective is to keep them from coming back, something much more difficult. This latter aspect—preventing reinfiltration by the guerrillas of a given district or village—is the essence of clearing and holding.

From the viewpoint of the counterinsurgent forces, during a clear and hold campaign the country consists of three parts: (1) the government's base area(s), usually the population centers along with any previously cleared or undisturbed districts; (2) the areas currently being cleared; and (3) contested areas, those places conceded for the time being to the guerrillas, usually the more remote and lightly populated regions of the country.

Protecting the government's base area will be primarily the responsibility of the police, assisted by army and militia units. In contested areas, the government should hold any large towns, if they can be supplied. Sufficient air power can prevent guerrillas from using a desert as their base. On the other hand, efforts to cordon off an extensive jungle area, especially if it lies on a border, will be a waste of time. But specially trained hunter units can penetrate a guerrilla-inhabited jungle and make life there stimulating.

Clearing a contested area means first to saturate it with troops. This is the easiest part because no well-led guerrilla unit will stand and fight against aggressive regular troops. But after the troops leave the newly cleared area, the guerrillas will return unless the government has previously accomplished two tasks. First, it has to uproot the guerrilla infrastructure. That means identifying and arresting or chasing out of the area active sympathizers or agents who are the eyes and ears of the guerrillas. Routine police methods can accomplish this, given time. Second, and simultaneously, the government needs to build a self-defense force to impede the guerrillas from infiltrating or attacking back into the area after the troops have moved out to clear another place.

Intelligently led guerrillas will attack only in overwhelming strength. Thus the main purpose of the self-defense forces in a village or district is to offer armed resistance to the guerrillas just long enough for a government rescue force to arrive and run the guerrillas off. The self-defense forces need not be very large, nor do they require the most sophisticated weapons. What they do need is to know that, if they call for help, that help will be forthcoming and in a timely fashion.

Workable village self-defense requires the government to maintain ready response forces that are mobile and linked with the self-defense units in the area by reliable communications. For linkage, two-way radios are much safer than telephone lines, and cheaper as well. Ensuring swift response may be difficult. In Vietnam, the Vietcong would attack a self-defended village at night; the village defense unit would send out the alarm; and the truck-borne government troops coming to the rescue would suffer heavy casualties in a carefully prepared ambush. Helicopters might appear to be the answer to this problem. Unfortunately, they are not difficult to hit from the ground, nor are they very effective at night, which of course is the best time for guerrilla actions.

Some villages already cleared may still be under grave threat because they are adjacent to an insecure border or an area currently being cleared. In such places the government might station small numbers of well-trained regulars to shore up the local defense group, as in the little-studied but lesson-laden Marine CAPs program in Vietnam.[2] In actual fire-fights with guerrillas, the training and discipline of regular troops are without exception incomparably more important than their numbers.

In those districts officially declared to be under government control (''cleared''), the government may legitimately impose the most severe sanctions on civilians who persist in actively cooperating with the guerrillas. But in contested areas, where the government is by definition unable to guarantee the physical security of the inhabitants, any civilian cooperation with the insurgents ought to be treated as a normal or at least pardonable activity.

## Blockhouse Lines: South Africa

The great weapon of the guerrilla is his mobility. Hence British forces in the South African (Boer) War eventually concentrated on depriving him of that mobility. This was the origin of the blockhouse lines.

In the beginning, the British erected blockhouses primarily to protect railroad lines. The construction of these small-scale forts began in January 1901. By then, the Boers had very few field guns with which to attack the blockhouses. Most of the blockhouses were constructed of two iron cylinders, one inside the other, with the space between filled with earth. Each cost about £16.[3] Telephone lines connected each blockhouse, surrounded by barbed wire, to its neighbors. Trip-wires festooned with tin cans partly filled with pebbles completed their outward defense. By May 1902, 50,000 white troops and 16,000 native Africans manned 8,000 blockhouses stretching over 3,700 miles. At first the blockhouses formed a cordon to keep the enemy out; later they became an offensive weapon to hem the enemy in. Armored trains patrolled tracks protected by these blockhouses. Lord Kitchener's massive cavalry drives often went from blockhouse line to blockhouse line, or from a blockhouse line to a railroad patrolled by several armored trains.

## Blockhouse Lines: Chiang Kai-shek

In his Fifth Encirclement Campaign against the Communists (October 1933–October 1934), Chiang Kai-shek introduced lines of blockhouses.[4] Rural laborers under supervision of the local elite constructed ultimately thousands of small fortifications, surrounded by trenches and barbed wire, with interconnecting fields of machine gun and artillery fire. Some of the biggest blockhouses were of brick and stone, three stories high, but simpler ones went up in from one to three days. After erecting a line of blockhouses, the troops would advance a few kilometers and, under the protection of the existing blockhouses, erect a new line of them, then advance again. To support all this building the Kuomintang (KMT) constructed hundreds of miles of roads.

The blockhouses choked Communist economic activities. They also allowed quick medical care for wounded KMT soldiers—very good for morale. But above all the blockhouse system deprived the Communists of their greatest advantage, the ability to maneuver. At the same time, the Communist forces could not meet the Nationalists in positional warfare because of the latter's superior weaponry.[5]

So undeniable were the successes of the Fifth Campaign that the CCP leadership decided to abandon its base in Kiangsi province and embark upon the famous Long March. This retreat began in the fall of 1934 and ended with the arrival one year later of the much-battered remnants of the Party in their new home in Shensi Province, in north-central China.

The Red Army had given a brilliant account of itself [on the Long March]. It is doubtful, however, that it could have continued to maintain itself if Generalissimo Chiang Kai-shek had pursued his policy of military annihilation of the Red forces. . . . At the end of 1936 [Chiang] was preparing a new "blockhouse-fortress" campaign around the [CCP] base in Shensi along the lines of the Fifth Campaign in Kiangsi. Had he decided to open this campaign, the Communist forces would almost certainly have been either "exterminated" or forced to begin a new "Long March," probably across Mongolia to Soviet Russia.[6]

## Impassable Barriers: The Morice Line

Morocco, to the west of Algeria, and especially Tunisia, to the northeast, were friendly to the Algerian insurgent FLN, which used the territory of these countries as sanctuaries. These might have played a militarily decisive role in the war. The French Army, however, negated their value by constructing barriers which drastically reduced traffic across the borders. The most famous of these barriers was the Morice Line, completed in 1957. Extending 200 miles along the Tunisian frontier, it consisted of an 8-foot high electrified wire fence, with mine fields on both sides, watchtowers at intervals, and constant patrols. Eventually 80,000 French troops deployed along the Line. Attempts by guerrilla units to break through set off electronic alarms, calling down upon them fire from French artillery as well as fighter planes and helicopters. After several quite costly failures, the FLN units in Tunisia gave up efforts to smash through the Line, and remained outside Algeria until the end of the conflict.

## Civilian Resettlement

Resettlement or relocation of civilians away from disturbed areas can be effective if it is done well. To do it well requires a good deal of money, planning, and skill. If relocation is carried out haphazardly, hastily, or on the cheap, or if civilians are removed to ill-chosen areas, it can alienate the population involved, and the relocation centers can become recruiting grounds for the insurgents. Resettlement, on the whole, worked well in the Malayan Emergency and was successful to a degree in the post-1898 Philippines and in post–World War II Greece. But there are also the unsatisfactory results of resettlement during the Boer War and the Algerian conflict, and in South Vietnam.[7] "Empirically the case against resettlement is overwhelming. . . . [R]esettlement cannot be regarded as a cure but as a symptom—a sign that government control over the people has so evaporated that the destruction of society is contemplated to protect it. . . . Perhaps future counter-revolutionary exponents would be wise to regard Malaya and [its] New Villages as aberrations rather than examples."[8] As a general rule, it seems a better idea to bring security to the peasants than to remove the peasants to a presumably secure area.

## MORAL ISOLATION OF THE INSURGENTS

Equally important to the physical isolation of the insurgents is their moral isolation. This involves two distinct components. The first is maintaining or creating a legitimate government.[9] The second is employing military tactics with the aim of doing the least possible damage to the society and keeping casualties as low as possible. Such tactics are herein called "minimal casualty tactics," or MCTs. Methods for establishing or increasing the legitimacy of the government lie outside the scope of this chapter. In the following section we will therefore concentrate on the tactical component of moral isolation. Once again, circumstances will vary but, clearly, an emphasis on MCTs automatically and irrevocably rules out such contrivances as "body counts."[10]

### Some Effective Minimal Casualty Tactics

The following list of MCTs derives from the well-known experiences of counterinsurgent forces in South Africa, the Philippines (post-1898 and post–World War II), Malaya, Tibet, Afghanistan, and Vietnam, among others.

- Commit sufficient troops to convince everybody—civilians, the insurgents, and the counterinsurgent forces themselves—that the guerrillas cannot win;
- Secure the government's base areas, through clearing and holding operations, constructing various types of obstacles and rooting out the guerrilla infrastructure;
- Provide security for civilians by establishing village militias and possibly U.S. Marine CAP-type programs;
- Close sanctuaries used by the insurgents through diplomatic and/or military means;
- Impede outside aid to the insurgents through diplomatic and/or military means;
- Construct an effective intelligence service, in part by recruiting indigenous personnel as guides, auxiliaries, etc.;
- Build roads to facilitate movement of troops and supplies;
- Control the storage and sale of local food supplies;[11]
- Promise amnesty to all except real criminals (and perhaps hard-core cadres);
- Publicize specific criminal acts committed by specific insurgent leaders;
- Offer huge rewards for insurgent leaders accused of criminal acts;
- Establish resettlement programs for long-time insurgents taking amnesty;
- Pay cash or release prisoners for guns, no questions asked; and,
- Separate insurgent followers from their leaders through well-conceived reforms and ethnic divide-and-conquer tactics.

## The Fundamental MCT: Rectitude

But the most fundamental minimal casualty tactic of all is the practice of rectitude: that is, correct conduct toward civilians and prisoners. One can hardly overestimate the importance of this factor. It is one of the most effective ways not only to ensure good intelligence but also to avoid making recruits for the insurgents. Beyond this, rectitude is essential to that pride in organization and belief in the cause, which are the foundations of good morale and discipline.

Consider these two examples of the importance of rectitude. In 210 B.C., the soldiers of Scipio Africanus, warring in Spain, had brought before him as captive a beautiful maiden. Scipio returned her unharmed to her betrothed, and sent along with her, as a wedding gift, the gold ransom her parents had given him. As a result of this magnanimity, the maiden's entire tribe came over to the Roman side.[12] Over twenty centuries later, Luis Taruc, the principal military commander of the Huks, persistently maintained that the main generative source of the Huk rebellion had been provocations and terrorism by government forces against peaceful civilians.[13]

Or consider the example of the rebellion against the French revolutionary regime that broke out in the Vendée in 1793. This was a purely popular movement in a small province without mountains and unsustained by outside aid. Nevertheless, by October 1794, the regime was deploying 130,000 troops in the Vendée and adjacent districts, compared to 180,000 left for fighting on the eastern frontiers against the Great Powers of Europe. The counterinsurgent campaigns in the Vendée were a series of atrocities comparable to anything in the grim record of the twentieth century. Regime forces committed mass rape followed by the deliberate slaughter of women and children, as well as the butchering of cattle and the burning of villages. The troops ignored political allegiances: any civilian, every civilian, was an enemy, a target. The fury of the regime turned the formerly prosperous and orderly Vendée into a howling waste. More Frenchmen died during the bloody frenzy in the Vendée than on Napoleon's Russian campaign. But these enormities did not go unavenged. In June 1815, renewed revolt in the Vendée forced Napoleon to send a force of 30,000 to repress it. Thus he had at hand but 72,000 soldiers on the climactic day of Waterloo.[14]

The road of military history is littered with the wreckage of counterinsurgent efforts that deprecated or systematically violated rectitude: the French in Napoleonic Spain, the Japanese in China, the Germans in Ukraine and Russia, the Batistianos in Cuba, and the Soviets in Afghanistan, to name a few. But in addition to proper conduct toward the civilian population, successful counterinsurgency also requires rectitude toward the enemy. As evidence for this statement, there is Mao Tse-tung's well-known insistence that prisoners of war be well-treated and then released. There is also the experience of the French Army in the Algerian conflict.

## Abandoning Rectitude: The French Army in Algeria

During their suppression of the Algerian insurgency, the French Army confronted terrorism aimed at the civilian population. To combat this terrorism, elements of the army employed torture of prisoners and suspects. Of course, these methods became known. The use of torture severely damaged the French Army in at least three ways: (1) it undermined morale, especially among younger officers; (2) it provided effective propaganda for those who opposed the Algerian war and/or the French Army; and (3) it set the stage for the rebellion of the army against constitutional authority in 1958, which within a few years had disastrous consequences for the army itself.

Regarding the moral ambiguities of insurgency and counterinsurgency, Raymond Aron once wrote that pacification cannot be imagined without torture, just as a war of liberation cannot be imagined without terror. Whatever the truth of this observation, the use of torture by French forces in the suppression of the Algerian revolution made it much more difficult for those forces to hold onto the victory that they had won on the field of battle.

Terrorism, in the cities and in the villages, was a basic technique of the FLN. Bombs went off in restaurants and near bus stops, with subsequent great injury or death for Europeans and Muslims alike. Muslims who cooperated with the authorities were marked out for especially grisly murder. In this context, many French officers found the usual justification for the forced extraction of information to be very persuasive. "Between two evils, it is necessary to choose the lesser. So that innocent persons should not be put to death or mutilated, the criminals must be punished and put effectively out of harm's way."[15] Or as General Massu phrased it, "the innocent [i.e., future victims of terrorist outrages] deserve more protection than the guilty."[16]

The use of torture, whatever its justification, was forbidden by French military law. General Pierre Billotte declared that "regarding torture, I am categorical: whatever its form and whatever its purpose, it is unacceptable, inadmissible, condemnable; it soils the honor of the army and the country. The ideological character of modern war makes no difference."[17] Many others in the army establishment issued similar statements. And "it would be wrong to infer that torture gangrened the army as an institution." These acts "being inadmissible, they were compartmentalized and secreted–known to all but apprehended by few, a dark cloud floating over the operational landscape."[18] However secret or discreet, "the well-established fact that certain members of the French military service, on their own initiative or on orders from above, methodically tortured FLN sympathizers and agents *contributed little to the unity of the army and much to its anguish* [my emphasis]."[19]

Of course, the fact of torture's practice by the army came to the surface. Its disclosure shocked many of the finest young officers. Inexperienced, idealistic, with a romanticized view of their profession, these young men imagined themselves as latter-day knights defending the ramparts of civilization against a bar-

barous and dishonorable foe. The morale sustained by this self-image began to disintegrate in a confrontation, even at secondhand, with the practice of torture, no matter how discreetly practiced or cleverly justified.

In addition, the revelations of torture played into the hands of those who opposed the whole French effort in Algeria, for whatever reasons, and also into the hands of the enemies of the French Army and of French foreign policy altogether. The torture issue gave all such elements an effective weapon with which to destroy support for the war in Algeria among groups that had not already become disaffected by growing casualty lists or the repellant attitudes of the *colons*.

Thirdly, and most importantly, the revelation of the fact of torture helped propagate within the army in Algeria the belief that institutional mutiny would be preferable to a surrender imposed by the politicians in Paris. The French officer corps in Algeria (and not they alone) opposed the idea of a negotiated peace with the FLN, for many reasons. They knew that they had won on the battlefield. They had become committed to their educational and medical projects among the Muslim peasantry. They could foresee what would happen to the many thousands of Muslims who had cooperated with the French. Above all, the army would not accept a negotiated FLN victory because if the war had been for nothing, then so had been the dishonor the army had acquired from the means employed to discover the terrorists. If the torture was to be more than a mere crime, then it had to have been for something great, it had to have been worth it. Thus the army set out upon the road that eventually led to the 1962 uprising against President de Gaulle[20] and the decimation of the French officer corps.

This tremendous damage that the employment of illegal means inflicted on the French Army appears all the more tragic if one reflects that the army obtained very little more information by these forbidden methods than it could have procured through the ordinary means of bribery, surveillance, and informers.

## REFLECTION

The argument of this chapter has been that the true objective of counterinsurgent operations is to end the insurgency by bringing the preponderance of its supporters to accept a lasting peace, peace through reconciliation. Those responsible for counterinsurgency planning should welcome this prescription, because absolute military destruction of a guerrilla movement is a very rare thing indeed.

The key issue is how the counterinsurgent forces conduct their campaigns. Conservative tactics are a key to reconciliation. Such tactics aim at the separation of the insurgents from the population on whom they depend and from foreign sustenance, while limiting the physical damage and moral offense to the civilian society. Experience shows that such tactics are both possible and productive.

Experience also shows that contrary conduct prolongs the insurgency, makes it much more expensive, and undermines the morale and discipline of the counterinsurgent forces. In democratic societies such as the United States, destructive tactics can also contribute mightily to congressional and public disillusionment with the counterinsurgent effort. Successful counterinsurgency consists of many elements, including luck; but the most effective political weapon in the armory of the counterinsurgents is rectitude. Rectitude is worth many battalions.

## NOTES

1. In this chapter, I follow closely the thinking of Sir Robert Thompson in *Defeating Communist Insurgency: The Lessons of Malaya and Viet Nam* (New York: Praeger, 1966).

2. See two works by F. J. West, Jr., *The Village* (New York: Harper and Row, 1972), and *Small Unit Action in Viet Nam* (Quantico, VA: U.S. Marine Corps, 1967); and Stuart A. Herrington, *Silence Was a Weapon: The Vietnam War in the Villages* (Novato, CA: Presidio, 1982).

3. Thomas Pakenham, *The Boer War* (New York: Avon, 1979), p. 569.

4. Credit for this new tactic should go to the KMT itself, not to visiting German officers, as is sometimes alleged. See William Wei, *Counterrevolution in China: The Nationalists in Jianxi during the Soviet Period* (Ann Arbor: University of Michigan Press, 1985), pp. 108ff.

5. The Japanese also employed lines of blockhouses in China; see also the conflict in the Vendée in the 1790s.

6. Lyman P. Van Slyke, *The Chinese Communist Movement: A Report of the U.S. War Department July 1945* (Stanford, CA: Stanford University Press, 1968), p. 33.

7. In Malaya, those who were resettled were poor and landless to begin with and had little objection to being removed to prepared villages. The record in Vietnam is, of course, complex, but negative on the whole. See Christopher Harmon, "Illustrations of Learning in Counterinsurgency Warfare," *Comparative Strategy*, Vol. 11 (1992).

8. R. Marston, "Resettlement as a Counter-revolutionary Technique," *Royal United Services Institute for Defence Studies*, Vol. 124, No. 4 (1979), p. 49. See also Richard A. Hunt, *Pacification: The American Struggle for Viet Nam's Hearts and Minds* (Boulder, CO: Westview Press, 1995), p. 230, and passim.

9. "Legitimate" here means "coming into and exercising power in accordance with the cultural norms of the society in question." It most certainly does NOT mean the mere mechanistic imposition of U.S.-style competitive elections.

10. "Casualty reports on either side are never accurate, seldom truthful, and in most cases deliberately falsified.... Losses incurred during the battle consist mostly of dead and wounded; after the battle they are usually greater in terms of captured guns and prisoners. While the former are shared more or less evenly by winner and loser, the latter are not. For that reason they are usually found only on one side, or at any rate in significant numbers on one side. That is why guns and prisoners have always counted as the real trophies of victory: they are also its measure, for they are tangible evidence of its scale." Carl von Clausewitz, *On War*, Michael Howard and Peter Paret, eds. and trans. (Princeton, NJ: Princeton University Press, 1976), pp. 232 and 234.

11. "The main and principal point in war is to secure plenty of provisions and to

weaken or destroy the enemy by hunger.'' Vegetius, *Epitoma rei militaris*, iii. This tactic was used to great effect against, for example, the Nien rebels in China, the Aguinaldo forces in the post-1898 Philippines, the Philippine Huks, and the Communists in Malaya. To attack the enemy's food and water supplies is unromantic but essential: even the bravest soldiers will be reduced to helplessness after three days without water. Controlling food requires effective civilian security, and also aggressive hunts for guerrilla food-growing areas and supply dumps.

12. Frontinus, *The Strategems* (Cambridge, MA: Harvard University Press, 1980), p. 191.

13. Luis Taruc, *He Who Rides the Tiger* (New York: Praeger, 1967), p. 144.

14. See Anthony James Joes, ''Insurgency and Genocide: La Vendée,'' *Small Wars and Insurgencies*, Vol. 9, No. 3 (Winter 1998).

15. Kelly, *Lost Soldiers*, p. 202.

16. Ibid., p. 201.

17. Ibid., pp. 200–201.

18. Ibid., p. 204.

19. Ibid., p. 198.

20. Whom the army mutiny of May 1958 had brought back to power; see Anthony James Joes, ''French Algeria: The Victory and Crucifixion of an Army,'' in *From the Barrel of a Gun: Armies and Revolutions* (Washington, DC: Pergamon-Brassey's, 1986), Chapter 7.

Chapter 5

# Sustaining Life, Relieving Suffering, and Regenerating the Economy

## Arthur E. Dewey

### EMERGENCY RELIEF, HUMAN RIGHTS ACCOUNTABILITY, AND ECONOMIC INTERVENTIONS— THE CONTEXT

Emergency relief is a distinctive phase and function in the crisis management spectrum, but it is not free-standing. Its effectiveness is inextricably linked to previously discussed public safety performance, and to isolation of belligerent influence on and off the humanitarian battlefield. Similarly, success in each subsequent lap of what amounts to a crisis management relay is linked to how well, or how poorly, the international humanitarian community runs the emergency relief lap. Emergency humanitarian assistance and accountability for human rights abuses are pivotal responses in what has become the pervasive threat environment of the post–Cold War era—that of the Complex Humanitarian Emergency, or CHE. The new trigger that puts troops in harm's way today is a humanitarian, human rights trigger. And it generally requires a solution to the root causes of human suffering and human rights abuses in order for the troops to leave.

A CHE, in a working practitioner's definition, is: "A major man-made disaster that may be complicated by natural disaster(s) and is often accompanied by a multinational military peace support operation." There are 28 CHEs in the world today. Eighteen involve military peace support operations. This current crisis tally of *twenty-eight* compares to an average of *three* CHEs at any given time during the Cold War (most notably Southeast Asia, Afghanistan, and the Greater Horn of Africa). By this measure the Cold War produced a much safer world, with peace virtually assured in large sections of the globe through nuclear deterrence. Today, few spots on earth are safe from the madness of warlords, crimelords, egomaniacal dictators, or terrorists.

The causes of CHEs are rooted in this madness. During the Cold War, it was fashionable for leaders of African socialist countries to attribute their crises to five politically correct "isms"—*Colonialism; Capitalism; Racism; Imperialism;* and (some added) *Zionism.* It was some time after the end of the Cold War before one of Africa's enlightened new leaders attributed Africa's crises to "bad leadership, and bad governance." That such leadership and governance, whether in Africa, the Balkans, or elsewhere, descends too often to levels of unmitigated evil, accounts for most of the unspeakable suffering and horrific crimes against humanity we have witnessed in our recent times.

There is a well-marked road to these humanitarian tar-pits. The signposts commence with the familiar "Bad Leadership" label, then proceed with haunting predictability to: "Economic Disruptions, Shortages of Essential Goods and Services"; "Civil Unrest, Government Crackdowns, Abuses of Basic (especially minority) Human Rights"; "Massive Human Dislocation, Internally and Externally"; "Acute Suffering from Hunger, Malnutrition, Starvation, Epidemics, and Disease"; and all too often, the ultimate effects of human rights abuses leading to these markers at the end of the road—"Ethnic Cleansing and Genocide." The traffickers on this modern "Street Without Joy" are literally the Four Horsemen of the Apocalypse.

The way the caring, civilized world community confronts evil leadership, and prevents and/or responds to its depredations, sets the stage for how the rest of the tragedy will play itself out. Timeliness, resolve, and effectiveness in this particular emergency humanitarian intervention (or non-intervention) phase is arguably more important to overall success than similar action in any other phase of the crisis life cycle. And what, after all, is "overall success" at the end of these tragedies? It is fundamentally provision for the needs of the emergency victims in ways that preserve their self-reliance and human dignity, and assist them in achieving sustainable versions of peace, security, and prosperity in a stable civil society.

### The Emergency Relief Phase—How to Get It Right

Political and humanitarian leaders may still plead incompetence in getting emergencies right; but they should no longer be able to plead innocence or ignorance. Down the tragic streets of each of our 28 CHEs we have gained enough experience, made enough mistakes, and identified enough lessons to begin to get it right. What does "getting it right" really mean for this vital phase that requires saving lives, relieving suffering, stopping human rights abuses, and restarting economic activity? Getting it right means emergency relief productivity that sets out a stable base for subsequent nation and society building. It means literacy and competence in all of the following:

- Knowing, using, supporting, and funding the internationally mandated *organizations* and *structures* that are accountable for emergency response performance. In brief, it means following the money, assuring the money follows the mandate, and holding designated agencies to their mandated accountabilities.

- Knowing, using, and supporting the established emergency response *systems* that provide most effective results in such lifesaving sectors as water, medical services, and food.

- Applying general *principles* and *best practices* that have proved successful in emergency response operations and rejecting those that have failed.

- In those cases where military troops are required to assist (not replace) civilian relief agencies in the performance of their emergency tasks, to understand how unity of effort is best forged out of organized, disciplined military leadership that is in support, and relatively less organized and disciplined civilian leadership that is in charge.

- Understanding *economic implications* and appropriate responses for victims of (a) complex humanitarian emergencies, where self-reliance and economic opportunity are vital to subsequent rehabilitation and development, and (b) emergency transitions from socialist to market economies.

*Getting the Structure Right.* Post–Cold War emergency experience indicates that humanitarian, human rights, and economic responses will normally be both *multilateral* and *multinational*. "Multilateral" means that a number of specialized international organizations (IOs), especially the United Nations operational agencies, will be involved and will constitute the main emergency response effort. "Multinational" means that rarely can a single country—even the United States—afford the financial and political costs of bearing civilian or military emergency burdens alone. When the United States is referred to as "the single indispensable country," its single indispensability must be gauged first by its competence to engage modern emergencies in concert with at least a few other like-minded states. Second, U.S. indispensability is tested through its behind-the-scenes ability to extract reform, productivity, and financial burden-sharing out of the United Nations emergency response system, and out of the international humanitarian community as a whole. (If "single indispensability" were confined to U.S. *unilateral* response, the world could well find too many of its human tragedies held hostage to U.S. unwillingness to bear the disproportionate material costs, or unilaterally to place its troops in harm's way.)

The Somalia CHE commencing in 1992 led many military and civilian leaders to believe that non-governmental organizations (NGOs) constituted the principal structure, and interface, for civilian humanitarian response. Such NGO prominence prevails where there is no government (U.N. agencies, even emergency operators, tend to intervene only at the invitation of a member host country). But the resulting practice of NGO independence and direct dealings with military forces left the unfortunate impression that such a chaotic, unstructured relief agency response was the norm.

Such "normative behavior" was reinforced in the Kurdish relief effort following the Gulf War. New emergency policy makers in the U.S. State Department and U.S. Agency for International Development were disappointed in U.N. performance. The new team members lacked the literacy and experience of their predecessors concerning how the U.N. system had worked, and how they could continue to make it work. So they tended to fall back on the more familiar U.S. unilateral procedures USAID had used for natural disasters or for development projects. They began to supplant the U.N. emergency framework with what has become, in effect, a new U.S. framework for engagement in man-made disasters. This new framework took the form of USAID Disaster Assistance Response Teams (DART) assessing needs, bypassing mandated IOs, and providing government funding directly to NGOs. Because these NGOs lacked operational accountability (having only a narrow financial accountability to USAID), and because the operationally accountable IOs had been marginalized, USAID was placing itself in the position of an operationally accountable prime contractor disbursing funds to its own universe of NGO subcontractors.

In this post–Gulf War period, the State Department's Refugee Bureau also began to shift much of its emergency funding away from the lead UN agency—the U.N. High Commissioner for Refugees (UNHCR)—to NGOs directly. The European Union's European Commission Humanitarian Office (ECHO), ready to show its own impatience with, and independence from, the U.N. system, quickly followed the U.S. lead and adopted similar funding arrangements.

To be sure, some military leaders that "parachuted" into such NGO-centric environments were both confused and skeptical. The military perception of NGOs as "takers" of military assets—transport, sleeping bags, jerry cans, and blankets—did not seem to be a rational allocation of assets or division of labor. Beyond the deep military-NGO cultural divide, the absence of either an NGO organizing, operating, or accountability framework annoyed and troubled many military persons. But lacking either schooling or experience in the way civil-military partnerships should and could work, most military persons seemed to conclude that, however regrettable, this "cat-herding" chaos was the norm. It soon became politically incorrect, even heretical, to suggest that it did not need to be this way. That a more functional NGO modus operandi had constituted the emergency norm of the 1980s. That this functional norm of the 1980s was characterized by:

- Donor governments giving primacy to IOs as solely accountable for operational success or failure, with NGOs working as their implementing partners;

- Obtaining quality NGO implementers through tripartite accreditation (U.N., host country, NGO) of competent NGOs for a particular emergency;

- "Carrots and sticks" that increased the likelihood that any independent NGO efforts were at least in harmony with the UNHCRs' (or other lead IOs') overall plan of action;

- Strong incentives for most NGOs to operate as UNHCRs' (or other accountable IOs') implementing partners; and,

- Clear understanding that U.S. responsibility consisted in leveraging IO reform and productivity through placing nearly all its funding with IOs, while being able to insist that these IOs implement the bulk of their programs through tested, competent NGOs.

The results of this former structure and funding system? Fundamentally, it represented the discovery of a future that worked. The value of that future, and rationale for trying to get back to it, are embodied in four important benefits:

1. NGO "cat-herding" can be largely eliminated. UNHCR can be required to provide direction and a functional operational framework for NGO implementing partners; and because of the funding channels, UNHCR and other IOs have little choice but to heed U.S. behind-the-scenes admonitions and "get-well" plans;
2. Donor states can receive a far better return on their investments through reduction of duplications, gaps, and inefficiencies;
3. Responsible, accountable IOs can be held to their operational and fiscal accountabilities—achieving both greater productivity and reform; and most important;
4. Emergency needs of the victims can be satisfied in a more timely, effective manner.

Even before the 1999 Kosovar refugee chaos in Albania, the structural and funding replacements to the practices of the 1980s began to show serious strains and limitations. The penchant of Western European states for "European-led emergency operations" resulted in replacement, and undercutting, of U.N. structures in Bosnia for several important emergency sectors. The European replacement of choice was the Organization for Security Cooperation in Europe (OSCE). Instead of enlisting and supporting the designated U.N. agency for human rights—the U.N. High Commissioner for Human Rights (UNHCHR)—OSCE was given, and continues to have, a major human rights monitoring role in Bosnia. At election times in Bosnia, the highly effective election administration and monitoring record of the International Organization for Migration (IOM) was ignored, and the inexperienced and less competent OSCE was given the election nod as well. Other structures newly created under the umbrella of the European-favored Office of the High Representative (OHR) in Bosnia further diluted human rights responsibilities, as well as UNHCR's responsibility and accountability for return of refugees and internally displaced persons.

But it was the previously noted funding practices that struck the heaviest blow to emergency response effectiveness in Bosnia. Take refugee/displaced person return as the prime example. This return solution was designated as the international centerpiece for 1998 (and again in 1999, due to disappointing performance in 1998). The security and political impediments to return were exacerbated by the fact that the United States, European Union, and other state donors provided UNHCR only half its financial requirements for 1998 and 1999. Instead of funding the internationally mandated and accountable IO with the minimal resources needed for the centerpiece effort in Bosnia, donor states and coalitions gave the bulk of their funding directly to NGOs. For example, out of ECHO's

130 million ECU emergency budget for 1998 in Bosnia, 80 million ECU went to NGOs, and only 18 ECU million to UNHCR.

During the same period, individual German states (i.e., lander) further complicated UNHCR's efforts by unceremoniously bussing refugees back to Bosnia and dropping them on UNHCR's doorstep. UNHCR not only lacked the funds to cope with these peremptory returns; the U.S.-led Multinational Division North also turned down UNHCR's request for security in the areas where UNHCR needed temporary resettlement space to house these unwanted victims—citing ''inappropriate conditions for return'' as the reason. Through this turn-down, MND-North effectively aggravated the misery of the victims it was in the country to assist, and it further postponed the date of its own exodus from Bosnia.

The dysfunctionality of these structural and funding arrangements was dramatized following the start of NATO bombing of Yugoslavia in March 1999 and the accompanying mass exodus of Kosovar refugees. Hundreds of NGOs were flooding into Albania and trying to help. Criticism was heaped on the High Commissioner for Refugees for failing to provide the organizing and operational framework needed to forge an effective NGO response. A senior U.S. refugee official, on seeing the results of the disorganized NGO monster that U.S. and EU funding practices had created, belatedly reminded the High Commissioner that UNHCR was in charge and was expected to provide the framework in which all these disparate NGOs could operate. With remarkable restraint, the High Commissioner reminded the world that the United States and the rest of the donor community had given UNHCR less than half the resources needed to cope with over a million needy persons inside and outside of Kosovo. She avoided reminding the United States, and other serious U.N. member states, that criticism of the U.N. must start with criticism of those member states that have allowed their own standards of funding, facilitation, and demand for effective U.N. performance to slip to such an abysmal level.

Why did the United States let this happen? Why did the most serious U.N. member state put itself in the position where the U.N. agency it most needed to do the world's emergency work could, in effect, tell the United States to jump in the lake? The answer from the refugee official above was that although the State Department did provide resources to UNHCR, the bulk of State's refugee funding (and all of USAID's) went directly to NGOs because State doubted UNHCR had the staff either to lead or to disburse large amounts of money to the number of NGOs involved. What, then, happened to the enduring truism that serious member states such as the United States can never put UNHCR on autopilot in an acute crisis? That U.S. refugee officials need to provide frequent behind-the-scenes monitoring, facilitating, and advisory services to make the U.N. emergency response system work? That the performance of UNHCR— and most U.N. agencies—is only as good as the standards the United States and a few other serious U.N. members *fund, facilitate*, and *demand*?

The unspoken reason for perpetuating this serious structural and funding defect is that there is no vocal constituency for change or return to the future that worked in the 1980s—not the U.S. Congress or administration, or the European Union; certainly not the NGOs; not even the IOs such as UNHCR that are now getting accustomed to being bypassed, undercut—and let off the accountability hook. It is a conspiracy of silence that must be broken—not least for the voiceless constituency that counts, and suffers, most—the haunting victims of tragedies such as Bosnia and Kosovo and others like them still to come.

*Getting the Emergency Response Systems Right.* Time-tested systems exist for emergency humanitarian response. Similarly effective systems are beginning to evolve for human rights programs in crisis situations. Early success and closure for the emergency relief phase of a CHE, together with a start toward reconciliation, depends to a large extent on emergency managers' understanding of, and respect for, these systems.

For the lifesaving emergency relief phase of a CHE, the U.N. Emergency Relief Coordinator (who is also Undersecretary-General, Office of the Coordinator for Humanitarian Affairs—OCHA) will often designate UNHCR as the lead agency for the international response system. Fundamentally, this means that UNHCR is expected to provide the planning guidance and the operational framework for the constellation of IOs and associated NGOs involved in the emergency. When donor governments and regional organizations in effect give up on the U.N. system and try to "play UNHCR" themselves, the costs and confusion mount and the emergency phase tends to perpetuate itself.

A simple psychology explains this: It is often easy to make a case for U.N. ineffectiveness. As previously noted, when serious member states flag in their material and facilitating support for U.N. agencies, U.N. ineffectiveness is almost always the result. Having established the case for U.N. ineffectiveness, governments and regional organizations can then conclude that they have to do it themselves; they must take charge, and in the process they will get the credit. Conversely, if they fail or perform poorly, they can conveniently pile the blame back on the United Nations. It is a vicious circle. And just at the time when we most need to break out of it—during the daunting Bosnia *cum* Kosovo crisis— we appear to be the most entangled.

Similarly disturbing dysfunctions have been adopted for several of the lifesaving sectors of emergency response, especially *water, medical services*, and *food*. The time-tested response system for *water* is to make UNICEF responsible and accountable for the overall purification and distribution system, using experienced NGOs such as OXFAM-UK as implementing partners. The system that works best for *food* is the UNHCR-World Food Program (WFP) cooperative agreement. Under this agreement, WFP mobilizes cash and in-kind food donations from donor governments and arranges the transportation and wholesale distribution of the food through the host country port of entry and on to retail distribution points where experienced NGOs receive it. These NGOs, such as Catholic Relief Services and CARE, then conduct the food retail distribution to refugee camps and needy communities of locally affected persons. The accepted system for *medical services*, especially immunization and preventive medicine needs of women, children and other vulnerable groups, is for UNICEF to take responsibility and implement these medical programs through such competent NGOs as International Medical Corps or Doctors Without Borders.

For human rights programs in CHEs, the responsible, accountable agency is the newest operational organization in the UN system—the Office of the High Commissioner for Human Rights (UNHCHR)—established just prior to the Rwandan genocide of 1994. Protocols for UNHCHR's performance began to take shape when High Commissioner Ayala Lasso was asked to field a U.N. human rights operation in Rwanda in the summer of 1994. Four major pillars for UNHCHR's work emerged:

• Field human rights monitoring teams to investigate abuses and provide a neighborhood watch.

• Teach and disseminate international human rights law and practice to militia, soldiers, magistrates, bureaucrats, and students at every level.

• Support the work of a U.N. Special Prosecutor by assisting in collection and verification of evidence for crimes against humanity.

• Provide material and professional cooperation with the host country in administration of justice.

Despite the newness of such U.N. human rights operations, and the low cost (about $10 million per year for Rwanda), this U.N. human rights effort was hailed as the most effective international intervention in the wake of the 1994 genocide—more effective than anything produced by the $700 million pledged by donor states for Rwanda's economic rehabilitation and recovery.

As seems the case for nearly everything in the international emergency response architecture, effectiveness of the structure and systems cited above depends upon constructive, behind-the-scenes engagement by serious U.N. member states—especially the United States. But lack of institutional memory, lack of literacy in "U.N. Course 101," and parliamentary/congressional short-sightedness make it all too easy to give up on the United Nations. We substitute the easier wrong of blaming the United Nations for its failures, for the harder right of blaming ourselves. This practice leads U.N. accusers into a trap of their own making. It is the already mentioned trap of substituting their own structures, systems, and even leadership for those already existing in the United Nations— core U.N. components from which they should, and could, be extracting productivity and cost-effectiveness.

For those still convinced that national/regional unilateralism is the answer to unsatisfactory U.N. emergency response, let us conduct a brief roll call:

1. However positive are some of the contributions of the Organization for Security and Cooperation in Europe (OSCE), its substitution in Bosnia for the United Nations as the human rights lead agency has led to diffusion of human rights accountability and delay in building the requisite human rights base for

a civil society. For election monitoring in Bosnia, substitution of OSCE for the experienced, highly qualified International Organization for Migration (IOM) has resulted in disorganized, substandard election administration.

2. Practices in official U.S. emergency response agencies and in ECHO that support nominally, but in effect replace, UNHCR and OCHA as the United Nations' emergency leaders tend to defeat unity of effort and increase the overall costs to national taxpayers. These practices have proved to be major impediments in moving on to sustainable rehabilitation and societal reconstruction in Bosnia. And unfortunately, they are succeeding in cloning the Bosnia experience in Kosovo.

3. "Service Packages" were introduced in Africa's Great Lakes Region crises as national in-kind executive agent responsibilities for key emergency relief sectors such as water, medical services, long-range transport, and air traffic control. Except for acute lifesaving sectors such as water and medicine, substitution of national agencies or military units for U.N. implementers can make sense on a short-term and case-specific basis. But when UNHCR assigned the most vital of all sectors for the 1994 million person exodus to Eastern Zaire—*potable water*—to Germany instead of to UNICEF, casualties of predictable proportions resulted. Tragically, when such national unilateralism fails, nations are predictably at a loss to produce a fix. It took the immediate action of an NGO—the Congressional Hunger Center (CHC)—to get the proven UNICEF/ NGO purification and distribution system back on track and to save tens of thousands of victims of waterborne disease.

4. A particularly instructive example stands out in the human rights area: As the newly created U.N. Human Rights High Commissioner was frantically trying to establish a field program in Rwanda in mid-1994, senior NGO leadership in the United States predicted failure and proposed that NGO human rights monitors be substituted for the United Nations. The U.S. State Department's Human Rights Bureau was even less forthcoming. Policy there was to withhold U.S. funding from UNHCHR until it proved it could do the job. It took an NGO, again the Congressional Hunger Center (CHC), to point out the fallacy of both positions. First, the Rwandan government had invited the UNHCHR; it would certainly not tolerate private groups performing this sensitive function. So the United Nations had to be made to work. Second, experienced CHC staff knew that the United Nations can rarely reform, or perform effectively, if left on its own. Literate, U.N.-savvy government emergency leaders must facilitate U.N. productivity from behind the scenes. In the absence of such official leadership, the private sector CHC got headquarters and field training programs started; helped organize the Kigali office; found excess U.N. vehicles in Kuwait; got the U.S. Air Force to fly them to Kigali so the human rights monitoring teams had transport; arranged with the U.N. peacekeeping element in Rwanda to maintain the UNHCHR vehicles; and in short, did what the United Nations is normally incapable of doing on it own, and what experienced, literate government

emergency managers must be prepared to do in order for the United Nations to work.

## BEST PRACTICES—KEYS TO SUCCESS IN EMERGENCY RESPONSE

Four fundamental considerations stand out as keys to success in emergency management and restarting economic activity. These are:

1. Putting the right person in charge;
2. Using comprehensive political-military planning and execution;
3. Using training, prior to and during, emergency relief response; and
4. Structuring emergency relief operations to facilitate sustainable solutions to victims' needs.

### Putting the Right Person in Charge

It should surprise no one that the right leadership was the single most important determinant for success in both Cold War, and post–Cold War emergency interventions. Correspondingly, when a U.N. member state would insist on seasoned, proven competence to lead these interventions, this insistence often constituted that state's most useful investment in the operation. Several of the finest hours of the United Nations dramatize this point:

1. Australia's Admiral Robert Jackson earned a reputation as one of World War II's premier logisticians. Sir Robert Jackson became humanity's "Great Captain" in the decades that followed. His legend grew through his leadership of major complex humanitarian emergencies—in Lebanon, in Bangladesh, and finally as Special Representative of the U.N. Secretary-General for the Thai-Cambodia border crisis in the early 1980s. As is too often the case, senior U.N. leadership frowned on Sir Robert's aggressive leadership style and resented his long string of successes in the midst of otherwise mediocre U.N. performances. When U.N. Secretariat detractors tried to remove Sir Robert for reasons of his age, the author, on U.S. Government instructions, succeeded in getting the Secretary-General to overturn the detractors' recommendations for three years running. This non-financial U.S. investment in perpetuating the Thai-Cambodia success story had, arguably, the greatest impact in making this emergency relief effort one of the finest hours of the United Nations.

2. Leadership for what is widely regarded as *the* finest hour of the United Nations also came about through a U.S. intervention. By late summer 1984 drought and civil war in the Greater Horn of Africa were creating a complex humanitarian emergency of biblical proportions. Concerned that the international humanitarian community would quickly be overwhelmed, and U.S. taxpayers would be left holding too much of the bag, State Department Refugee Bureau

Director James Purcell called in the author one evening and directed him to go to U.N. headquarters the next day and "fix it." The next morning in New York was spent in enlisting the help of a trusted colleague, and Executive Director of UNICEF, the late Jim Grant. The rest of the package was done in the afternoon with Secretary-General Perez de Cuellar. The result? The creation of the Organization for Emergency Operations in Africa (OEOA), with the world-class team of Bradford Morse and Maurice Strong to lead it. Largely because the United States insisted on the right organization and leadership, OEOA stands to this day as the finest hour of the United Nations.

3. Effective *U.N.* leadership usually depends on effective *U.S.* leadership. During the 1980s, the State Department Refugee Bureau provided that leadership for man-made crises and the USAID Administrator provided it for natural disasters. With personnel changes in the 1990s, U.S. leadership more often needed to be prompted from outside the government. Getting the United States to lead and generate international leadership for Africa's most intense disaster—the precipitous million-person exodus of Rwandan refugees to Eastern Zaire in July 1994—was prompted by an NGO, the Congressional Hunger Center. Neither U.N., nor U.S. leadership seems to generate automatically, or from within. There may well be a new niche for experienced NGOs, providing both the U.S. government and the United Nations with facilitating, advisory services for CHE leadership.

### Comprehensive Civil-Military Planning and Implementation

Comprehensive prior planning can contribute significantly to a better run of the emergency relief lap portion of the CHE civil-military relay. It can assist in identifying and clearing most of the interim hurdles prerequisite to a prudent military exodus from the civil-military relay team. A central consideration for both political and military emergency managers should be use of such a civilian master plan of action—a comprehensive campaign plan.

Narrower military planning is second nature to those in that profession. Wider comprehensive political-military planning appears to be second nature only to a very few. Only recently have military leaders admitted to the limitations and inadequacy of their planning for real-life operations absent the larger political picture. They are beginning to sense that only such master planning can offer the advantages of: (1) utilizing timely political-military deterrence measures that could reduce requirements for last minute, desperation-type military deployments; (2) limiting the acute emergency phase, both in terms of time and human/material cost; (3) facilitating more rapid and orderly progression to the recovery, rehabilitation, civil society, and development phases; and most important for the military planner; (4) providing greater assurance of reaching that point of sustainable security that will permit military forces to leave.

A military appetite for such political-military "big picture" planning was stimulated first in a 1994 U.S. Pacific Command peacekeeping training exercise.

There the author tried to answer the questions of what military forces were supposed to do with, for, and against whom by sketching out a master civilian concept for the overall operation. The author outlined the plan in the familiar five paragraph military operations order format. In 1995 the "civilianized" five paragraph format was further refined in the U.S. Southern Command's *Fuerzas Unidas* and *Fuerzas Aliadas* peacekeeping exercise series with Latin American civilian and military colleagues. Former Foreign Service officer Walter Clarke contributed the valuable Political Annex to the plan. This remarkable constellation of civilian and military planners quickly took ownership of the concept and gave it the name it bears today—the Comprehensive Campaign Plan (CCP). (The CCP was, in effect, the forerunner of the much less inclusive and less functional political-military plan that was mandated for U.S. use in complex contingency operations by Presidential Decision Directive 56 of May 1997.)

The Comprehensive Campaign Plan not only engages military leaders, along with key civilian agency heads, in mission planning and mission analysis; it then derives from mission planning and analysis the potential range of tasks that military units *should be prepared to perform*, as well as those tasks the military *should not* perform. Inappropriate tasks include direct delivery of relief goods and services that are performed far more cost-effectively by the mandated and designated civilian agencies. (Military performance of relief tasks costs on the average ten times as much as it would for the designated civilian agency to do the same thing.) Generic tasks that the military should be prepared to perform include: *security* for relief convoys, for medical and food distribution activities, for human rights teams, and for forensic experts exhuming mass grave sites. Increasingly, military *civil affairs capabilities* for community-based assessments assist UNHCR in managing refugee/displaced person returns. And these assessments are valuable to USAID and other national development agencies in pinpointing infrastructure rehabilitation projects that will facilitate transition out of the emergency and hasten the day when military forces can exit the "humanitarian battlefield." Military *information operations* (public information and psychological operations) can fill an important gap for civilian relief agencies that lack such capabilities. In employing information operations capabilities, either internally to the military or on behalf of civilian participants, it is imperative that the civilian emergency managers in charge exercise political quality controls over the products and methods of dissemination.

Transfer of the comprehensive planning appetite in training to adoption of comprehensive planning and implementation in real operations failed most notably in the crafting of the Dayton Accords for Bosnia. There, comprehensiveness was intentionally shattered with the erection of a high, nearly impenetrable firewall between a strong military component and a weak, almost invisible civilian structure. By the time military planning for real-life operations in Kosovo came around in the Spring of 1999, it was clear that little if anything had been learned from the lack of comprehensive planning for Bosnia. When a senior military officer in the Pentagon was questioned about military task specificity in the military operations plan recently drafted for Kosovo, he immediately shifted to the urgency of getting a workable political-military plan for Kosovo. Absent such a civilian master planning construct, it was impossible for military planners to be very specific about what military force was supposed to do, how it was supposed to do it, and with, for, and against whom it was expected to support some unknown overall mission objectives.

## THE VALUE OF TRAINING PRIOR TO AND DURING THE EMERGENCY RELIEF PHASE

Participatory, interactive workshop training became the foundation of UNHCR emergency effectiveness for the "Refugee Decade" of the 1980s. Beginning in 1986, new UNHCR leadership strengthened emergency management training and created a training culture embedded in staff points of contact in every section, both at headquarters and in the field. The staff owned it; they were empowered by it; and it became the irreversible underpinning for UNHCR's highly professional response to the daunting proliferation of refugee crises in the post–Cold War period. The energy of training could not be contained in UNHCR alone. It quickly spread to UNICEF, then to the U.N. Development Program and to the former U.N. Disaster Response Organization.

In the late 1980s, then U.N. Director of Human Resources, Kofi Annan, was handed the short fuse requirement to train civilians deploying as staff of the U.N. Transition Assistance Group (UNTAG) for Namibia. Equipped with a large training office, but no operational training capability, Annan called on UNHCR's Deputy High Commissioner for help. Two weeks of intensive workshops, facilitated by UNHCR's Philip Sargisson and attended full-time by UNTAG chief Marti Ahtassari, contributed substantially to making the Namibia operation one of the United Nations' finest hours. A culture of training, beginning in UNHCR and rapidly spreading to key agencies and operations elsewhere, also became the United Nations' most important reform initiative for the decade of the 1980s.

UNHCR's leadership team in the mid- to late 1980s used training for four important functions:

- In the conventional sense, to impart and develop skills.

- To improve communication within the organization and build an operational team (organizational development).

- To reduce conflict and reconcile tensions and differences.

- To train with associated IOs and NGOs so as to facilitate UNHCR's *coordinating* role as the usual lead agency in an emergency relief operation. (While associated relief agencies loathe coordination, they tend to welcome training because it empowers them. De facto coordination is easier to accept if done under the guise of participatory, interactive workshop training, conducted regularly during the actual conduct of an emergency.)

A major challenge after the Cold War is creation of a culture of joint, combined, civil-military training in and among all of the principal civilian and military participants in modern CHE operations. Military leaders have long been in the lead in moving toward this comprehensive training culture. But for the U.S. Army, training for today's complex contingency operations has become a "just-in-time" culture. Army training for peacekeeping, in particular, is left to the last minute—just before deployment to an operation such as Bosnia or Kosovo. The problem is that just-in-time training falls far short of giving both officer and enlisted personnel the literacy and competence they need to work with, and adequately support, the complicated constellation of civilian actors involved in today's peace support operations. The army must face up to the fact that peacekeeping comprises much of what it is doing today—and what it is likely to be doing for at least the next quarter century. Such a predictable requirement argues for conducting intensive courses in civil-military operations at every level of the military school system—from basic training to post–senior service schools (capstone). At the Washington level, there is clearly a need for an "inter-agency university" to qualify civilian and military leaders to plan and operate within a comprehensive political-military framework.

## STRUCTURING EMERGENCY RESPONSE TO FACILITATE SUSTAINABLE SOLUTIONS

### For Complex Humanitarian Emergencies

While serving as U.N. Deputy High Commissioner for Refugees, the author discovered how difficult it was to avoid responses at the start of an emergency that contributed to a dependency syndrome for refugees and other assisted populations. The sense of pity felt by U.N. relief agencies and relief NGOs for the victims was understandable. But the dependency resulting from trying to do everything for them—water, food, medical care, and living quarters—often exceeding the levels they were accustomed to, was troubling. Emergency victims tended to lose the energy and industry that enabled them to flee in the first place. Many were dehumanized by dependency. Moving refugees back home, or to other durable solutions, or even to self-reliance economic enterprises in place was often delayed or frozen. Similarly, some NGOs resisted change or solutions that would cost them their jobs by reducing dependency of beneficiaries on them as caregivers.

One of the few cases where UNHCR avoided such dependency is instructive: In 1988 Sudanese troops swooped into a Blue Nile village of evangelical Christians, killing some and forcing hundreds to flee across the border to southwestern Ethiopia. The author happened to be in Addis Ababa at the time and took personal charge in an attempt to start this relief effort on the right path. He listened to the refugees' version of their needs and started by giving them the materials they requested to build their own huts, rather than permitting NGOs to do it for them. Then the refugees asked the author to try to get more land from the Ethiopian government to provide space around each hut for fire protection and planting of kitchen gardens. This was done immediately. After getting the camp expansion, spreading out their own huts, and using the seeds and tools they received for kitchen gardens, the refugees asked for additional land to grow more of their own food, together with cash crops that would enable them to buy the rest of what they needed in local markets. Because these measures were taken in the first few days after the refugees arrived, dependency was avoided and relief costs to the international community were either avoided or sharply reduced. Urgent efforts were made with the Sudanese government to permit their safe return and in a few months they were experiencing the best of all solutions—going home. The author only regrets the scarcity of such emergency success stories during his watch at UNHCR.

This fundamental principle of listening to refugees' wishes and preserving their native industry and independence seemed to have been forgotten by the U.S. policy makers in responding to the mass exodus from Kosovo in the spring of 1999. In an emotional rush to do good, they offered temporary resettlement for 20,000 Kosovar refugees in America. This offer overlooked the fact that most refugees prefer staying close to their homes and their missing loved ones so as to return as soon as possible. And it overlooked the likelihood that those persuaded to settle temporarily in a third country such as the United States are likely to make it permanent.

## For Transition Emergencies, as in the Former Soviet Union

Emergency actions that seem to fall farthest short of facilitating sustainable solutions are post–Cold War responses to so-called *transition emergencies.* Western market economy efforts to restart economic activity in the former Soviet Union are prime examples. To this day, the definitive ''how-to'' book is yet to be written for such transitions from centrally controlled to market economies. Following are some lessons identified (none should use the term ''lesson learned'' anymore) from this painful period commencing in 1991:

1. *Lack of Leadership.* The United States produced giants to secure the peace and implement worldwide recovery after both First and Second World Wars. The roll call includes Woodrow Wilson, Herbert Hoover, Harry Truman, George Marshall, and George Kennan. Where were the leaders we needed even more to try to rebuild a world order after the Cold War? The leaders we did have merely talked about a ''New World Order.'' None of them have been able adequately to plan for it, shape it, or achieve it.

2. *Donor Coordination and Competition.* In late 1991, the United States convened a donors conference in Washington to discuss the former USSR's transition emergency. Instead of rationalizing or harmonizing donor efforts, however, the conference had the effect of irritating European colleagues with the U.S. announcement of a massive emergency airlift (composed largely of

leftover Gulf War rations and medicine). By concentrating much of this airlift on Russia, the U.S. unilateral response overlooked European competitive advantages of also concentrating their relief efforts on their Russian "nearer-abroad." This fact of competition, and the absence of true coordination, left many gaps, caused significant overlaps, and produced some dismay among victims most in need of help.

3. *Absence of a Comprehensive Transition Plan.* The competitive spirit of unilateralism noted above effectively ruled out comprehensive planning by, or among, any of the major donors. Instead, each pursued its narrow interests and did "what was right in his own eyes." Neither Russia, nor any of the other newly independent states, was in a position to transfer their socialist central planning skills into workable comprehensive plans for transition to a whole new economic world. So what was needed most—a comprehensive, realistic economic plan of action—never materialized.

4. *Inadvisably Applying the Western Economic Template.* Western economists, notably Harvard's Jeffrey Sachs, counseled Russia's reformers to strike while the iron was hot and immediately discontinue such socialist practices as central pricing and distribution controls. This lurch to capitalism, absent any safety nets for fixed income and other vulnerable groups, tended to exacerbate and prolong the transition emergency.

5. *Resort to Supply-Driven versus Needs-Driven Emergency Response.* Rather than assessing and responding to highest priority needs, donors—especially the United States—tended to ship what was in greatest abundance, in this case, leftover rations and medicines from the Gulf War. This was a mistake lost in silence; victims in need of *everything* are unlikely to complain when they at least receive *something*.

6. *Cultural, Religious Insensitivity.* While it was widely known that U.S. leftover military rations contained pork, some senior emergency managers noted that Central Asian practice of Islam was not all that rigid and that hungry Muslims would learn to like it. Undoubtedly some Muslims did. But it gave an opening to Islamic extremists in nearby Iran to exploit "U.S. religious insensitivity." (Apparently this lesson was respected more recently in the shipment of "pork-free" U.S. rations to Kosovar Muslims in 1999.)

7. *The Value of End-Use Monitoring.* The flood of relief articles during this transition emergency was understandably tempting to the emerging Mafia groups in several of the Newly Independent States. Noting losses from early European donations in 1991, the first act of the U.S. Emergency Humanitarian Relief Coordinator was to contract with a proven relief articles monitor—CARE—to oversee the full length of the emergency pipeline for U.S. donations. Whereas the Europeans had lost whole trainloads of supplies to the Mafia, CARE's professional monitoring precluded any significant diversions of U.S. supplies. Russian officials, though initially skeptical, came to appreciate monitoring as confirmation that they were facilitating an honest relief effort.

8. *The Value of Training in a Transitional Emergency.* Training's greatest

emergency value was demonstrated most dramatically in the former Soviet Union's most severe economic basket case—Tajikistan. Tajikistan's critical transition emergency was exacerbated by the even more acute emergency of its own civil war. The U.S. Emergency Relief Coordinator was in Tajikistan trying to help in October 1992 when the fighting extended to the heart of Dushanbe and the American Embassy was evacuated. The coordinator's first act on arrival in Western Europe was to contract with the International Organization for Migration (IOM) in Geneva to train Tajik staff to manage the massive needs of their own emergency victims that had flocked into the capital. Despite sporadic shooting, IOM trainers managed to arrive and start work the following week. They developed a cadre of emergency managers to deal with the relief needs of 200,000 displaced persons in the capital; then they trained trainers to train additional Tajik staff to work in the war-ravaged regions of the south and southwest.

Then Tajik officials came to IOM, noted their new capacities to manage the emergency, and suggested expanding this interactive, participatory workshop kind of training to empower Tajik planning and development representatives to build and manage their country. Both IOM and Tajik participants enthusiastically joined in this challenge to use organizational development training as a vehicle for nation building.

The results were heartening. And the costs were minimal—only $100,000 each for the full cycles of emergency response and national development training. Where only millions merit a place on senior USAID officials' screen, this remarkable $200,000 nation-building success long went unnoticed. And it remained even longer unheralded for fear the U.S. Congress would discover how inexpensive it could be in some cases to accomplish USAID's primary mission.

## REFLECTIONS

A lesson from all of this should be that both emergency victims and national taxpayers deserve better performance. If we are satisfied with the way our nation and the international humanitarian community deal with post–Cold War crises, then our standards are too low. Past success stories have revealed to us much of a workable future for crisis response. The key now is to get back to that future through better leadership in that handful of nations that actually shape the way the international community thinks and acts. "Single indispensability" anywhere, but particularly in the United States, must depend substantially on the quality of its leaders' engagement with, and ability to extract, operational and burden-sharing productivity from the international emergency response system.

Where we let our leadership standards slip, there are still some measures for damage control. A treatment for shortsightedness, callousness, and irresolution in geopolitical policy makers could be the requirement, either in legislation or executive decree, for "humanitarian impact statements" for major national decisions they take—or fail to take. It could focus a spotlight on the "people" effects of leadership failures that were as obvious in foresight as in hindsight, including standing by while Germany recognized Croatia in 1991; failure in 1994 of the United States and United Nations to act on hard intelligence of impending genocide in Rwanda, U.S. delay in labeling it genocide when it happened, and four months of merciless killings while the United States dallied in delivering armored personnel carriers to U.N. peacekeepers; and, finally, ignoring the intelligence predictions of accelerated ethnic cleansing in Kosovo associated with bombing Yugoslavia—with no alert or assist to the U.N. High Commissioner for Refugees to prepare for the inevitable mass exodus of Kosovars.

Why not a national "Impact for Humanity" movement to work alongside the highly visible environmental movement? In our current "impact culture," should not "people hugging" be as politically correct as "tree hugging"?

There is another important crutch for identifying both the fact, and the implications, of humanitarian impacts. We came close to realizing this vital capability in the once promising, but now flagging, political-military planning requirements of U.S. Presidential Decision Directive (PDD) 56. Now we must go beyond PDD 56 to the more useful and powerful Comprehensive Campaign Plan (CCP) instrument used so successfully over the last five years in civil-military training for complex contingencies. The CCP reaches beyond U.S. unilateralism to include international organizations that are such important parts of the total civil-military response force. And the CCP goes beyond the Washington Beltway to embrace our own civilian and military operational agencies that have so much to contribute to planning for contingency interventions. Yet all these crutches and tools profit us little unless someone is in charge. The missing dimension in both U.S. government reinvention, and in U.N. reform is someone in charge of, and accountable for, productivity in the inter-agency planning and implementation process.

At the end of the day, it is leadership accountability that counts. Simple contrition when things leaders are responsible for go badly wrong is not enough. Apologies neither cleanse their own hands nor bring back what has been lost. Mea culpas become both too easy and too cheap when used as fallbacks in the event of culpable outcomes all too predictable early on in the decision-making process. There needs to be a new leader accountability code for our times, where being truly presidential or prime ministerial can mean never having to say you're sorry.

# Part III

# Moving from the "Defense" to the Offense

It must be remembered that the achievement of an enforced peace is only the beginning point from which a sustainable peace with justice might be generated. Once law and order are established, belligerents brought under control, and people taken care of, it is time to refocus thinking and resources from the defensive action of peace enforcement to the offensive action necessary to secure a durable peace.

Civil affairs and other military personnel involved in "defensively" controlling the population, providing intelligence for the conflict, and involved in information and public diplomacy efforts directed at generating support for the peace or stability operation must be reoriented and directed toward the mandated peace. This involves a transition from "war" to "peace" and, sooner or later, from military to civilian control.

Thus, we discuss the widening of the parameters of involvement in peace and stability operations and argue that intelligence will become increasingly important to the civilian component of a peace or stability mission (Dolman). Transferring these functions smoothly from military to civilian control and from international to local authorities are essential elements in the evolution of a peace or stability operation. Militarily strong forces unwilling or unable to share their formidable contact skills and sophisticated assets to help facilitate a smooth and positive transition are poorly prepared to win "the savage wars of peace" (Fishel).

Again, declaring victory and going home is not enough. If that should be the decision, however, the intervening powers face the unhappy prospects of having to perform their intervention tasks again and again, and again; staying in a "peace maintenance" or quasi military occupation role, either in place or "over the horizon,'' for protracted periods of time; or simply hoping that the problem ''will stay the hell off CNN.''

Lieutenant General William G. Carter III, USA (Retired), is blunt and frank: ''The only viable exit strategy is a nation-building strategy'' (interview).

It is at this point that the search for a sustainable peace begins in earnest. The defensive neutralization, control, or destruction of an ''enemy'' military capability is no longer of paramount importance. Shifting from the defense to the offense requires substantive changes of thinking and action. In this context, the ''enemy'' now becomes violence and the causes of violence. Power becomes more than the effective maneuver of aircraft, tanks, and troops. Traditional power gives way to predominantly ''soft'' power, and a combined political-economic-psychological-military/police effort that can be subtly, carefully, and surgically brought to bear on the causes and perpetrators of violence. And ''victory''—or success—should now be redefined as the achievement of a durable peace.

A successful ''offensive'' to secure a just peace requires strategic clarity. That clarity, first, requires civil-military agreement and cooperation to achieve the desired end state (Fishel, again). Second, strategic clarity requires a carefully prepared and implemented ''ends, ways, and means'' grand strategy to achieve the desired end state (Herrick). Finally, a successful ''offensive'' to achieve peace with genuine stability and justice requires the nurturing of a legitimate civil society (Maxwell).

Boutros Boutros-Ghali had it right when he said:

> Only sustained, cooperative work to deal with underlying political, economic, social, cultural, and humanitarian problems can place an achieved peace on a durable foundation.
>
> —*An Agenda for Peace*

# Chapter 6

# Military Intelligence and the Problem of Legitimacy: Opening the Model

## Everett C. Dolman

Military intelligence can be defined as timely, accurate information useful in the attainment of military objectives. It is in this chapter inextricably bound with support to military operations (SMO). Nonetheless, the intelligence community (IC) is additionally tasked to collect, analyze, and disseminate information at the request of non-military intelligence consumers, to include a wide range of needs like diplomatic support, narcotics and terrorist activities surveillance, economic information, and technology proliferation. "SMO is, to some extent, a contingent need," aptly demonstrated in the Cold War and post–Cold War eras, "thus, a balance needs to be struck [so that shifting SMO needs are met without running] the risk of leaving many other ongoing policy needs partially or completely unfulfilled."[1]

Still, it is hard to determine which, if any, of the above missions do not have at least tangential impact on military operations. So long as the military or military assets are involved, some impact on operational readiness is manifest. The continued growth of so-called operations other than war (OOTW) "peace-keeping, peacemaking, humanitarian efforts, etc., [that are] putting US personnel into harm's way much as if they were in combat, call for different intelligence priorities overall."[2] This brief chapter will look at some of the emerging dilemmas facing the IC, and suggest a model for action that is based on the growing importance of legitimization now evident in all phases of U.S. military activity abroad.

The challenge for the IC is to satisfy the needs of a demanding and highly varied set of consumers, while maintaining a clear priority on missions of military concern. Significant changes in what constitutes a national security threat, and U.S. responses to them, will determine the shape of the international milieu in the next century as well as define the scope of America's leadership and participation. Until recently, the greatest threat to the United States has been a highly sophisticated, technologically proficient enemy that organized its resources and fought its wars in much the same manner that we do.[3] A similar emphasis on order of battle, supply and mobilization, and strategy and tactics made the jobs of intelligence professionals more focused, if not generally easier. The new threats to the United States, as outlined in the opening chapter of this text, share few if any of those familiar characteristics, and the IC will be hard pressed to accurately assess them. Effective planning, management, and deployment of appropriate intelligence resources will be crucial to the establishment of a new intelligence standard.

To state that international relations have fundamentally changed since 1989 has become fashionably axiomatic. It has been equally stylish to denigrate the intelligence professionals who seemed so completely surprised at the rapid collapse of the Soviet Union and who now appear to be scrambling for new missions. The many years of relative success since 1945 seem forgotten. When the IC is doing its job, no one notices. When it fails, too often solutions are overreactive. The first part of this chapter identifies some of the problems of revising the traditional IC purpose and scope in an era of rapidly changing mission requirements, foremost among them the task of legitimizing operations. The second part suggests a prefatory solution to some of these problems through a separation of classified and open source intelligence production.

The formidable chore in such an endeavor is that the implied question is always a variant of: ''What unforeseen challenges threaten the next century?'' The question is a first-order paradox. Neither I nor anyone else can reliably predict the unforeseen (by definition), but we can identify trends and broad changes that seem likely to impact U.S. foreign policy and military operations for the next several decades. I begin with the rapid transformation of the world from bipolar antagonism to unipolar ambiguity.

## LEGITIMACY IN THE NEW WORLD ORDER

When George Bush declared a ''New World Order'' following the allied victory over Sadaam Hussein in 1991's Gulf War, the profound changes embedded in that statement still resonate. This New Order has generally been perceived as the final triumph of the era of collective security envisioned in the Charter of the United Nations, but its true meaning is subtler, and far more profound, than that standard interpretation.

The collective security approach was established on the principle that no one state can guarantee its sovereignty against a determined set of adversaries. Therefore, by banding together in a massive permanent alliance, participating states hoped to create an unfavorable balance against any and all that might arise to oppose them. This approach was the culmination of years of high politics diplomacy based on the variegated concept of balance of power. In the multipolar Great Powers period (1815–1914) and bipolar Cold War period (1947–1989), such balancing behavior was thought to promote peace through fear of an overwhelming opposition coalition.

In the current period, the United States stands essentially unchallenged by traditional great power rivalry. No state or coalition of states can effectively threaten the sovereignty of the one remaining superpower. In a real and meaningful way, the international system has been transformed. Now, *aggression* is opposed not because it upsets the extant balance of power but because it is *morally wrong*. Aggression itself is the antagonist; it is illegitimate.

Within this framework, military operations are judged first on the *legitimacy* of the contextual application of force and on the *effectiveness* of that force second. Military intelligence must be similarly judged. It must have both a legitimate goal and it must employ legitimate means. The problems that ensue for military intelligence addressed in this chapter applies only to the democratic state in the New World Order. Legitimacy has become the primary motivating factor in decisions to intervene abroad, and to maintain intervention over time. Overriding questions include: Does the state have a *right* to intervene? Does it have an overwhelming *humanitarian* or *economic* interest? Are efforts being made to ensure a *minimum loss* of civilian life?

The constraint does not apply to authoritarian states that base the justification of their governance and legitimacy on perceptions of efficiency. For these states, so long as the social order is maintained and external sovereignty is defended, the public has no basis for complaint. When criticism does occur, it is put down by force. Indeed, the legitimacy of the authoritarian state is enhanced by effective and efficient suppression of its own, as well as enemy, populations. Here, military intelligence resources are often inwardly focused, in support of the reigning government, and are in this use indistinguishable from the police power of the oppressive state. The public does not need to know the basis for government decisions, nor should it desire to know.

To the contrary, the democratic state receives legitimization through public *consensus*. The public not only has a right to know the intention of its government, without its estimable backing, the state is unable to marshal the resources necessary to enact its policies. Efficiency is a factor and can temporarily assuage a fickle public, but in the end government is responsible to the people and must provide justification for its actions. In this environment, intelligence collection is constrained in a manner not shared by its authoritarian foes. Information gathered using cruel, morally corrupt, or domestically illegal means *may not* be acceptable. Secrecy is mistrusted. Openness is therefore vital in the consensus society. Without it, support dwindles, and the state is weakened.[4]

The process can be viewed as having domestic and international components. On the domestic stage, the democratic state must be perceived as having a moral purpose for intervention. War, especially, must be for a just cause.[5] Above all, the democratic state must be able to sustain support for the conflict. When operations are going well, casualties are light or nonexistent, and a suitable enemy body count or BDA (Battle Damage Assessment) can be shown on TV, the public is less capricious. But when returns are mixed, or the war seems to be going badly, then the opposition must be shown to be a direct national threat. The incentive in this situation would seem to be to give the public what it wants. Manufacture good news and shield bad as necessary. The problem is when the news is found out to be false or misleading, the public backlash can be overwhelming. Depending on the seriousness and directness of the threat, a democratic public may be willing to support a failing operation. When the life of the nation is at stake, democracies have been shown capable of accepting tremendous sacrifice. When the threat is difficult to perceive, or the combatants are remote and apparently unrelated to the public interest, very few setbacks are tolerated.

The international challenge is to broaden the perceived number and support of allied nations through multilateral rather than unilateral action. The more states that willingly participate, the more legitimate the action appears, but the more problematic any intelligence decision to share sensitive data. Ideally, in the New World Order, rogue states are to be isolated. A unanimous coalition of morally outraged states is to condemn the announced atrocities and participate in the destruction of the perpetrator's capacity to make violence.[6] In most cases, this means accepting as at least temporary allies previous collaborators and in all probability future friends of the target state as well as non-involved states of dubious character in other regional or issue specific areas. Intelligence shared cannot be assured of staying secret, and so intelligence will not be widely distributed. Coalition states may see this as a refutation of their reliability, but more importantly, may harbor doubts as to what other countries know, when they knew it, and how they plan to use the information. Information released asymmetrically can in this way destabilize the coalition.

Thus, the problem of intelligence in the next century is situational. There is no "one size fits all" solution. The intense and extraordinarily sophisticated intelligence collection and analysis effort that helped end the Cold War in our favor cannot be allowed to atrophy. Should a militarily equal opponent unexpectedly emerge, the United States should not be in the position of having to reinvent the wheel. The Cold War IC must be cut back, to be sure, but a cadre structure capable of maintaining the institutional knowledge and quality training of that extraordinary era should survive. The most effective use of this smaller, professional IC is to support operations in the now seemingly endless progression of small or limited wars that show no sign of abating. Still, the success of the intelligence establishment in these situations is at best equivocal.[7] Where the old IC seems clearly unable to cope effectively is in the new problem areas of OOTW, where the security threat is ambiguous, the antagonists neither good nor evil, and the mission requirements rarely spelled out.[8] The existing IC needs more than a facelift. It needs a new mindset. One way to begin a proper analysis is to assess the capacity of the current process to operate in the new environment.

**Figure 6.1**
**The Intelligence Cycle**

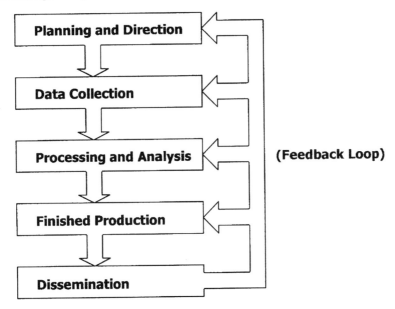

**Planning and Direction**

**Data Collection**

**Processing and Analysis**        **(Feedback Loop)**

**Finished Production**

**Dissemination**

## ASSESSING MILITARY INTELLIGENCE OPERATIONS:
## THE INTELLIGENCE CYCLE

The traditional intelligence cycle is composed of five parts, each connected via feedback loop (see Figure 6.1). There are three to five steps in the cycle (depending on the source[9]), and they generally cluster around the following:

The first step of the cycle is *planning and direction*. It is the major input area for policy makers and intelligence consumers (through requests for information or RFIs). Here, targets are identified and prioritized, funds and resources allocated, and timelines for data acquisition and finished intelligence dissemination prepared. The key point for the planning and direction step is the recognition that the United States cannot, and therefore should not, attempt to fully cover and exploit all potential security risk situations everywhere and at all times. To endeavor to do so would be a waste of resources and an unacceptable financial burden. Targets must be selected and prioritized with recognition that excellent coverage of highest concern targets will provide a better intelligence return than mediocre coverage of all targets. This is not to say that regional or issue areas should be abandoned. It simply must be recognized that there inevitably will be intelligence gaps.

The entire intelligence cycle is politicized, to be sure, but perhaps nowhere more noticeably than in this first step. Guidance comes from policy makers in the executive office, oversight and funding are dependent on the wishes of Congress, and mission needs are zealously protected by the military. Not least important is the generation of new requirements stemming from the results of finished intelligence, follow-ups, or new avenues for exploitation. The allocation of scarce intelligence resources based on competing mission needs means this step probably cannot be depoliticized, but it should be clarified.

When the legitimization priorities of broadly varied mission tasks are disaggregated and matriced with the intelligence cycle, we see that total war, limited war, and OOTW have distinct and incompatible priorities (see Figure 6.2). Total war planning requires a narrow focus on victory. Enemies are clear and allies must be suspect. Maximum resources are devoted to intelligence, subject only to the limitation of other complementary military missions. Legitimacy is gained through victory alone; anything that enhances the speed and margin of victory is acceptable, even laudable.

In limited war, focus is extended to include an end game (completion of hostilities and what is to be done after victory). Enemies are clear and allies *should* be trusted. Legitimacy is garnered through policies that limit the loss of life (military and civilian in the home country, at least civilian in the target country). Intelligence resources must compete not only with military missions but domestic, non-military priorities. Note that it is quite possible, even likely, that one side will view the conflict as a total war (of national survival), while its opponent will view the operation as a limited war.[10] In this case, intelligence priorities and legitimization will be different for each side.

In OOTW, the focus is extremely broad. One may not know precisely who the enemies are and may be equally unsure of one's friends. Legitimacy is gained through both respect for loss of life (a negative requirement) and surety that the intervention has a humanitarian purpose (a positive requirement). This is the most difficult arena for intelligence to compete for resources, as the case must first be made that a significant threat may exist before popular support for a search for threats is palatable. Each of the simplified categories of military operations place differing demands on the policy and decision makers, as well as the IC.

The second step in the intelligence cycle is *data collection*. Raw information gathered from high and low technology sources is compiled and categorized. High-tech sources today generally involve ground-, air-, sea-, and space-based assets. They include electronic and communications intelligence (ELINT and COMINT), photographic or digital imagery intelligence (PHOTINT and IMINT), radar or multispectral imaging (RADINT and IMINT, again), and unique signature data from electronic emitters (MASINT). Low-tech intelligence collection is provided by field agents and area specialists (HUMINT), and increasingly from open sources that include newspapers and periodicals, multimedia broadcasts (TV and radio), the Internet, and independent think tanks.

High-tech data collection is desirable in the information age because of the massive amount of information that can be collected and machine processed. An imaging satellite, for example, can take thousands of high-quality photos in

**Figure 6.2**
**Intelligence Matrix for Operations Legitimacy**

## Support to Military Operations

| Intelligence Cycle | Total War | Limited War | OOTW |
|---|---|---|---|
| Planning and Direction | Narrow Focus; Enemies/Allies Differentiated; Max. Damage | Extended Focus; Limit Casualties, Min. Collateral Damage | Broad Focus; Limit Loss of Life and Property; Un-Knowable Enemies |
| Data Collection | Any and All Means Incuding Espionage | High-Tech Low-Tech Mix; Open Source | Limited High-Tech; Max. Open Source; Low-Tech Reliance |
| Processing and Analysis | Wide Area Coverage; BDA, Targeting | Narrow Area Coverage; BDA, Targeting | Global/Specialized Coverage; I&W; Treaty Verification |
| Finished Production | Highly Classified and Compartmented | Highly Compartmented | Minimum Classification and Compartmentation |
| Dissemination | Highly Asymmetric | Selectively Asymmetric | Symmetric |
| **Legitimacy Measurement** | Victory; **Effectiveness** | Minimum Allied Losses; **Efficiency** | Humanitarian Focus; **Morality** |

a single 90-minute orbit and pass the information via data link to ground stations in near real time. ELINT collectors can theoretically log and store every telephone conversation that transits via airwaves and electronically search the database for keywords and tip-offs in real time. The absolute magnitude of the information collected is a boon to the IC, which can automate many of the collection and processing steps. It is not a panacea, however. More information has two inherent problems: (1) the greater the amount of information, the more analyst time needed to assess and interpret the data, even with machine processing (see the data analysis example below), and (2) the greater the amount of information and information potential, the more difficult it can be to act decisively. There is always a fear of making a decision before all the information is in, but in this brave new world, all the information may never come in.

Low-tech data collection is more sporadic, less standardized, and vastly more subjective. Sources can be in grave danger, and the cost of data is correspondingly high. Nonetheless, some information can *only* be obtained from human sources physically located in the target area. The emotional state of a national leader, for example, or one's propensity for arbitrary and violent decisions can still not be determined accurately through automated means. High-tech and low-tech means are both vulnerable to deception, and both have different means to verify accuracy, but low-tech information has a much higher propensity to be accurately assessed with intuition and experience. If high-tech intelligence collection is state of the art, low-tech collection is still the art of intelligence.

Nonetheless, while high-tech data collection and analysis consumes the lion's share of the annual intelligence budget (the CIA, which runs most HUMINT operations, receives only about 10 percent of the $30 billion currently spent), low-tech means cannot be allowed to languish. Numerous arguments in support of the latter can be formulated. One of the more discriminating problems of data collection is a general one, long recognized. The mere act of collecting data, even when using relatively nonobtrusive methods such as space surveillance, changes the phenomenon under study. When individuals know they are being watched, or might be watched, they change their behavior. For example, if the target understands the IC's ability to intercept and exploit wireless phone conversations, the target will likely use a more secure method to transfer information.[11] Indeed, one should assume any information that is intercepted under these conditions to be bogus, an attempt at misdirection. The greater our high-tech capabilities, the more likely the target will use low-tech means to avoid them. In low-tech environments, or against an opponent who eschews high-tech command and communications, HUMINT is not only the best but possibly the only potentially reliable source available.[12]

In total war, all collection means to include active intelligence engagements of the enemy (i.e., sabotage, espionage, double agents, assassinations) are acceptable. In this chapter, passive collection methods are the only ones seriously considered, but the decision not to include active means is based on a limit of space and time, and not meant as a policy recommendation. Once again, victory is the legitimizing agent in total war. In a limited war, great care is taken to restrict human intelligence to passive collection means and eschew the more active use of spies. This limitation on the home country helps to insure legitimacy for the cause—we will use honorable means even if the other side chooses not to. In OOTW, high-tech sources must be limited to protect the innate rights of privacy of individuals. Low-tech means that emphasize open source collection and community contacts are acceptable, so long as attempts are not made to manipulate the target countries or unduly influence their preferences. Still, in any legitimacy war, *covert* high-tech surveillance of foreigners is generally viewed as less invasive and hence more agreeable to a democratic state than *covert* low-tech ones, in light of several highly publicized active intelligence atrocities in third party states.[13] Note, too, the risk factor of human life for HUMINT collection. The legitimacy of the operation is compromised in limited war and OOTW operations if the covert operative is found and publicly paraded.

*Data processing and analysis* is the third step in the intelligence cycle. Here raw data is decrypted or decoded (if needed), sorted, translated, and compiled. It is at this step that the promise and the problems of high-tech data collection are realized. Machine processing of raw data still requires a human analyst to make sense of the mass. In photo interpretation, for example, hundreds of pictures can be generated in an hour from one imaging satellite, but it takes a human analyst several minutes (at least) to scan the image for useful or irregular information, even after the image has been machine processed for the same material. Once an image is identified as significant, it may take an analyst several hours to completely scan and correlate the information with other sources and to verify the intelligence on the image. For each imaging platform in orbit, hundreds of human analysts are necessary to fully exploit its capabilities.

Which brings up a response to an interesting criticism of the IC, exemplified by overhead imaging (and referred to in data collection above). With all its magnificent resources, why can't the IC find a specific individual (such as Saddam Hussein or Slobodan Milosovic) for targeting? If we can read a license plate from space (arguable, but an accepted assumption in order to respond to the question), why can't we find a particular person at a particular time with an imaging satellite (presumably so we could then launch a cruise missile at that location)?

The answer is relatively straightforward. The wider the field of view of the camera, the less detail in the image. The greater the detail, the less the field of view (think in terms of a variable zoom telephoto lens). The greatest detail, of course, comes from air-based platforms that include aircraft and remotely piloted drones (they come physically closest to the target). These are also the most susceptible to enemy action and the most obvious to the target. It is difficult to hide from a satellite that can't be seen, much less shoot it down. In order to get an image resolution high enough to identify individuals and read license plates, the field of view can only be about $10m^2$ or less. In order to point a camera that precisely one has to know what one is looking for.

Here is the problem. Hussein could be anywhere in Baghdad. At less than one-half foot resolution, not quite enough to identify the dictator through facial characteristics, we would need to take over 16,000 pictures (with a field of view of $10m^2$) to blanket the city. By the time analysts have had a chance to scan the pictures, even after machine processing, Hussein will be long gone. Essentially, we have to know where an individual *will be* in order to direct our intelligence asset to look at that point at that precise moment. In other words, we need intelligence to do intelligence. ELINT could possibly pinpoint a location through an intercepted telephone conversation, say, and relay it to imaging satellite controllers in time to get a useful photograph, but that eventuality is based on luck. A reliable HUMINT agent familiar with the dictator's schedule would provide much more time for satellite guidance and targeting preparation.

High-tech imaging assets, then, are much better suited to real time identification of large equipment (airplanes, tanks, ships, industries, and infrastructure) and military units than individual persons. This is especially applicable to the traditional war scenarios against an enemy using equipment and tactics similar to our own. Against guerrilla armies and non-traditional foes, who would be difficult to identify in wide-angle broad search techniques, low-tech HUMINT seems the most cost-effective instrument—if for nothing else than to key our high-tech assets where and when to look.

Thus for total war, wide area coverage is most needed, especially informing the state of preparations for troop and equipment movements and other assaults. Targeting and Battle Damage Assessment (BDA) (for retargeting, if necessary) are the primary needs of the military commander. In limited war, coverage is area dependent, though targeting and BDA are still the most prevalent needs. In OOTW, coverage may need to be global, but primarily for indications and warning (I&W) of new or emerging threats. Higher resolution targeting is also more necessary to the OOTW environment, working in close collaboration with low-tech means.

The conversion of processed and analyzed data into useful formats is the *finished production* step of the intelligence cycle. In this step analysts compile data from multiple sources (called all-source analysis), assess the validity of both the data and the analyst's conclusions, and package the information for specific intelligence consumers. In the intelligence field, sensitive classified information is compartmentalized, which means a consumer must have both the security clearance necessary to view the material and the "need to know," that is, an implicit or explicit requirement for the intelligence product. The problem is that the analysts cannot know what they have a need to know, or what potentially available data is relevant to their problem. The data controllers determine it for them. In a total or limited war scenario this is done to protect sources. In an OOTW scenario it severely constrains analysis.

The available data can be presented to show a dire problem, a moderate problem, or a nonexistent one. Data can be manipulated to avoid giving policy makers bad news. It can be massaged to give a favorable impression of current operations. In all three areas of war, the exposure of fraudulent or manipulated data will lead to a deligitimization of the intelligence process. In OOTW, as will be argued below, the more open the process, the more likely intelligence will be presented in a balanced and fair manner and the greater will be public support for the IC.

The final step in the intelligence cycle is *distribution* of finished intelligence. The primary problem to be addressed here is the symmetry of disbursed information. In total war, the goal of the intelligence agencies is to have the maximum amount of accurate information on the enemy while the enemy maintains a minimum amount of accurate information about you (or a maximum amount of inaccurate information). This is *highly* asymmetric. The enemy will have the same goal, naturally. In such a situation, between equally competent intelligence agencies, we can expect a perverse sort of symmetry to develop as each agency has a modicum of accurate and inaccurate information about its adversary. The intent, and important for perceptions of legitimacy, is to strive for maximum asymmetry even while recognizing in the aggregate it may not occur.

In this situation, information and disinformation in the form of propaganda is highly anticipated. This feeds inaccurate information to, or at a minimum, hides bad information from the public to increase support for the war effort. In total war, no intelligence effort is disallowed unless it is ineffective. Winning creates legitimacy, losing illegitimacy. In limited war, the rationale is similar but not so Machiavellian. Accurate information must be fed to the public because inaccurate information will ultimately be found out and will reduce war support. The gathering of accurate information for us and the denial of accurate information to the enemy will be lauded as a means of limiting friendly casualties or reducing resource expenditures. Active espionage will be tolerated only so long as it can be shown as necessary to save lives, and intelligence sharing can be expected among allies to bolster coalition support. Indeed, some accurate information may be sent to the adversary to show the untenable nature of their position.

In OOTW, asymmetric information causes distrust and limits the effectiveness of operations. Often, there are no clearly identified enemies and no sure enemy state. The intelligence host country may be intervening in areas where hostilities are entirely between third parties. In these situations, the maximum amount of accurate information is desirable, and that information should be as broadly dispersed as possible. Only in this manner can the two sides be coaxed into meaningful negotiations. Victory is not the goal of OOTW. A stable and enduring peace, made so by mutually acceptable terms and conditions, is.

Think of the information symmetry problem in intelligence dissemination as similar to the problem of buying a used car, often depicted as adversarial negotiation. Under what conditions is a buyer more or less likely to come to the table and negotiate with the seller for a mutually advantageous contract? I maintain this is best done when information is readily available to all sides and all information is perceived as accurate. Let me continue the analogy. Assume you are driving by a car lot and see a beautiful Mustang convertible for sale. Having the price and mileage boldly written on the window assists you in deciding whether to stop or not. Thus, *some* information is helpful in prodding first steps at negotiation. Further assume that you stop to look at the car and a salesperson approaches and offers the following account—the car had only one owner and is priced below market value. You may be suspicious of such a tale, but if the salesperson provides you with a Blue Book and title history to back up the claims, you may be very likely to purchase the car at or near the window price.

Naturally, in the above example, maximum profit is gained from providing the other side as little accurate information, even deliberately misleading or false information, while keeping as much accurate information hidden as possible. But in such an instance, the two sides will be very wary of entering into binding negotiations. In total war, maximum gain is the desirable end to negotiations, and so they are not entered into freely but only when one side feels compelled to do so by force. To continue our analogy, assume the purchaser accepted the seller's claims but later found out that the odometer had been turned back. The buyer would not be satisfied with the deal and would attempt to return the vehicle, seek court redress, or in some other way get back at the seller. This is not a stable and enduring, much less mutually satisfactory, outcome.

Unique to the OOTW scenario, then, is the general imperative for widely dispersed, readily available, highly accurate information—but not in all cases. Intelligence sharing in some OOTW arenas is especially problematic—for example, in the case of international crime. Often the agencies receiving information have been infiltrated by the criminal element under investigation or are on the take. In this case, maximum dissemination of accurate intelligence information compounds the law enforcement problem. Still, this is an unusual context-specific problem, and it highlights the complication of using military forces for traditionally policing actions.[14] The more military units find it their function to act as police auxiliaries, the more apt they are to treat intelligence gleaned in all OOTW missions as privileged information. The less forthcoming they are, the more they treat target states as criminals.

## INTELLIGENCE CONTRIBUTIONS IN THE POST-WAR/ POST-OOTW ENVIRONMENT

One of the implicit functions of all limited war and OOTW campaigns in third party states is the establishment of a stable peace. The likelihood of that occurrence is enhanced if the peace is perceived as just, and if the resulting government is both responsive to its people (preferably democratic) and sparing in its use of force. For this beneficial scenario, the IC may have to take on a previously nonexistent role, that of nation builder within its sphere of expertise.

In virtually every case of necessary intervention in the last 30 years, the United States has been faced with a corrupt state that uses its intelligence service as a surveillance and subversion tool against internal enemies. The intelligence assets are wholly integrated into, and indistinguishable from, the police state. It may even seem to the members of the state that this is a normal and legitimate role.

Such a disposition is wholly consistent with the move from external to internal focus that has been ongoing in several military organizations over the past decades, particularly in Latin America and developing states. The change has been associated with the evolving notion of military professionalism, from the classic view described by Samuel Huntington and Morris Janowitz to the modern notion revealed by Alfred Stepan.[15] This dichotomy corresponds fairly neatly to the general theme of offense and defense described in this book. The old professionalism was outward in its focus, concerned solely with the requirements of international conflict. Concern for domestic problems was beyond the purview of the professional officer, who could take no time from preparation for war. Huntington argued that the professional soldier, engaged in issues of external threat only, manifests no interest in domestic politics and would never be a threat to the state. The new professionalism is internally focused. Stepan countered that the emerging military officer was concerned primarily with internal development. In other words, the state, as supplier of the military, must develop at a rate sufficient to meet the perceived materiel requirements of the military. If the civilian governors of the state cannot fulfill their obligations, then military leaders may feel compelled to intervene. In this conception, the offensively oriented military will be less inclined to interfere in domestic politics in normal or nonwar conditions.

Even when a state's military is outwardly focused, an argument can be made that a professional officer has a vested interest in securing for the military the necessary supplies and troops to achieve victory. Nonetheless, a domestically aimed military will use its intelligence sources much differently than an internationally focused one, and here is the entry point for post-OOTW IC intervention. The IC will have, at a minimum, two functions after a working peace has been established.

First, it must help to professionalize and modernize indigenous intelligence operations so that they will serve the state in the monitoring and surveillance of external enemies and non-legitimate domestic political opponents. This is the instillation of classic military professionalism. The members of the indigenous intelligence establishment must understand their roles as external monitors and be prepared to refuse orders that compromise that mission. To make such a change palatable, the U.S. IC will have to share modern intelligence methods and techniques. This openness will be extraordinarily difficult, but is vital to the success of the new state. The indigenous IC must perceive itself as competent if it is to maintain itself separate from domestic political activity. In this manner, whoever is in charge of the government will see the advantage of a proficient IC and will value its contributions. Budget authority will be based on the value of information provided and not on blackmail, treachery, or perceived levels of support for the extant state.

Second, the IC must assist in the transition from international/foreign military peacekeeping to domestic military functionality, and along with it, from international civilian control to domestic civilian control. In the transition period of professionalization above, the U.S. IC will need to provide accurate data to the new government IC, and ideally to legitimate rival political factions. This may include raw data but will certainly include symmetrically released finished intelligence. This will assist in making the transition government and its political opponents feel more secure, hence more likely to let the political system handle ideological conflict and differences of opinion.

The intelligence function does not end when the troops come home. Indeed, good intelligence is as vital in peace as in war. Forewarned is forearmed. The IC needs to assist the new or reformed state in the establishment of a proper intelligence community for its own use, and for its own security. It is wholly naïve to think the target state can do this alone.

## PROBLEMS IN IC STRUCTURE AND A PRELIMINARY SOLUTION

The preceding discussion of the traditional intelligence cycle and its components shows that change in routine operations from a focus on total and limited war to OOTW is necessary. In the model for intelligence needs (refer to Figure 6.2) the problem of symmetry in OOTW stands out and is the basis for the recommendations that follow, but numerous other difficulties are evident. High-tech information is too important for the most precious of national security interests to be compromised. Yet if accurate information is not available, regional trouble spots could ignite into genuine national security threats. Low-tech information, including the human in the loop and the traditional covert operative, are expensive assets and relatively vulnerable because of their access to classified information. Nonetheless, they cannot be disposed of and replaced solely by high-tech collectors for the reasons listed above. The problem simply put is how can we reconstruct the IC to deal with the challenges of the next millenium, which will span the range of total war to OOTW scenarios, within a reasonable and limited budget?

It seems clear that the current IC is well organized and adapted to supporting the type of total warfare envisioned as a constant threat in the post–Cold War environment. Despite a rather poorly anticipated end game, the IC was instrumental in winning the Cold War. The potential damage in total war makes it imprudent to disband the capacity for such support even if the possibility of total war is remote. Where the IC has been arguably less effective is in the limited war and OOTW scenarios, and reviews are certainly mixed. Indeed, the further from total war the scenario, the less appropriate the current IC appears. Rather than try to adapt the existing system to fish-out-of-water applications, and in the process degrade the capabilities of the IC to conduct total warfare support operations effectiveness, it may be time to envision a new, parallel intelligence agency.

This new entity would rely totally on unclassified and non-government open sources. It would make OOTW operations its primary mission. It would disseminate its findings to the broadest possible audience, with the principles of guaranteed access and maximum information dispersal as its foremost guidelines.

Information from the new agency would be freely available to the current IC structure, while high-technology and covert operations remain secret and unshared with the new one. For the lack of a better name, I'll call this entity the International Information Agency, or IIA.

The IIA would publish its findings in the broadest possible media spectrum, to include the Internet. Current unclassified operations supported by the existing IC, such as the Foreign Broadcast Information Service (FBIS), would be transferred to the IIA's control. The IIA would be free to disperse its data and assessments to everyone, including the current IC. The IC could in turn give critical intelligence information, such as battle damage assessment or evidence of international criminal activity, to the IIA for public release. This would assist in keeping sources relatively safe, and the IIA could rate its validity just as it does from any other source. If the IC feels the information cannot be released without compromising source data, then it does not have to do so. The IC could still selectively release information to allies and other combatants as needed.

This dual information/intelligence structure would allow the United States to cut back funding in traditional IC activities without stripping the current CIA-DIA-NSA troika of their much needed classified missions and resources. Consolidation of some agency activities could also be promoted and overlap reduced. The traditional intelligence problem of a truly centralized intelligence agency, which would limit the number of intelligence estimates available to decision makers, is reigned in with the creation of the IIA. Ideally, academics and journalists could be accessed by the IIA for both their knowledge and direct foreign area expertise, something many are loathe to do today for fear of compromising their objectivity, their access to foreign individuals and groups, or their personal safety. Since the new organization would not classify any of its work, the specialists who provide their judgments would be free to disseminate them on their own if the IIA failed to do so. This would assist in making the IIA appear truly nonpartisan.

It would further make the problem of using military assets in essentially policing situations much less insidious. When soldiers are impressed into policing duty they become cops. Civilians who are regulated by them can and do see them as supporters of a corrupt regime, often with good cause. When military intelligence assets are transferred from military support to police support missions, these assets begin to violate the fundamental legitimacy of the liberal state. The IC begins to look more like Big Brother than a legitimate military force multiplier.

The IIA could also help lessen the dual dilemmas of the domestic and international constraints referred to above. As for the domestic context of sustainability, adequate public preparation assists in making palatable difficult, costly, and sometimes deadly foreign interventions. The IIA could become a type of foreign policy CNN, providing continuous expert reports on regional atrocities and government breakdowns. The public would feel decisions of their government to intervene are less arbitrary, less propagandized, and truly needed. As the United States moves toward intervention, accurate and timely information, broadly dispersed, can help reduce casualties as military planners have more accurate data available to them and are less likely to enter a conflict zone unawares.[16] At the very least it can prepare the public to accept casualties should the violation of international morality be egregious enough. But only if the information is disseminated and perceived to be nonpartisan.

In international context, the problem of multilateral action and sensitive dissemination is reduced. The dilemma here is simple. In limited war and OOTW, the more allies the better/more legitimate the action. The more allies, however, the more difficult to keep the coalition unified in the face of adversity. Along these lines, we can reiterate the need for both a classified IC and an entity like the proposed IIA. While unilateral effort is decisive, multilateral effort is desirable in a moral war climate. In this case, decisiveness is in direct contravention to legitimacy. In total war, decisiveness is legitimate if it is effective, and there is no problem with unilateral action. In OOTW and limited war, the IIA would be faithfully pumping the most accurate, time-sensitive assessments possible to all combatants, including the enemy. All sides would know the reasons for joint action, the justifications given, the probability for casualties, costs, and outright victory if need be, and of course, the prospects for stable peace. Indeed, for OOTW and limited war, good intelligence may be more valuable to winning the peace than prepping the war. We undoubtedly need better intelligence to get out of a bad situation than to get into a morally justified one.

The most provocative formation of the IIA would be to eventually make it a truly international organization, established along the principle of regimes such as is evident in the World Trade Organization and International Monetary Fund.[17] In this conception, the IIA would be operated by participating countries, each agreeing to fund the organization on a percentage basis equal to their ability to pay, the amount of material they either contribute or take out, or on some other acceptable basis. The principles of uniform information sharing, oversight of noncompliance in participating states, reciprocity and nonrecrimination would apply. The United States would be freed of the full burden of financial support and the perception of pushing partisan propaganda and would gain the knowledge, opinions, and support of the many nations which choose to participate—as well as diverse assessments on the many who don't. The IIA would become over time the purveyor of an international public good.

## CONCLUSIONS

Ultimately, the problem of perceived IC failures in the Cold War end game and in numerous limited war and OOTW operations can be boiled down to the inability of the current intelligence structure to fully disseminate information. Part of the problem lies in the obsolete maxim that in the intelligence world, knowledge is power. Analysts and agencies jealously hoard their stash of compiled data in the mistaken belief that to freely give it away is to hand over their very source of strength.[18] Analysts who spend years learning the intricacies of foreign state politics or technical capacities of foreign weapons systems occasionally fear putting themselves out of work by the communal dissemination of their labor. Academics and journalists realize that in an information age, it is the *dissemination of knowledge* that is power. In total war and in active engagements of the host states in limited war, the former adage may be true, but in OOTW and in the rest of the limited war scenarios, the latter observation is profound. Hence the need for two separate intelligence communities, the classified one and the unclassified other.

One of the most pervasive criticisms of the IC is that it can't seem to project the political climate in various states. Why didn't Vietnam back down when we began unrestricted aerial bombing? Why didn't the Haitians greet our military liberators with open arms? Why did Hussein attack this time and not that time? Why can't we seem to be able to withdraw from Iraq? Part of the problem is a public that seems unable to digest anything but absolutes. This is why we all too often paint the Sadaams and Slobodans of the world as reincarnations of Hitler and lament the loss of every minor state as a domino in a line moving to topple the extant power structure. This can be explained with the analogy of the public to an ignorant child. It doesn't understand the subtleties of the very complex situation, so that when we must finally take action, we justify it with either an oversimplified explanation of right or wrong in the liberal mode (''bad dictator'') or a simple decree (''because mommy said so'') in the authoritarian mode. In the former case, as the child grows and gains knowledge, explanations are more nuanced, some rebellion is accepted, and the authority of the parent becomes based on honesty and forthrightness. Arguably, the practice of keeping the public ignorant of global situations until an action is already decided upon and then flooding it with oversimplified explanations to gain their support is the reason that we seem to make every contested transgression the moral equivalent of ''making the world safe for democracy.''

The problem with such a policy is that when the public finds out the nemesis is not Hitler, that the world is no more safe for democracy than it was before, it reacts with understandable resentment. It no longer trusts any of the government's justifications. It begins to believe that the enemy was not so bad. But then again, when we must act, we must act. If we let even minor infractions go unpunished, each successive one ratchets up the cost of punishment in the next confrontation. An educated public knows this and will accept the use of force even for minor infractions if they are honestly and openly presented and both the means and end are legitimate.

Intelligence is still the best bang for the military buck. Knowing when and where the next problem will arise allows us to maximize and concentrate our resources. In a world where everyone admits a fundamental change is occurring, the intelligence process should change as well.

## NOTES

1. "IC21: The Intelligence Community in the 21st Century," Staff Study Permanent Select Committee on Intelligence House of Representatives 104th Congress, http://www.milnet.com/milnet/usint/ic21011.htm, viewed May 7, 1999.

2. Ibid.

3. See Jeffrey B. White, "A Different Kind of Threat: Some Thoughts on Irregular Warfare." http://mprofaca.cro.net/mainmenu.html, viewed April 24, 1999; see also Richard Kuglar, *Toward a Dangerous World: U.S. National Security Strategy for the Coming Turbulence* (Santa Monica, CA: Rand Corporation, 1995); and Max Manwaring and William Olson, eds., *Managing Contemporary Conflict: Pillars of Success* (Boulder, CO: Westview Press, 1996).

4. Stephen Cimbala presents a complementary view in *Intelligence and Intelligence Policy in a Democratic Society* (New York: Transnational, 1987).

5. There is still no better discussion than Michael Walzer's *Just and Unjust Wars* (New York: Basic Books, 1977).

6. Not for the purpose of marshalling military power, as in the collective security era, but for creating maximum moral capacity for action.

7. See Stanley Taylor and Theodore Ralston, "The Role of Intelligence in Crisis Management," in *Avoiding War: The Problems of Crisis Management*, Alexander George, ed. (Boulder, CO: Westview Press, 1991), pp. 395–412.

8. Starting with Richard Betts, "Why Intelligence Failures Are Inevitable," *World Politics*, Vol. 31 (1978), pp. 61–89; and Walter Laqueur, *A World of Secrets: The Uses and Limits of Intelligence* (New York: Basic Books, 1985); Mark Perry, *Eclipse: The Last Days of the CIA* (New York: William Morrow, 1992), presents a series of insightful comments; and Bob Woodward, *Veil: The Secret Wars of the CIA, 1981–1987* (New York: Simon and Schuster, 1987), persists in detailing the problems of a government estranged from its people.

9. General examples are pervasive. The description used here can be found in Norman Polmar and Thomas Allen, eds., *The Encyclopedia of Espionage* (New York: Random House, 1997), p. 283.

10. Vietnam, for example, fought a total war against first the French, then the United States, who fought limited wars. The failure of the United States to recognize that the legitimacy factor was different for its military and intelligence operations than for the Vietnamese contributed mightily to the public dissatisfaction that eroded support for the war.

11. The U.S. Space Command provides satellite ephemeris data, orbital characteristics free to anyone who asks, including via the Internet. A sophisticated target could simply avoid operations when photo satellites are overhead, but this would severely degrade operations.

12. Even if the target is not aware of the surveillance, the data may be changed by the simple act of observation. This is a variant of Schroedinger's Cat paradox, long appreciated in the social and physical sciences but underdeveloped in military intelligence.

13. See, for example, Howard Jones, ed., *The Foreign and Domestic Dimensions of Modern Warfare: Vietnam, Central America, and Nuclear Strategy* (Tuscaloosa: Uni-

versity of Alabama Press, 1988); and Shaun McCarthy, *The Function of Intelligence in Crisis Management* (Aldershot: Ashgate, 1997).

14. See Everett Dolman, "War and the Democratic Peace," in *Citizenship Studies* (1999) for a discussion of concerns about the legitimacy and application of democratic states using military forces as auxiliary police units.

15. Samuel Huntington, *The Soldier and the State: The Theory and Politics of Civil-Military Relations* (Cambridge, MA: Harvard University Press, 1957); Morris Janowitz, *The Professional Soldier: A Social and Political Portrait*, rev. ed. (New York: Free Press, 1971); and Alfred Stepan, "The New Professionalism of Internal Warfare and the Military Role of Expansionism," in *Authoritarian Brazil*, Alfred Stepan, ed. (New Haven, CT: Yale University Press, 1973).

16. See, for example, Charles Cogan, "Intelligence and Crisis Management: The Importance of the Pre-Crisis," *Intelligence and National Security*, Vol. 9 (1994), pp. 633–650.

17. This would be based on the utility of regime theory begun by Robert Keohane and Joseph Nye, *Power and Interdependence* (Boston: Little, Brown, 1977); and developed in Stephen Krasner, ed., *International Regimes* (Ithaca, NY: Cornell University Press, 1983), and Friedrich Kratochwil and Edward Mansfield, eds., *International Organization: A Reader* (New York: HarperCollins, 1994).

18. William Corson, *The Armies of Ignorance: The Rise of the American Intelligence Empire* (New York: Dial, 1977).

Chapter 7

# Beyond Jointness: Civil-Military Cooperation in Achieving the Desired End-State

## John T. Fishel

### WAR'S END: A STRATEGIC CONCEPT FOR POST-CONFLICT OPERATIONS

International law in general, and the law of land warfare in particular, provide that the victorious nation in war has specific responsibilities toward the people of the vanquished nation.[1] Some of these are the maintenance of law and order, the provision of food and shelter, the care of displaced civilians, the provision of health care and services, and the reestablishment of public education.[2] It takes very little extension of this concept to conclude that a "liberating" power has most of the same responsibilities as does an "occupying" power. This conclusion is even more valid if the government of the nation being liberated is totally unorganized.[3]

Two recent cases point this out clearly. In Grenada in 1983, the United States was de facto responsible for all government services until a new government could be organized. At the time of the "rescue mission," Grenada was governed by one man, Sir Paul Scoon, the governor general. Eighteen months later, U.S. forces left the island with a new government fully responsible for its own affairs. Similarly, in 1989, Panama demonstrated that three elected officials do not make a government, and the slogan "Liberation, not occupation" failed to relieve the United States and its military forces of responsibility for the welfare of the people of the nation.[4] Thus, U.S. efforts did address assisting the new government to establish itself and provide the required services.

The American and allied experiences in the Gulf War represent a third example of the varying degrees of responsibility that the victor must assume for the inhabitants of conquered or liberated territory. In Kuwait, which had a government in exile but numerous financial resources and coalition partners, the responsibility of the United States, while less, still remained. In southern Iraq, U.S. and allied forces were responsible for the welfare of inhabitants and refugees until those forces were withdrawn. Finally, among the Kurds of northern Iraq, the United States and its allies accepted the moral, if not the legal, responsibility for the welfare and survival of these people by initiating Operation Provide Comfort.

In practice, immediate responsibility for conquered and liberated territory devolves upon the military commander on the ground. It remains there until other agencies of the government, international organizations (such as the United Nations), and the host government assume that responsibility. Again, in practice, this often means that the military commander, as the person controlling the key resources, will have to continue exercising the responsibility long after the U.S. State Department and other agencies have arrived and begun to function. This situation also marks the transition from military-dominated warfighting or peace "enforcement" to civilian-controlled "peace building" or the development of civil society.

### Occupation History

If liberation and occupation are related concepts, and not antithetical, then it is important that one consider the major historical experiences of Americans as occupation forces. Modern American occupation history is that of being the occupying power after World War II. That experience provides a basis not only for lessons learned in planning and executing both occupation and liberation but also in the structuring of the U.S. military organizations that conducted what army *Field Manual 41–10* calls "civil administration" functions, the civil affairs units of the U.S. Army.[5]

While the World War II occupation experience is not likely to be repeated, contingencies similar to events in the Dominican Republic (1965), Grenada (1983), Panama (1989–1990), Kuwait (1991), southern Iraq (1991), or northern Iraq (1991) are highly probable in the near future. As the leading nation in former President George Bush's vision of the "New World Order," the United States will most assuredly have the major role in any crisis where American interests are at stake. Equally important is the fact that, although other nations are developing some capability in this area, only the United States has significant military forces specifically designed, configured, and trained to conduct the wide array of relevant civil military operations. Contingencies have arisen from scenarios as diverse as peacekeeping in Yugoslavia and peace enforcement in Haiti.

### Civil-Military Operations Strategy

The effective conduct of civil-military operations (CMO) in the aftermath of conflict, whether as liberation, occupation, something in between, or something else entirely, depends on the existence of strategy at both the national and the theater levels. If there is any lesson common to all our recent experiences, it is that the lack of a full-blown strategy raises grave doubts about the long-term success of the enterprise. Strategic success thus depends on the three pillars of strategy: ends (objectives), ways (concepts), and means (resources).

*Ends.* The first issue is defining the ends or goals to be achieved. This is often where the strategic process breaks down because at the beginning of an operation, the national strategic (political-military) objectives generally are obscure. Indeed, while national policy goals often are reasonably well articulated, rarely are they translated into strategic political-military objectives expressed as end states and attainable supporting objectives.[6]

Perhaps the key to resolving this problem is the concept of the strategic objective as an end state. An end state is a description of what we want the battlefield to look like when the campaign is over. In the political-military realm, however, that description will include a range of acceptable outcomes—hence, the picture of the terrain will be fuzzy around the edges. If the national policy in Panama was the restoration of democratic government as a result of Operation Just Cause, then what were the specific political-military objectives that, if achieved, would together describe the desired end state? If the restoration of the legitimate government of Kuwait was the policy goal, and if the restoration included some liberalization of the government, then what were the specific political-military objectives that together would constitute the desired end state? In neither case was the end state adequately described, so in neither case was there a clear national strategic objective.

World War II provides yet another set of examples of a lack of clarity of objective. We obviously wanted the absolute defeat of Germany and Japan and their unconditional surrender. However, even though much effort was devoted to planning for the post-war era in both countries, we remained unclear as to the policy goals we desired in each.[7] While we described Germany in end-state terms in the Morgenthau Plan, we really never committed our nation to achieving that particular end state. With changed circumstances, the policy goals changed as did the acceptable outcomes. An agrarian, disarmed Germany gave way to an industrialized, rearmed Germany, which was federal, democratic, and firmly committed to the West as a member of the North Atlantic Treaty Organization (NATO) and the European Communities. While the extreme end state envisioned for Germany was abandoned, the core of a democratic nation bound to the Western Allies was the central objective achieved.[8]

The case of Japan was somewhat different. While there was no Morgenthau Plan to be rewritten and therefore the envisioned end state was hazier, the vision that General Douglas MacArthur, as proconsul, had of a democratic, prosperous Japan that had renounced war as an instrument of national policy clearly set the tone of the occupation.[9] In both cases, however, a great deal of planning had gone into how to administer conquered territory as well as the appropriate ways to provide what has come to be called civil administration assistance to liberated governments.[10] In addition, effort went into accessing and training appropriate civil affairs personnel, detachments, and larger units to provide military government and civil administration.

At the time, what we now call the inter-agency environment was hardly conducive to a smooth transition from military to civilian operational control. General George C. Marshall and the U.S. War Department wanted as little to do with military government as possible.[11] The State Department, however, asserted that it lacked the capability to plan and execute an occupation.[12] That left the military as the only organization able to carry it out.

Given the predispositions of the U.S. Army, civil affairs and military government units were designed around a concept of self-sufficiency and the ability to interface with remaining civilian infrastructure rather than with military combat, combat support, and combat service support units. The underlying idea was that these civil affairs/military government soldiers should be prepared and able, on very short notice, to remove their uniforms and function, intact, as subordinate organizations of the State Department.[13] While this never came to pass, the organization of post–World War II civil affairs units continued to reflect this concept through the Table of Organization and Equipment (TOE) used during Operation Desert Storm.

The subject of means will be addressed in greater detail later in this chapter. However, what is clear from a reflection on the end of World War II is that the appropriate end state represented a range of alternatives organized around some core objectives. If we consider several post-war contingency operations in the Dominican Republic, Grenada, and Panama, we find as common core policy goals, democratic, stable, and friendly nations. The details and supporting objectives were unclear and often unstated, which left room for significant amounts of conflict, not only about ways and means but also about appropriate ends.

This pattern suggests that there may well be an important lack of connectivity between national policy, national strategy, theater strategy, and operations. While the linkage among these levels may be broken, it is not at all clear at what point the break occurred. In Panama, there were breaks all the way down the chain of command.[14]

The linkage is, first and foremost, one of policy goals, national strategic objectives, theater strategic objectives, and operational objectives, all of which should be analyzed as end states. The question that should be asked at the policy level concerns what kind of world we want to see when this policy has been implemented and its goals have been achieved. At the national strategic level, we wish to know what the landscape will look like with the achievement of the national strategic objectives. In Panama, for example, we should have been prepared to state with a great degree of specificity what a democratic government would look like, how its institutions would be organized, and what they would be capable of accomplishing at any given time.

At the theater strategic level, we should have been able to state as objectives those actions that would yield the kind of institutions we wished to see in Panama, while at the operational level, we should have conducted an analysis of the probable consequences of our actions. In no case was this, or anything like it, done adequately.[15]

A similar analysis of goals and objectives as end states would appear to have been required in the wake of the Gulf War. However, while an end-state analysis was conducted at U.S. Central Command (CENTCOM), it was not carried to the point of establishing the full range of essential links from policy through operations. Moreover, it never went directly beyond the CENTCOM staff.[16]

*Ways.* Even with goals and objectives defined as end states and linked from the policy through the operational levels, what exists is only a partial strategy. There are two other components of strategy—ways and means.[17] Critical among the ways to achieve an objective on any level of the equation is unity of effort. However, achieving unity of effort for post-conflict operations is extraordinarily elusive because at least three separate games are being played at the same time, each one under different rules.

The first game is the inter-agency game. In every contingency, the game will clearly encompass multiple agencies of the U.S. government. Always among the players will be the Department of Defense, Department of State, the military forces on the ground, the Agency for International Development (AID), the U.S. Information Agency (USIA), and the Central Intelligence Agency (CIA). In addition, one often finds players from the Department of Justice, the Department of Commerce, and the Federal Aviation Administration (FAA), among many others. Normally, the control of this inter-agency hodgepodge lies with the U.S. ambassador to the host nation, by virtue of his letter of instruction and appointment as the president's personal representative. This normal control is invalidated only in time of war, when the president clearly directs that the military commander in theater is the senior U.S. representative, when the U.S. embassy in a country is not operational (as in Kuwait during the first week following liberation), or when activities take place across the boundaries of several nations. The latter two conditions occurred in the Gulf War; the former did not. Thus, there were times when clarity of control was obscured at the working levels of the inter-agency players.[18]

A second aspect of the interagency game is that no player except the military has the means to carry out those activities required to achieve post-conflict objectives. As a result, the military—especially its civil affairs units and other combat support and combat service support units such as the military police (MPs), engineers, medics, transportation, and logistics organizations, among others—will provide the bulk of the assets to achieve objectives at all levels. To these military organizations must be added the other U.S. government agencies involved, including AID, its Office of Foreign Disaster Assistance, the U.S. ambassador and his Country Team, and such agencies as the International Criminal Investigative Training Assistance Program of the Department of Justice. Achieving unity of effort in the inter-agency game means developing effective command, control, and coordination mechanisms that are adaptable to a wide variety of circumstances.

A third aspect of the inter-agency game is the involvement of non-governmental organizations (NGOs) and private voluntary organizations (PVOs) that render humanitarian service. These can be as varied as the Red Cross and the American Friends Services Committee. Invariably, issues involving NGOs and PVOs spill over into the second, or "combined," game.

The combined game refers to coalition military activity involving the armed forces of two or more nations. This narrow, technical, military definition must be expanded in post-conflict operations to include the activities of the civilian agencies of those governments and, often, the activities of NGOs and PVOs. If one adds the involvement of the United Nations, its specialized agencies, and other inter-governmental organizations (IGOs), the combined game becomes very complex indeed.

In most of the recent U.S. operations, the combined game has been relatively simple. In Panama, for instance, it was generally bilateral, with only limited IGO, NGO, and PVO involvement.[19] By contrast, the Gulf War produced an extremely complicated combined game, which, at its most complex, was played in northern Iraq as Operation Provide Comfort. Somalia and Haiti provide similar examples of complexity.

The issue of the combined game is one that compounds the inter-agency game of who is in charge. In the combined game, the answer depends on the circumstances in which the question is asked and whether one expects the answer to be de jure or de facto. This is not to argue that it cannot be both, but rather that it may well be different. For example, in Panama, Commander in Chief (CINC) General Maxwell R. Thurman resolved his problem by placing the commander of his Civil Military Operations Task Force under the operational control of the U.S. embassy in support of the Panamanian government.[20] While the de jure arrangement was coordination between the two governments and control of all U.S. activities by the chargé d'affaires, the de facto arrangement was that the U.S. military controlled everything that was done in Panama by either government. This was a result of having the resources required, whereas the embassy was severely understrength and the Panamanian government consisted only of the elected president and two vice presidents.[21]

By contrast, the de jure situation in Operation Desert Storm had all U.S. effort unified at the level of the CINC and coordinated with the coalition forces. Generally, this was the de facto situation as well, however, there appear to have been moments when members of the U.S. Country Team in Kuwait had questions as to whether the CINC was usurping the authority of the ambassador.[22] As in the Panama experience, there was no apparent conflict among the principals, but such conflict did arise at the action level.[23] Operation Provide Comfort gives the best example of congruence between the de jure and de facto organization for unity of effort. In Turkey and northern Iraq, all coalition forces, both civilian and military, were under the "tactical control" of the task force commander, U.S. Lieutenant General John Shalikashvili.[24] Coordination with the United Nations and other IGOs and NGOs and PVOs was effected in order to prepare for a handoff to the former, but there never was any question of who was in charge.

The third game is what we will call the joint game, which is the game most controlled by doctrine—a purely military game dominated by such terms as attachment, operational control, and direct support. All the U.S. military players understand the terminology and what it means, but this makes it no less difficult to establish unity of effort in cases where the players are unclear over ends, ways, and means.

One example of the kind of confusion that was possible came during Desert Storm where the Army Component (ARCENT) of U.S. Central Command (CENTCOM) perceived that CENTCOM had ordered it not to establish any refugee camps, and therefore, was doing next to nothing to assist refugees.[25] Meanwhile, CENTCOM was insisting that the refugees be cared for in accordance with international law.[26] The net result was confusion, both over who was, in fact, in charge and over what was expected.

In spite of these difficulties, it seems clear that achieving unity of effort among the various U.S. military organizations is a much easier process than achieving it between agencies and governments. However, because the joint game has been far more institutionalized than any of the other games, it is far more subtle. The joint game has been played in the U.S. military for years, and even such major rules changes as the Goldwater-Nichols legislation of 1986, which reorganized the Department of Defense, have only changed the game at the margin, although in some very profound ways.

As a result, few would ever question the fact that the CINC commands all military forces in the theater. Even such situations as took place during Desert Storm, where U.S. European Command (EUCOM) forces provided combat search and rescue over northern Iraq, were covered by agreement and doctrine which made EUCOM the supporting command to CENTCOM. This, in turn, put EUCOM forces under the operational control of CENTCOM.[27]

Considering all three games, a central question is where unity of effort—or stated as the military principle of war, unity of command—is to be achieved. Critical to the response is which game is dominant as well as the circumstances in which the games are being played. If the joint game dominates, then the Joint Force commander (usually the CINC) commands. If, however, the inter-agency game is dominant, then command and control generally will be exercised by the chief of the U.S. diplomatic mission (the ambassador). One exception to this generalization is that when the game crosses international boundaries, it becomes far less clear who should be in charge. In the case of the combined game, command and control of U.S. elements usually will rest with the U.S. military commander (again, the CINC).

If the United States is the leader of a coalition, then its military leadership should exercise command and control over coalition forces. This, however, may not always be the case. It is perfectly possible to envision a combined game under U.N. auspices where the coalition force commander will be from some other nation. Another possible approach to command and control in both the combined and inter-agency game is that of appointing a civilian as the person in charge. This raises many questions about the capability of civilian leadership to command and control large military forces and civilian organizations, but it should in no way be impossible.

*Means.* This discussion should lead to the third leg of the strategy stool— means or resources. These are best considered in terms of the principles of war, *mass* and *economy of force*.

The evidence of our recent contingency operations and wars is that the forces required to fight only have a partial overlap with the forces required to terminate a conflict. The latter forces are primarily combat support and combat service support, as opposed to combat. The most important of the forces required for war termination are military police, engineers, medical, and transportation types including air, and most critical of all, civil affairs (CA). Ninety-seven percent of the latter personnel are in the U.S. Army Reserve (USAR).

Getting these military forces into the theater and properly organized to accomplish the war termination mission effectively was a major problem in both Panama and Operations Desert Storm and Provide Comfort. In neither case was civil affairs doctrine adhered to. Rather, as in Panama, Kuwaiti and northern Iraqi task forces were created that followed more closely special operations doctrine than anything else, resembling the Security Assistance Force (SAF). In each case the task force had at least two major components, one of which was a civil affairs task force.[28]

The common thread in these three operations with respect to doctrine is that civil affairs doctrine does not account for how CA forces will interact with the rest of the army.[29] Rather, it addresses how CA forces interact with host country civilians and civil government. The gap that existed in these operations was that what needed to be done could only be accomplished by military forces—mostly, other combat support and combat service support units.

As a result, commanders on the ground chose to organize composite task forces that contained what they perceived as the correct mix of forces to carry out their assigned and implied missions during war termination. This situation continued to persist through the U.S. involvement in U.N. peacekeeping in Haiti.

Obviously, not all, or even most, of the resources required for war termination are military units and civilian organizations. Many resources can be accounted for in terms of the dollars required and authorized to procure their equipment as well as to support and sustain them. Each of the operations considered here suggests different problems and solutions in acquiring resources.

Operations Just Cause and Promote Liberty in Panama were defined as liberation. Only a month into the operation, this resulted in a prohibition being placed on U.S. forces from spending any further operational funds on restoring the Panamanian infrastructure.[30] The further result of this ruling was to thrust necessary funding activities into peacetime systems that were ill suited to the task. Only the fact that some very skilled professionals were in positions to make things happen permitted the degree of efficacy in the acquiring and disbursing of funds that prevailed.[31] Finally, two emergency appropriations by Congress resulted in some new funding finally becoming available three and a half months after it was required.[32]

Operation Desert Storm illustrates two different situations. First, with respect to operations in southern Iraq, the United States and its coalition partners constituted an occupying power under international law. As such, U.S. forces were required to provide for the well-being of the local population, including any refugees, of which there were ultimately some 30,000. Since this was a legal obligation, operational funds could be used; indeed, any order cutting off their use without compensating funds being made immediately available would have been patently illegal.

A second situation existed in Kuwait. There, the coalition forces entered as liberating armies. This situation was analogous to Panama with one overriding difference. Kuwait had the wealth to pay for any services it received, and agreements to this effect had been made with the government in exile. As a result, all actions taken by U.S. and coalition forces to restore the Kuwaiti infrastructure were paid for by Kuwait.

Operation Provide Comfort in northern Iraq illustrates a third example of obtaining resources. In this case, the operation fell under a different rubric—disaster assistance. It was a humanitarian relief mission. As such, it was funded by the various donor nations and agencies (for the United States, the Department of Defense and AID's Office of Foreign Disaster Assistance).[33]

In these instances of war termination operations, economy of force only applies to the Panama case. During Operation Promote Liberty, and especially after the Department of Defense (DOD) cutoff of operational funds for restoration on January 20, 1990, U.S. forces were used quite effectively to carry light engineering projects and medical civic action to many rural villages in the Panamanian interior—all under the auspices of the Joint Chiefs of Staff (JCS) and U.S. Southern Command (SOUTHCOM) exercises.[34] These "exercises" served to carry the message that the U.S. and Panamanian governments cared about the people of Panama while the normal peacetime funding was winding its way through legislation and bureaucratic disbursement.

### Organizing to Implement a Strategic Concept

This part of the chapter has focused on developing the background for a strategic concept of post-conflict operations. It rests on the three components of strategy—ends, ways, and means. More than ever in future operations we need to determine what our political-military objectives will be when war is finally terminated. Not only must we know what our objectives are, we should be able to describe the desired landscape—at least in general terms.

Our strategy must develop the ways in which we intend to achieve our objectives. We need to develop the proper organizations to achieve the requisite unity of effort in the environments of the inter-agency, combined, and joint games. Such organizations will, of necessity, be task forces built around the CA forces of the U.S. Army (mostly found in the reserves) and other combat support and combat service support units. To these will be added a variety of other government agencies, IGOs, NGOs/PVOs, and military and civilian organizations from other nations. Command and control, to be effective, will require innovative thinking and flexibility, coupled with more knowledge of the underlying political-military reality among military and civilian leaders than presently exists.

Adequately resourcing these efforts will require new legislation and streamlined bureaucratic procedures to get resources where they are needed in a timely fashion. As with organization, open minds and flexibility associated with strong planning capabilities will be essential.

The concept outlined here is not yet national policy. The failure to make it so almost certainly will condemn us to live with significantly less than optimal ways to address the challenges of conflict termination. Consequently, there is a requirement for national policy to produce a strategic concept for war termination, but there is also a requirement to institutionalize that concept. The joint community needs to do this as well as develop implementation doctrine. Although the term *doctrine* may carry negative connotations for civilian agencies, it is not dogma. Rather, military doctrine represents general rules for how operations are conducted. Doctrine is modified to fit the circumstances in which one finds oneself.

Additionally, civilian agencies operate within a doctrinal framework. The difference is that they do not call their procedures doctrine. Whatever it is called, however, a doctrine for post-conflict operations that embraces this strategic concept is essential. Such doctrine will be best produced with the joint doctrine system and further developed by the individual services. Finally, there will be a need to disseminate it beyond the military for adoption by other government agencies. In the end, if useful, the concept will provide the means by which the community of IGOs and NGOs/PVOs will be able to most effectively coordinate their activities with those of the U.S. government, should that be the mutually desired goal.

## STRATEGIC IMPLICATIONS OF CIVIL-MILITARY OPERATIONS

The study of civil-military operations in the contexts of liberation, occupation, peacekeeping, and complex human emergencies underlines the transcendental importance of the requirement for strategic vision. Here, strategic vision means that the political and military leadership must have a relatively clear picture of the desired end state—what the leadership desires the battlefield and the surrounding political landscape to took like when the war is over—and it represents a range of acceptable political-military outcomes. Moreover, end states suggest descriptions, in fairly great detail, of the goals of national policy.[35]

### National Policy Goals and Strategic Objectives

In the Persian Gulf War, the U.S. articulation of its policy goals was mixed in terms of its effects. The picture is one of a president rhetorically stating his goals, followed by members of his administration providing interpretations that at times had little relationship to the words uttered by President Bush.

Two cases will serve to illustrate the point. First, when the president uttered the words, ''This will not stand,'' it became American policy and from that moment on meant that Iraq would be ejected from Kuwait in one way or another. This policy clearly implied that, if necessary, offensive military operations would be used. It took no genius to make this analysis, but CENTCOM and the Joint Staff gave the strong impression that all military efforts were focused only on the defense of Saudi Arabia. While offensive planning was taking place at this time, it was so closely held within CENTCOM (for reasons of operational security) that much of its own army component, especially the civil affairs officer, was in the dark. As a result, all of ARCENT's early civil-military operations and civil affairs planning focused exclusively on defensive operations and host-nation support within Saudi Arabia. This focus reinforced the predisposition of the active-component civil affairs personnel supporting ARCENT to minimize any role for reserve CA units, thereby depriving ARCENT of the robust civil affairs CMO planning and execution capability that it required until very late in the process. It also seemed to cause ARCENT to fail to look toward Washington, where the Kuwait Task Force (KTF) was planning for precisely the operation that ARCENT would have to execute.

That presidential rhetoric was policy did not escape the key player in establishing the KTF, Colonel Randall Elliott, nor the notice of the Assistant Secretary of Defense for Special Operations and Low Intensity Conflict, James Locher, and his assistants. Together, Elliott, Locher, and their associates in State and Defense developed the conditions whereby the Emir of Kuwait requested army CA assistance and the KTF was established to provide it. That it took nearly two months from the time of the Emir's request until the establishment of the KTF is explainable only in terms of bureaucratic reinterpretations of presidential statements and an unwillingness to recognize the strategic and operational implications of the fact that rhetoric is policy.

The second example of rhetoric becoming policy is found in the numerous calls by President Bush for the overthrow of Saddam Hussein. In this case, however, CENTCOM clearly recognized the danger at the political-military level and repeatedly advised that a definition of the policy goal of regional stability required an Iraq that, while weakened, not be dismembered.[36] What CENTCOM failed to do as successfully was to examine the consequences of ''rhetorical'' policy with respect to its impact on CMO in the occupied areas of southern Iraq and direct aggressive CMO planning for the refugees produced by the consequences of the Shiite rebellion.

EUCOM, which was responsible for operations from Turkey in support of Operation Desert Storm, did anticipate that there might well be some undefined CMO mission or requirements, and General Galvin asked for support from his CAPSTONE CA command, including its general officer commander. However, there is nothing in the record that would indicate that EUCOM predicted the Kurdish revolt or did anything to specifically prepare to deal with its consequences. Like the Shiite revolt in the south, the rebellion of the Kurds was eminently predictable. No matter what its outcome, the requirement for a major CMO effort should have been anticipated.

The presidential rhetoric that launched Operation Restore Hope in Somalia convinced the CENTCOM planners that they were dealing with a mission not unlike the rescue of the Kurds in northern Iraq. Given the significant humanitarian component, they felt a need to have a robust civil affairs element. This, in turn, required the call-up of reserve civil affairs units, which CENTCOM requested but backed away from when the Joint Staff questioned the need. Thus, CMO was conducted only by active-component CA personnel, who were designated military personnel with other special ties—some related to CA, some not, operating out of the civil-military operations center (CMOC). Much was ad hoc and improvised. That it worked as well as it did was due to the integration of the Office of Foreign Disaster Assistance's Disaster Assistance Relief Team (OFDA/DART).

As these examples show, military leaders and staffers in a unified command, including action officers, need to be extremely sensitive to the strategic and operational implications of policy made by presidential public declarations. Such sensitivity would allow for the development of policy options to be carried to the Chairman of the Joint Chiefs of Staff (JCS) and Department of Defense (DOD) as well the development of theater strategies and campaign plans to address the contingencies brought on by these rhetorical flourishes, which become policy whether well thought out or not.

In general, CENTCOM did well in developing its strategic objective as end states. Interestingly, the principal national strategic objective ejecting the Iraqis from Kuwait was the same as the theater strategy objective. A definition of the end state based on the policies enunciated by the White House was relatively simple and led directly to clear and specific supporting objectives. Only at the margins did the objectives become fuzzy, exactly as they had in Panama and would become again in Haiti. Somalia contrasts with these cases by both the lack of an agreed end state and the changing of policy as administrations changed.

### Well-Defined End States—Were They Good Policy?

CENTCOM defined its objectives as end states in terms of two fairly clear policy goals: the restoration of the legitimate government in Kuwait and regional stability. To achieve the restoration of the legitimate Kuwaiti government required that the Iraqi army be forced out of Kuwait City in one way or another. CENTCOM's preference was that Saddam pull out peacefully in response to the U.N. resolutions, and failing that, if he had to be ejected by force, it was felt that fighting in the city could be limited so as to minimize the number of casualties and damage. This desire to limit casualties and damage led to discussions about leaving an open escape route from Kuwait City which, in turn, came to pass by default.

CENTCOM also recognized that it had to plan to provide emergency services to Kuwait in the immediate aftermath of liberation. This task was fulfilled in the several annexes (labeled G) to the OPLANs of both CENTCOM and its army component, ARCENT. It was also included in Annex G developed in Washington by the KTF which, however, was not coordinated with either ARCENT or CENTCOM. This lack of coordination meant that a significant amount of rewriting was required when the KTF finally arrived in-theater.

None of this should be construed as criticism of any of these organizations for failure to identify the supporting objectives required to achieve the identified end state. The organizations did plan the courses of action necessary to achieve the objectives as well as the resources required. Finally, the KTF planned for the long-term reconstruction of Kuwait in coordination with the Kuwaiti government's special planning agency.

The U.S. government, however, had another political objective for Kuwait, which was not at all reflected in the end state derived by the military planners— to move the Kuwaiti government, upon its restoration, to a more democratic mode.[37] The specific objective to be achieved was the restoration of the Kuwaiti legislative assembly, and the way to achieve this objective was to extract a promise from the Emir. This was the mission of Ambassador Gnehm, whose means were to apply the resources he had, or could tap, through the military and AID to enhance his diplomacy. The objective of restored (or newly established) democracy also was central in Panama, Haiti, and even in Somalia.

The fact that the end state envisioned by the military planners did not reflect this political agenda resulted in a disconnected policy and strategy between the military and civilian agencies of the U.S. government. This is not to say that the military strategy contradicted the policy addressed by Ambassador Gnehm, but rather that there was a far more insidious result. Civil military operations in Kuwait never directly supported this larger policy goal in any coordinated way. The closest they came to doing so was in their focus on preventing human rights violations.

As discussed elsewhere, democracy in Panama was left largely undefined.[38] Therefore, the assumption on the part of the military units charged with carrying out civil-military operations was that the restoration of the elected civilian government equaled democracy. The only attempt to get beyond that simplistic equation came in the draft U.S. government strategy, which called for community participation through the venerable Latin American tradition of the *ca-*

*bildo abierto* (town meeting) for decisions on civic action projects. That strategy was never implemented as a whole.

Somalia saw similar, but very sporadic, scattered, and localized efforts to introduce elements of democratic participation, but there was no clearly stated strategy of democratization enunciated either by UNITAF or UNOSOM II. Haiti, in turn, reflected the experience of all the previous cases. The restoration of the elected civilian government was equated to democracy. Scattered and localized efforts to bring about greater participation in decision making took place, but without any coordinated national strategy. In contrast to the other cases, the one clear democratization objective was to hold a series of free and open elections that would culminate with the election of a new president and the transfer of the office from one freely elected leader to another. That this happened was all to the credit of the United States and the rest of the international community. That the elections were less than models of democratic participation, while not unexpected, is evidence of a certain distancing of the international community from its responsibility to achieve its own stated goal of democratization. Finally, it is evident that the U.S. government's perception of democracy had not evolved beyond the necessary, but insufficient, condition of free and fair elections.

The fact that the envisioned end states of the civil government and the military were not in complete congruence made for less than effective policy. Had CENTCOM been directed to incorporate strengthened democratic institutions into its view of the end state of a restored legitimate government of Kuwait, additional objectives in support of that end state would have been incorporated into the CMO planning at all levels.[39] In turn, this might well have made for greater policy success than we have had to date. However, the lessons of the other cases give one pause. The U.S. military, along with the rest of the U.S. government, appears not to know how to establish self-sustaining, effective, democratic governments.

While the congruence of government policy and military strategy with respect to Kuwait was not fully synchronized, there was a definite lack of congruence between the end state of regional stability as envisioned in the military strategy and the end state as seen in U.S. government policy. The military strategy saw regional stability in terms of an Iraq whose military capability had been so degraded that it could not threaten its neighbors, but not a dismembered Iraq consisting of a Shiite state in the south, a Kurdish state in the north, and a Sunni Arab Mesopotamian state in the center, all at war with each other. While government policy rejected this nightmare, it never was clear from the president's rhetoric just what it was that he did want. Different audiences could deduce from his statements almost any outcome they desired. As a result, the CENTCOM-defined end state became just one of several competing visions of the future resulting from U.S. policy. The results, of course, were the revolts of the Shiites and the Kurds, the collapse of the revolts under pressure from Saddam who, although defeated, represented the unified Iraq of the CENTCOM end state, and the ensuing refugee rescue operations. Lack of congruence within the

U.S. government made for confused policy and undesired (and, in some cases, unanticipated) outcomes. A similar lesson that appears not to have been learned was the consequences of the lack of congruence among the participant nations of UNOSOM II. In that case, the result was failure.

## THE STRATEGIC WAYS—ORGANIZATION, COMMAND, AND CONTROL

The establishment of the KTF resolved one problem that had plagued the Panama planners—inter-agency coordination. The KTF, however, was a creation of the inter-agency process and, as such, served its inter-agency masters well. In fact the KTF used its inter-agency status to support its mission, and there was close and effective coordination through the KTF between State and Defense. The inter-agency coordination developed with the KTF carried over into Operations Provide Comfort and Restore Hope and reached new highs in Operation Uphold Democracy.

The very fact of its inter-agency status was also the major problem associated with the KTF. As an inter-agency creation, it was not under any single chain of command and control. Its master was the Steering Committee Group, which was made up of senior officials from State and Defense, with day-to-day monitoring being handled by the Working Group, which was staffed by action officers of both departments on a part-time basis. In other words, the KTF supervisors served to support the activities of the KTF as determined by its commander, Colonel Elliott. Thus, no other organization of the U.S. government or its military was in command, or exercised control, of the KTF. This situation clearly is contrary to the recent development of effective command and control under the unified command system. Moreover, the problem did not develop in the subsequent operations.

To a certain extent, the KTF command and control arrangement evolved from the de facto abdication by CENTCOM of its authority to command any organization that would operate within its Area of Operational Responsibility (AOR). Had CINCCENT insisted, it is highly likely that the KTF would have come under his command, if not his operational control, until it deployed to theater. This would have increased the opportunity for the KTF to have received CENTCOM guidance on planning for CMO and required the KTF to have its plan reviewed by the CENTCOM staff early in the process. In other words, the principal command and control lesson of the KTF is that, while such an organization is required to work in the inter-agency arena (and the combined arena, if appropriate), it must come under the command of the Unified Commander. During the Washington stage of its existence, the KTF was appropriately under the operational control of the inter-agency Steering Committee Group but should, at the same time, have been under the command of CENTCOM. The proper arrangement for CMO planning within a theater is an inter-agency group under the command and control of the CINC.[40] Although this solution was not adopted in northern Iraq, Somalia, or Haiti, inter-agency coordination has much improved, resulting in a limiting of the associated problems.

Within CENTCOM, planning for CMO was divided between ARCENT and the Directorate of Policy and Plans (CCJ5). ARCENT had full responsibility for CMO planning by virtue of its designation under standing procedures as executive agent for civil affairs. CCJ5, however, retained more than mere staff supervision of CMO planning since the CINC had not designated a land component commander, which made him such by default. In his capacity as combined commander with General Khalid, the CINC also retained authority for CMO that he simply could not delegate.

Indeed, under the Goldwater-Nichols Act (1986), which significantly strengthened the role of the unified commander, it is clear that executive agency no longer is a proper command relationship, if it ever was. If the CINC desired to delegate responsibility for CMO or civil affairs, it should have created a Joint or Combined Civil Military Operations Task Force (J/CCMOTF) directly subordinate to himself. That General Schwarzkopf never created such a task force caused significantly more confusion with respect to CMO than was necessary. This confusion carried over from planning through execution. By contrast, such an organization (first COMCMOTF, and later the MSG) was developed for Panama, and similar planning was undertaken with respect to Haiti.

### Organizing to Execute CMO

Two major organizations to execute CMO came out of Operations Desert Storm and Provide Comfort. These were Task Force Freedom and Combined Task Force Provide Comfort. The similarities between both organizations and the Military Support Group in Panama were so striking that they suggest the need to inquire into the doctrine in which they were based and to incorporate the lessons of those experiences into new doctrine for the conduct of CMO.

The inspiration for the MSG was found in the Security Assistance Force (SAF), which is found in the doctrine in *Field Manual 100–20; Low Intensity Conflict* (1981 edition). The SAF has been renamed in the 1990 edition as the Foreign Internal Defense Augmentation Force (FIDAF), and its structure has become more generic (see Figure 7.1).[41] When the FIDAF is compared with the organizations of TF Freedom in Kuwait and southern Iraq and Operation Provide Comfort (CCTF-PC) in northern Iraq, the similarity is remarkable.

However, the inspiration for TF Freedom was not wholly doctrinal. Rather, its establishment was the result of General Yeosock's rejection of the ARCENT civil affairs officer's proposed organization for the conduct of CMO, followed by the adaptation of the logic of the ARCENT staff. While the inspiration for the organization of the Combined Task Force-Provide Comfort (CTF-PC) is unclear, given that the initial forces on the ground that set the tone were the special operations forces (SOF) under Special Operations Command–Europe, it is reasonable to suppose that CTF-PC was adapted from the SAF/FIDAF con-

**Figure 7.1**
**Type of Foreign Internal Defense Augmentation Force**

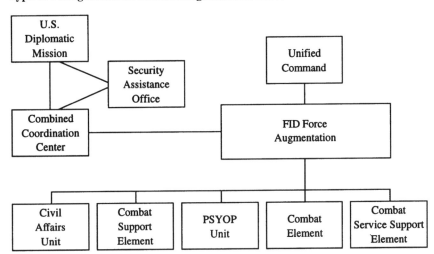

cept. Several adaptations of the concept were consistent in each of the three organizational structures created. First, each organization was commanded by an army general officer (or selectee) whose career had been made in the conventional combat arms. That is, he was not from another service or from the special operations community. In Panama, the initial organization for CMO was under an air force general, as it was in the first stages of Provide Comfort. In both instances this initial command was a result of the circumstances prevailing on the ground and not of any particular preference. Moreover, in each case, one of the first changes made was to replace the air force commander with an army commander. The rationale would appear to be that the vast majority of the forces required to execute this kind of operation are ground forces.

The decision not to use a special forces or civil affairs commander requires more explanation. In Panama, the original civil-military operations plan had called for a CMO task force under the command of a principal staff officer responsible to the CINC. His deputy was to be the senior civil affairs officer in-theater. Under the circumstances of execution, no civil affairs personnel arrived in a timely manner, and when they did, they were organized as subordinate task forces, as called for in the plan.

When reorganization became desirable, it was clear that the proper commander of the organization to carry out long-term CMO was a general officer. No such individual was represented among the civil affairs officers in the CMO task force. Moreover, analysis had shown that the mission called for an organization that was CA-heavy but included far more than civil affairs. Thus, the new Military Support Group was patterned after an adaptation of the SAF.

Since a Security Assistance Force is doctrinally built around a special forces group, it was not illogical to conclude that the right commander for the MSG would be a special forces general. That, however, was not General Thurman's choice. Instead he selected a cavalry officer who had served as commander of an augmented security assistance organization in the region. While Thurman's rationale can only be supposed, it was clear from the nature of the MSG that its significant component of conventional combat support and combat service support forces played a major role in the decision.

Task Force Freedom represents a similar decision for similar reasons. Although the ARCENT civil affairs officer proposed that a CMO task force be established to carry out the emergency restoration of Kuwait and that Brigadier General Howard Mooney, USAR, be its commander, General John Yeosock rejected the proposal. Instead he created TF Freedom under his Deputy Commanding General. Again, although General Yeosock's specific rationale can only be speculated about, it was clear that the forces required to conduct the emergency restoration mission included much more than civil affairs. In fact, there was a sufficient combat service support element to require a second subordinate task force in addition to the civil affairs task force. It should also be noted here that nowhere in civil affairs doctrine is the issue of coordination with U.S. military forces addressed. However, it is precisely those forces that have the necessary capabilities to carry out the kinds of activities required during both occupations and liberations. Until the occupied or liberated country has its government in place and functioning, the occupying or liberating military forces will, of necessity, provide the services that are normally provided by government.

The issue of command in Combined Task Force-Provide Comfort did not involve a civil affairs general but rather special forces. It would have been logical in following the SAF/FIDAF concept to have named the SOCEUR commander, Brigadier General Richard Potter, as commander of CTF-PC. After all, he was already on the ground and was the commander of a subunified command. Again, however, the CINC—in this case, CINCEUR—decided on a conventional forces general, John Shalikashvili, the DCINC of U.S. Army Europe. One reason may have been the perceived need for a senior general: Shalikashvili wore three stars. Another reason may have been the requirement to control a wide variety of forces that were not Special Operations—or SOF—related. These included both army and Marine aviation, army engineers, medical personnel, and military police, in addition to air force, Marine, and allied units.

The conclusion that one draws from an examination of the organization for CMO and its command and control is that low-intensity conflict doctrine provides a useful conceptual model. However, that model is best when modified in a number of significant ways. First, the concept is much broader than augmentation for security assistance or foreign internal defense. Rather, it is applicable to scenarios ranging from occupations and liberations, through disaster relief and other humanitarian assistance missions, to foreign internal defense.

Second, the base of organization should not be tied to any particular combat organization (such as an SF group in the older SAF configuration). Instead, the organization should be built from the kinds of units needed to execute the specific mission in the particular political-military context. In this regard, the FIDAF model represents a significant improvement over the SAF.

Third, the commander of a task force charged with a CMO mission should not be selected for his technical specialization as a CA, SF, engineer, medical, or artillery officer. Rather, the essential criteria for command of this type of organization should include broad background, command of other fairly large military units, regional familiarity, and political-military sensitivity. Such an individual may be found in CA or SF but is equally likely to be found in one of the combat arms or combat support branches.

The operations in Somalia and Haiti differed from those in Panama and the Gulf in that, like Provide Comfort, they were predominantly civil-military in character, and what combat orientation they had was in support of political and humanitarian objectives. Unlike Operation Provide Comfort, the military forces required were large combat formations organized as traditional joint task forces (JTFs) and built from the army corps and its Marine counterpart, the Marine Expeditionary Force (MEF). While these organizations were appropriate, the supporting organization for CMO was wanting in both cases.

In Somalia, because there was no reserve call-up, CA units and personnel were stretched thin. Elements of the 96th CA Battalion were attached to special forces teams throughout the operating area. CMO was coordinated by the Civil Military Operations Center (CMOC), where UNITAF's principal CA staff (Colonel Kennedy) colocated with the OFDA/DART (Mr. Garvelink). They, in turn, coordinated CMO with the U.N.-sponsored Humanitarian Assistance Coordination Center (HACC). These arrangements generally continued in this form through UNOSOM II.

Haiti followed a similar format. It began with a corps as JTF, downsized to the Tenth Mountain Division as JTF and Multinational Force headquarters, with subordinate JTFs in the JSOTF, JPOTF, and 2d BCT. Neither JTF 180 (the corps) nor JTF 190 (the Tenth Mountain) created any organization to command and control CMO. Instead, they and the follow-on UNMIH took the model that had been developed in Somalia of the CMOC and HACC and applied it without thinking through the consequences of substituting a location for a command and control headquarters.

### The Civil Affairs Component

Another element common to each of the three organizations tasked with the conduct of CMO in these contingencies was the hefty civil affairs component. In the case of the MSG, it was called the Civil Affairs Task Force (CATF); in TF Freedom it was the Combined CATF (CCATF). In CTF-PC the civil affairs component was the CA Command with its attached units under the control of Task Forces Alpha and Bravo. In each case, the CA elements performed the principal interface between the military and the civilian elements of the U.S.

government and those of the military and the host government. In the case of Operation Provide Comfort, one modification to this generalization was that the CA elements provided the interface between the military and the various international relief agencies (IGOs, NGOs, PVOs) whose role was somewhat analogous to the role of the host government in other contexts.

Somalia contrasted with the other operations considered here in that the CA elements assigned to the mission were extremely limited. For this reason, the military used the CMOC as the place to coordinate CMO, working with the U.N. HACC. The fact that this system worked as well as it did was due to the inter-agency nature of the CMOC with the OFDA/DART taking up much of the slack created by the limited number of CA personnel.

In Haiti, the same system was adopted but with the addition of a robust CA element. Here, the CMOC was colocated with the tactical operations center "inside the wire," while the HACC was located at the old USAID building in the center of the city of Port-au-Prince. Moreover, the HACC was staffed by U.S. CA personnel, deviating somewhat from the pattern in Somalia. The result was a duplication of coordination effort without any effective CMO command and control headquarters, complicated, to some extent, by confused command relationships between CA elements and the units they supported.

In Panama, Kuwait, and Haiti, civil affairs elements played a major role in the reestablishment of civilian government through teams of functional specialists who worked closely with the newly named ministers. In Panama, the Ministry Support Teams provided the initial staffing for the various ministries moving quickly to an advisory role. In Kuwait, the KTF served in much the same way. In Haiti, the Ministry Support Teams were again used, and by that name. In each instance the last role played by some members of these teams was to augment functional sections of the U.S. embassy, which were very much understrength until some time after combat ceased.

It should be noted that ministry and embassy support are missions that are especially appropriate to civil affairs units, especially in view of their origin in World War II as civil affairs and military government units.[42]

## The Inter-agency Imperative

One of the major lessons of the Panama experience was that CMO is inter-agency business. Typically, the lesson was learned in several different forums and in several different forms. Colonel Randall Elliott, the founder and chief of the KTF, did not see this as a lesson at all but rather simply as common sense. Consequently, he structured the KTF under the inter-agency Steering Committee Group, with the strong and positive support of allies within State and the Office of the Assistant Secretary of Defense for Special Operations and Low Intensity Conflict, among others.

Lieutenant General Michael Carns, the Secretary of the Joint Staff, felt strongly that, after Panama, DOD had been left to pay the bills despite informal commitments from other government agencies. As a result he insisted that Elliott and the KTF involve other government agencies in a manner such that they would have to share the bill-paying. Elliott responded in a number of innovative ways, which did bring some 27 agencies of the government into the play. The most obvious and, in the long run, important example was AID's Office of Foreign Disaster Assistance (OFDA), whose director, a USAR major, became Elliott's executive officer but also brought his civilian agency checkbook.

The OFDA/KTF connection became important in the field in other ways. A few OFDA personnel were attached to the KTF, as were personnel from the OFDA-contracted consulting firm, Intertect. These individuals made the KTF a field-operating inter-agency organization. When the KTF was absorbed by the CCATF, it, too, became inter-agency, as did its parent, TF Freedom. Thus, the OFDA-contractor section played an important role in the restoration of Kuwait and the refugee operations in southern Iraq.

The lessons learned by OFDA during Operation Desert Storm served the country well when it became necessary to execute Operation Provide Comfort. The OFDA director dispatched his deputy to work with CTF-PC, thereby re-creating the OFDA-contractor section in the CTF such that it more or less duplicated the experience of TF Freedom. The organization of the CTF into two operating task forces did make the OFDA-contractor section less effective in some ways than it had been in the south, but it generally served well and greatly enhanced the overall effectiveness of Operation Provide Comfort.

The contrast between the organizations charged with carrying out the CMO mission in Panama and the Gulf with respect to their incorporation of an inter-agency element clearly argues strongly in favor of this approach. The staff of the MSG recognized that the lack of inter-agency organization significantly hampered their efforts but were unable to do anything to change the situation.[43] By contrast, the far-sighted approach taken by Colonel Elliott to implement General Carns' guidance made the field aspect of inter-agency organization essentially a nonproblem. This particular lesson gives the appearance of having been institutionalized by Somalia and Haiti—with significant expansion in the latter.

The one area where the inter-agency requirement was ignored was in planning at the theater and army component level. Closely held plans, that initially did not admit to anyone outside a very narrow circle that there was any intention to eject Saddam from Kuwait, certainly did nothing to further inter-agency planning. More important, this approach withheld from the KTF information it required to make its plans conform to those of CENTCOM and ARCENT. Since KTF plans were developed without theater input, they were clearly less than wholly usable and so were rejected by the ARCENT and CENTCOM staffs. Not until the KTF arrived in-theater and came under the CINC's control were these discrepancies reconciled. While compartmentalization remains a problem—significantly so in Haiti—it has been ameliorated to a limited degree since Panama and the Gulf. Nevertheless, Haiti saw the first-ever effort at inter-agency political-military planning. Although it was hardly a success, the Clinton administration has attempted to institutionalize the lessons with the promulgation of Presidential Decision Directive (PDD) 56.

### The Means (Resources)

The conduct of CMO during war, in the termination of war, and in transition to secure a sustainable peace requires the application of significant organizational and material resources. Organizational resources come in two models—military and civilian. The first of the military organizations to be considered is the civil affairs community. It is made up of five USAR Civil Affairs Commands, their supporting brigades and battalions, and the active component 96th Civil Affairs Battalion.[44] In addition, there are two civil affairs groups in the U.S. Marine Corps Reserve.

The origins and development of U.S. Civil Affairs are discussed above. Here, it is sufficient to state that U.S. civil affairs units, particularly those in the USAR, provide capabilities and expertise in thousands of permutations of the 20 CA functional areas that are largely unknown in the active military. Further, these CA units are more than capable of interacting effectively with the U.S. and allied military command, as well as with U.S. and other governmental civilian agencies. CA units are designed to, and do, bridge the gap between the military and the variety of civilian government and private organizations involved in the zone where military operations are taking, or have taken, place. CA units, however, do not have the capability to command and control other types of military units charged with executing portions of the CMO mission. Nor are CA units alone fully capable of planning the entire range of civil-military operations.

The numerous tasks involved in civil-military operations go far beyond the capabilities of CA units. Typically, there are tasks that call for engineer units, medical units, transportation units (air, ground, and sea), quartermaster units, and others. Often, an area support group is essential to the effective execution of the mission.

What has not been mentioned previously is the security mission so often associated with CMO, especially during the war termination process. This was a critical factor in Panama, Kuwait, southern and northern Iraq, Somalia, and Haiti. Infantry, MPs, and special forces were essential to the success of the CMO mission in all these cases. In Operation Provide Comfort, armed air assets, both rotary and fixed-wing, provided much of the punch that kept the Iraqis from interfering with the humanitarian assistance mission. Often overlooked in considering the CMO mission are the assets represented by civil agencies. This was a concern at the Joint Staff level during the planning for Operations Desert Shield and Desert Storm, which resulted in significant consideration and involvement by, and with, U.S. civilian agencies in Kuwait. A very similar situation developed in Haiti. The fact that the KTF, in conjunction with the Kuwaiti government, constituted a combined planning group brought into play the various host government agencies and institutions. Most of these were government ministries which did, as in Panama, need to be reconstituted before they could begin to exercise their functions effectively.

Operation Provide Comfort brought a whole new set of organizational resources into play. These were the various IGOs, many of which were members of the U.N. family, and NGOs, such as the International Committee of the Red Cross and Doctors without Borders. Each organization brought certain expertise that needed to be coordinated with the whole effort but often was best coordinated through the informal mechanisms developed in shared experiences in countless disasters. However, Operation Provide Comfort was the first time that most of these organizations had ever worked with the military of any country. Subsequently, Operation Restore Hope greatly expanded dealings with IGOs and NGOs, and by the time of Operation Uphold Democracy, many such relationships were being routinized.

Material resources, especially including finances, largely were the responsibility of the involved governments. Most of the NGOs, for example, were funded for the purchase of necessary materials, such as tubing for potable water and medicines, by grants from the various governments involved. In the U.S. case, these grants generally were funded by OFDA at the discretion of its Disaster Assistance Relief Team chief. U.N. agencies are, of course, funded by member nations' governments, which pay regularly assessed quotas as well as supplemental emergency quotas.

Only in Kuwait, of all the cases under consideration, was the funding of operations significantly different. Kuwait, as an incredibly rich, oil-producing state which has invested its oil profits wisely and well for a number of years, contracted with the U.S. government, the U.S. Army Corps of Engineers, and U.S. and other private firms to provide the necessary materials and services, both for emergency restoration and for long-term reconstruction. However, one would be hard-pressed to think of any probable future scenarios where the liberated or conquered nation will be able and willing to pay for the material resources required. Thus, planning for future operations will have to take a long and hard look at resourcing if the operations are to be successful.

## The Strategic Implications

War termination and transition to a post-conflict peace-building development effort are phases of military operations that must be planned in full coordination with war fighting. To be successful, its objectives need to be defined in end-state terms with clear supporting objectives that are both military and civil-military in nature. This, in turn, suggests that civil-military operations in the post-conflict period—post-conflict activities—may be a necessary condition for victory. Thus, when the political-military and the exclusively military end states are not fully synchronized, strategic victory is that much harder to achieve.

For the United States to effectively terminate a war requires that unity of effort be achieved within the entire U.S. government. This demands inter-agency coordination from the beginning, at the highest levels. It further requires that the concept behind the Goldwater-Nichols legislation be adhered to throughout DOD as well as in the inter-agency arena. The use of executive agency within CENTCOM, as well as for the reconstruction of Kuwait, violated the intent of the legislation and served to further complicate relationships that already were quite complicated.

The best example of the intent of Goldwater-Nichols being ignored in the inter-agency arena is the case of the KTF in Washington. It was wrong that the KTF was not under the command of CINCCENT until deployed to theater; this is not to say that the KTF should have been under CENTCOM operational control, but rather that the lack of any kind of command relationship was a complication that could easily have been avoided.

Inter-agency planning only took place because of the existence of the KTF and because it was operating under inter-agency auspices. CENTCOM planning was closely held and not shared in the inter-agency coordination forums. Had it not been for the creation of the KTF, CMO related to Desert Storm might never have seen any inter-agency coordination prior to execution, as occurred in Panama. It is hardly laudable to fight a war and win a peace if the only way that all elements of power can be brought to bear on the problem is through pure serendipity. However, that is precisely what happened in the creation of the KTF—and did not happen in Panama, with predictable consequences.

American military doctrine is changing rapidly to recognize the inter-agency imperative. Already, the Joint Staff has published a manual on inter-agency operations. Inter-agency operations are being taught in the staff colleges. Operationally, two counterdrug JTFs (JTF 4 and JTF 5) have been renamed and reconfigured as Joint Interagency Task Forces East and West. Although there has been significant progress in this area, the military still has not realized institutionally that the problems of war and peace are too complicated for either the military or civilian agencies of the U.S. government to address without the participation of the other as a full partner. There remains far too much compartmentalization in the name of operational security, resulting in a lack of critical input by civilian governmental agencies to OPLANS and OPORDS.

The same three operations tell us that in organizing to execute CMO, we are on the right track. The SAF/FIDAF provides a good model organization to conduct CMO. The model, however, lacks a major and essential component: it fails to integrate civilian governmental agencies. The negative consequences of this failing were found in the operation of the MSG in Panama.[45] The positive effect of such integration was shown by the operations of TF Freedom and the CTF-PC; however, neither of the latter two organizations provides an appropriate model. In both cases, the integration of the OFDA-contractor team was done ad hoc. Rather, what is required is an organizational construct that views the entire task force charged with the conduct of CMO as being fully integrated with civilian government agency personnel in the command group and on the staff, and generally operating sections organized by individual agencies.[46] The

SAF/FIDAF model is not appropriate for conducting a major operation like those in Somalia or Haiti. There, the SAF/FIDAF might well have been incorporated as a subordinate JTF.

Command and control has been addressed to some extent in this chapter and elsewhere. The questions remaining are for whom the CMO commander should work, as well as who he should be. These operations clearly suggest that the CMO commander should be under the command of the senior commander having responsibility for whatever goes on in the area of the operation. In Operation Desert Storm, this should have been the CINC rather than the ARCENT commander. In Operation Provide Comfort, it was the CINC. In Panama, it was initially the CINC, and then, with reorganization, it became the Joint Task Force Commander. In neither instance did command of CMO violate the dictum stated here. This discussion clearly supports the notion of the SAF/FIDAF model for a subordinate JTF.

Control, however, is sometimes different from command. In some instances, control should be exercised by the president's senior personal representative in-country. Most often, this is the American ambassador. In Panama, the ambassador was given operational control of the CMO task force by the CINC. Later, when the MSG was established, it was a de facto member of the country team, and embassy suggestions were treated as orders. In Kuwait, TF Freedom specifically did not come under the operational control of the ambassador, for some good reasons. Potential problems were solved by effective coordination without conflict. Later, however, as the Defense Reconstruction Assistance Office was being established, there were some interesting, if minor, battles to resolve who really was in charge—it turned out to be the ambassador, to nobody's surprise. Command and control in an environment like Kuwait with a functioning embassy and an ambassador in-country, but with coalition operations taking place across international borders, require some doctrinal thought and clarification. Nevertheless, the president needs to designate one individual as being unambiguously ''in charge.'' Anything less will produce needless conflict and confusion.

The final, and most important, strategic implication of this study is that it confirms the observation that civil-military operations are significantly larger than civil affairs. CMO represent the centerpiece of the termination of war on terms that achieve the end state identified by our national objectives. CMO also may be the essence of the operation itself, going well beyond war and conflict termination.

**NOTES**

This chapter is a revision of chapters 1 and 17 of John T. Fishel, *Civil Military Operations in the New World* (Westport, CT: Praeger, 1997).

1. Headquarters, Department of the Army (HQDA), *Field Manual [FM] 41–10: Civil Affairs Operations* (Washington, DC: HQDA, December 17, 1985).

2. Ibid.

3. See John T. Fishel, *The Fog of Peace: Planning and Executing the Restoration of Panama* (Carlisle Barracks, PA: Strategic Studies Institute, U.S. Army War College, April 15, 1992).

4. Ibid.

5. HQDA, *FM 41–10.*

6. Fishel, *Fog of Peace.*

7. See Robert Wolfe, ed., *Americans as Proconsuls: United States Military Government in Germany and Japan, 1944–1952* (Carbondale: Southern Illinois University Press, 1984).

8. John H. Backer, "From Morgenthau Plan to Marshall Plan," in Wolfe, *Americans as Proconsuls,* pp. 155–165.

9. Ralph Braibanti, "The MacArthur Shogunate in Allied Guise," in Wolfe, *Americans as Proconsuls,* pp. 77–91.

10. M. J. Mayo, "American Wartime Planning for Occupied Japan: The Role of the Experts," and Earl F. Ziemke, "Improvising Stability and Change in Postwar Germany," both in Wolfe, *Americans as Proconsuls,* pp. 3–66.

11. Ziemke, "Improving Stability," p. 59.

12. Ibid.

13. Lucius D. Clay, *Decision in Germany* (Garden City, NY: Doubleday and Company, 1950), p. 56.

14. Fishel, *Fog of Peace.*

15. Ibid.

16. Interviews with CENTCOM staff officers, October 1991–May 1992.

17. Arthur F. Lykke, Jr., ed., *Military Strategy, Theory and Application* (Carlisle Barracks, PA: Strategic Studies Institute, U.S. Army War College, 1989).

18. Interviews with CENTCOM/ARCENT, State Department/AID officers, October–December 1991.

19. Interviews with SOUTHCOM/COMCMOTF/MSG officers, April–May 1991.

20. Fishel, *Fog of Peace.*

21. Ibid.

22. Interviews with CENTCOM/ARCENT/KTF/Country Team officers, October–December 1991.

23. Ibid.

24. Interview with Lieutenant General John Shalikashvili, October 31, 1991. Note that while U.S. government civilians were under the legal jurisdiction of the U.S. embassy, they operated under the control of General Shalikashvili (Operational Control [OPTCON] and Tactical Control [TACONI]).

25. Interviews with ARCENT and CENTCOM officers, October–December 1991.

26. Ibid.

27. Interviews with CENTCOM and USSOCOM officers, October–December 1991.

28. Fishel, *Fog of Peace*; interviews with CENTCOM/ARCENT/KTF/TF Freedom and Provide Comfort officers, October–December 1991.

29. HQDA, *FM 41–10.*

30. Fishel, *Fog of Peace.*

31. Ibid.

32. Ibid.

33. Interviews with Operation Provide Comfort and State Department/AID officers, October–December 1991.

34. Fishel, *Fog of Peace*.

35. The Army War College recently has integrated into its curriculum the study of post-conflict activities as a way to successfully terminate war, as have the Command and General Staff College, the Air Command and Staff College, and the Canadian Armed Forces Staff College.

36. Douglas Craft, ''Operational Analysis of the Persian Gulf War,'' draft paper, Strategic Studies Institute, U.S. Army War College, 1992.

37. Colonel Randall Elliott, interviews, September–December 1991, February 1992.

38. See Fishel, *Civil Military Operations in the New World*, especially Part II.

39. See Fishel, *Fog of Peace*. An example of the kind of things the military can do in CMO planning to strengthen the basis for democracy is consulting the local populace in establishing priorities for restoration of services. In Kuwait, this would have meant calling together local assemblies—in the Kuwaiti tradition of its legislative assembly, establishing an electoral mechanism, and training the assembly. A similar concept based on Panamanian traditions was included in the strategy proposed by the MSG to the U.S. embassy.

40. See Fishel, *Fog of Peace*.

41. Headquarters, Department of the Army (HQDA), *Field Manual [FM] 100–20; Low Intensity Conflict* (Washington, DC: HQDA, 1981).

42. Headquarters, Departments of the Army and Air Force, *Field Manual 100–20; Air Force PAM 3–20, Military Operations in Low Intensity Conflict* (Washington, DC, December 5, 1990).

43. HQDA, *FM 41–10*. See also Chapter 1 of this study.

44. Fishel, *Fog of Peace*.

45. It should be noted that USAR CA companies have been upgraded to battalions.

46. Fishel, *Fog of Peace*.

Chapter 8

# A Grand National Security Strategy for Legitimate Governance and Crisis Prevention

## Robert M. Herrick

The Cold War victory of legitimate governance over authoritarianism provides the first feasible opportunity in history for the world to embrace the principles of legitimate governance and human dignity as a basis for preventing crises and realizing global peace.

Expanding U.S. national security strategy from its current predominantly defensive posture to a profoundly more proactive and principled grand strategy emphasizing legitimate governance and crisis prevention would be a visionary and historic political evolution for the United States and world affairs. A principled grand strategy that reinvigorates U.S. national purpose while securing national interests will require implementing legislation to enhance national security policy and planning and implementation of institutions and resources.

This chapter develops a strategic framework and rationale leading to a concrete approach for responsible intervention in failing or failed states. In making the case that leads to implementing legislation, a story about national security strategy insights since Word War II is told. The argument begins with a discussion of strategy itself, followed by the rationale for legitimate governance, including dimensions and stability factors. Then, strategic insights from Cold War and post–Cold War milieus substantiate the need for change. Finally, the current strategy is viewed to determine specifically what must be done, leading to the required legislation.

## PART I: STRATEGY, STRATEGY CONSIDERATIONS, GRAND STRATEGY, AND VISION

Before delving into the ''grand and principled strategy'' argument itself, it is appropriate to briefly establish a common basis for discussing strategy, strategic concepts, and considerations for evaluating strategies, grand strategy, and vision. An acceptable definition of strategy is *Webster's*: "the science and art of employing the political, economic, psychological, and military forces of a nation or group of nations to afford the maximum support to adopted policies in peace or war." Strategic theory traditionally explains strategy as a system with three major components: ends, ways, and means. With variations in specific terminology, these components have stood the test of time. Unfortunately and too often, they are appreciated only retrospectively because national leaders and politician authors seldom consider them adequately before making earthshaking decisions.

### Strategy Ends

The first strategic component is the "objective," "end," or "end state" to be achieved. History warns, at the peril of would-be strategists, kings, and leaders, that the strategic objective(s) must be clearly stated and, where appropriate, defined comprehensively. Obviously, clarity of objectives is critical when considering alternative plans and resource requirements, the inadequacy of which may well spell disaster.

Recent strategic thinking about objectives has evolved toward greater consideration of end states or the specific conditions that must be achieved before exiting a situation or for recognizing when victory has been achieved. Advanced thinkers are considering "stable end states" that are self-sustaining, thus limiting the probability of future crises. These end states involve the achievement of legitimate political, economic, social/legal, military/security, and psychological/informational states that are resilient to corruption or internal and external threats by being properly representative of, and responsive to, their societies. Again and again, history is clear: governments that are not legitimate are not stable. They inevitably devolve into crisis.

As the most advanced theorists examine the empirical evidence flowing from the great and unique American experiment, they are increasing their appreciation of the strategic insights of history's notables such as Confucius, Sun Tsu, Sophocles, Cicero, St. Augustine, Machiavelli, Napoleon, Clausewitz, Lincoln and Grant, MacArthur, Marshall, Mao, Giap, and King. The American experience, with its democratic and human rights impact on the world, illuminates the strategic linkage between international, national, local, and individual interests. It validates the notion that, indeed, the legitimacy of a government ultimately is derived from the consent and support of the citizens—with the conclusion that human dignity and inalienable rights transcend both borders and the sovereignty claims of despots. The strategy implication for objectives and end states is that individual rights must be a strategic consideration because an illegitimate end state is unstable and unsustainable.

## Strategy Ways

The second component of strategy is the "plan" or "way" in which the objective is to be achieved. In theory, all the elements of national power—political, economic, military, and informational—are appropriately used in a coordinated and synchronized way to achieve strategic objectives. There may be intermediate objectives, certain sequences of actions that need to be accomplished, excursions into situations that unexpectedly crop up or perhaps actions in seemingly unrelated areas to shore up international support or deter external foes. Of course, ways should be reassessed continuously during implementation based upon the facts on the ground.

The president is responsible for national security policies and strategies. With the assistance of the National Security Council (NSC) and the State Department as the lead agency, foreign policy is supposed to be formulated and then implemented with coordinated strategies to achieve national strategic objectives. As will be discussed in some detail later, important aspects of U.S. strategic planning have been in disarray for many years, with a penchant for the ad hoc. The principal reason, despite the NSC's coordination role, is that U.S. strategic planning and implementation capabilities are weak across the board and dangerously inadequate in the State Department.

## Strategy Means

The third component of strategy consists of the resources or means necessary for implementing the strategic plan. Here, even in the abundant United States, priorities and tradeoffs are in order. But without sound objectives and plans, the U.S. administration and Congress are often forced to make priority and resources decisions based upon insufficient information including overreliance on the supposed wisdom of the executive branch political appointees and personnel occupying strategic policy positions, who are not strategists. Vietnam is one costly example where strategic planning was inadequate. Millions of Vietnamese and Cambodians were victims as well as the 60,000 U.S. lives lost and a trillion dollars expended.

## Considerations for Evaluating Strategies

The rule of thumb for evaluating strategic alternatives and plans consists of three broad questions that should be satisfied. Is the strategy "feasible," "practical," and "suitable?" These are hard questions about the ends, ways, and means of a strategy that when not answered satisfactorily, set the stage for failure.

Vietnam is an appropriate example of a failed strategy that can be used to discuss feasibility, practicality, and suitability considerations. Was the Vietnam

War strategy a feasible, practical, and suitable strategy with (1) the "end" of providing the corrupt and illegitimate South Vietnamese government the opportunity to determine South Vietnam's own future; (2) the "way" of convincing North Vietnam to stop fighting through a constrained bombing and interdiction campaign and a war of attrition conducted in South Vietnam without conquering North Vietnam; and (3) the "means" of an open-ended commitment of massive amounts of U.S. resources and lives?

We are slowly coming to grips with the answers. Yes, it was suitable from a geopolitical, containment, and human rights perspective to save South Vietnam from communism. The United States dismissed the direct option of conquering North Vietnam as unsuitable because of no overt North Vietnam provocation and the risk of provoking China. Also, the direct option was considered impractical and infeasible in light of the French debacle and other worldwide commitments. Therefore the United States chose supporting and assisting South Vietnam as the seemingly suitable, practical, and hopefully feasible option, even while recognizing that Ho Chi Minh, the leader of North Vietnam, enjoyed great political legitimacy throughout Vietnam as a nationalist leader responsible for the Vietminh victory over the French.

As confirmed by the Johnson tapes, the tragic error in U.S. strategic considerations was the lack of wisdom about legitimate governance as a critical end state for South Vietnam. Had this strategic objective been pursued with diligence early on, it would have been feasible and practical to defeat North Vietnam's efforts to subvert the South. Unfortunately, when furtive efforts to improve South Vietnamese legitimacy became frustrating, the United States turned to the military, supporting military coups and a succession of corrupt and illegitimate South Vietnamese governments. With a weakening South, the United States chose to take over the war to avoid early military defeat, an action that further damaged the credibility of the South. Despite battlefield losses as the war progressed, the North became even more convinced of their ultimate victory because their claims of a legitimate nationalist cause were reinforced by the heavy U.S. involvement and no effective moral challenge by the obviously corrupt South Vietnam government.

The U.S. public supported the U.S. effort in Vietnam when they believed the strategy had a legitimate government in South Vietnam as the end state. Moreover, had early legitimacy efforts been more productive, the canceled 1956 election would have occurred. North Vietnam would have lacked the provocation for massive subversion and would have realized it would be impractical and infeasible to win against a legitimate government. A diplomatic solution would have been possible.

Strategically, the Vietnam War was lost early because of the lack of South Vietnamese legitimacy. At the time, even those with standing such as Sir Robert Thompson and those in important positions such as General Edward Lansdale, who warned that the strategy was fatally flawed for legitimacy reasons, were not only ignored, they were ridiculed and pushed aside. Unfortunately, the les-

sons about legitimate governance still have not sunk in, and the United States
is on the road to making monstrously greater mistakes in the post-Cold War
period.

**Grand Strategy and Vision**

Grand strategy involves achievement of an overarching global vision or end
state embodying national values and interests. "A world safe for democracy,"
"world communism," and "containment" provided global objectives to measure the feasibility, suitability, and practicality of regional strategies, tactics, and
national decisions. The backdrop provided by a grand strategy is important for
ensuring that near-term actions are in consonance with, and not dysfunctional
to, the achievement of the ultimate goal.

A grand and global strategy is now feasible for enhancing world peace by
promoting legitimate governance and thus ensuring the American way of life
for centuries. As the dominant, unchallenged military and economic power with
one of the most legitimate and respected governments on the globe, the United
States not only has the capacity but also the moral responsibility to undertake
this mission. Beyond the imperative of ensuring survival, the United States has
a principled legacy of sacrifice for freedom and a revolutionary vision for humanity and the world. American vision is expressed in ideas and deeds from
pre-Revolutionary Puritan Governor Winthrop's shining city on the hill; the
Declaration of Independence's profound premise of the inalienable rights of all
people to life, liberty, and the pursuit of happiness; Jefferson's view for spreading democracy throughout the world; the aspirations of the League of Nations
and United Nations (U.N.); Cold War containment; and now the Organization
for Security Cooperation in Europe's (OSCE) and the North Atlantic Treaty
Organization's (NATO) concern about democracies. It is from this positive legacy, with due consideration given to the current and projected world milieu, that
a vision for the future and the outline of a grand strategy is built.

"Legitimate governance" or "democracy" is the feasible, suitable, practical,
and principled grand strategy to succeed "containment." The vision and end
state of the principled grand strategy is peace maintained and strengthened
through cooperation among countries in a world dominated by a growing number of nations with legitimate governance. The rationale and implementation
aspects of the grand strategy for legitimate governance are examined in the
discussions that follow.

**PART II: RATIONALE OF HISTORY AND THE CURRENT
MILIEU**

**Ancient Wisdom**

The rationale for legitimate governance as an essential tool for peace is as
old as history itself. Over two thousand years ago Sun Tzu observed that "those,

who excel in war, first cultivate their own humanity and justice and maintain their laws and institutions. By these means they make their governments invincible."[1] Sun Tzu's direct meaning is clear. A government with the support of its people will be strong, and foes need be wary.

More important, full understanding of the wisdom of Sun Tzu's admonition comes not from the explicit but from the implicit message—the converse of his admonition. Illegitimate governments are doomed to failure. Without the support of their people and fear in the hearts of their foes, illegitimate governments inexorably are brought down by either internal or external forces, or both. Ultimately, the illegitimacy of both suppressive and seemingly benevolent authoritarian governments leads to their destruction.

### Legitimate Governance

Before going further, it is appropriate to define the term "legitimate governance." John Fishel's 1986 study of the subject examined its relationship to stability and respect for human rights. His study broadened the meaning of the term "legitimate" as it relates to government from de jure, with its traditional national sovereignty rights, to the now widely accepted meaning that embraces the concept of "moral legitimacy," and thus the term: "legitimate governance." There is legitimate governance when government exists to serve the people. The measure of this involves three essential ingredients: consent, rectitude, and accountability.[2]

- Consent means that the people determine the form of government and the method by which officials are chosen to serve. Constitutions are a way for achieving consent of the governed.
- Rectitude means that the government must make good on its contract with the people it serves.
- Accountability means that the people have the ability to change peaceably the form of government and those who serve. Referendums, constitutional amendments, elections, and fair representation of the people are ways.

It is clear that elections do not a democracy or legitimate governance make. Elections are essential in legitimate governance but not sufficient in themselves for legitimate governance. This is because many elections are held by forms of government that do not serve the will of the people in terms of consent, rectitude, and accountability.

### Legitimate Governance Dimensions

Legitimate governance may be described more specifically in normative terms relating to political, social-legal, economic, and military-security dimensions of government. This normative approach, which is adaptable to different cultural contexts, provides an important criterion for measuring the relative legitimacy of governments or actors in instability situations.

The political dimension considers constitutional, representative, pluralistic government with bills of rights and rules of law; civil government supremacy over military with mechanisms for peaceful transition of power; professional, noncorrupt civil service; appropriate distribution of power and services from national to local levels.

The social-legal dimension considers religious tolerance and special considerations, including special autonomy where appropriate; equitable justice system; franchising of all ethnic groups; social mobility including special efforts to enhance opportunity for the historically disadvantaged; and social services including health and education.

The economic dimension considers economic opportunity for all segments of the population; actions to eliminate economic control by oligarchy and corruption; support for small business, including economic incentives; privatization of statist industry; support for a free market system.

The military-security dimension considers professional law enforcement in the service of the people; professional military subordinate to civilian authority capable of accomplishing national defense and treaty responsibilities. In an internal threat or insurgency situation the military dimension is additionally measured by its ability to defeat insurgency rapidly with professional forces operating in support of national legitimacy objectives, and its ability to organize and train forces to defeat the threat by attacking insurgent vulnerabilities emphasizing superior intelligence, operations/exploitation, and security capabilities.

### Lessons from Recent History

In 1984, the U.S. Army, still confounded by what happened in the Vietnam War, directed a research effort to determine the critical national stability factors leading to victory or defeat in conflicts since World War II. The formal work, led by Professor Max Manwaring and Colonel Al Baker, took two years to examine 69 situations around the world through research and face-to-face discussions with internationally known experts and principals on both sides of the conflicts. Following this research, Manwaring spent several years in South America continuing the research and assisting Southern Command's Small Wars Operations Research Directorate (SWORD) in the resolution of Latin American conflicts and crises.[3]

The background research for the project revealed that the effort was actually the first attempt to examine the critical elements of national stability through rigorous analysis. When the research data and relationships were analyzed, it became evident that the findings supplanted many previous notions and anecdotal theories about national stability, including economic determinance and prerequisites for democracy. Over 100 variables were factored down to seven national stability factors, each so important that failure in any one factor meant almost sure defeat. Affectionately, the factors have become known as the "Max Factors."[4]

The stability factor that dominated all others was legitimacy. In almost every case, the results showed that the relative legitimacy of competing causes and the legitimacy of actions by antagonists were dominant factors in determining victory or defeat. The six factors other than legitimacy were: unity of effort or congruence, plans and programs, competence, and three categories of support, which were assistance from a major external supporter, internal support, and actions to stop external support to internal adversaries. The results were validated by successfully applying the seven factors to the 69 original cases. Subsequently, the factors were used to analyze ongoing conflicts in Latin America and elsewhere, where they successfully predicted outcomes.

It is important to note at this point that the 1984–1986 research was conducted during the Cold War with no preconceived ideas or theories. The emergence and validation of legitimacy as the dominant national stability factor in peace and war was neither obvious nor anticipated by the researchers. Essentially, legitimacy or legitimate governance was shown to be the new stability paradigm for analyzing root causes and solutions for national stability situations.

During the 15 years since the study, thinking in the military doctrine, academic, and national policy communities has moved rhetorically toward understanding the legitimacy imperative for national stability. But the movement has not been sufficient to overcome traditional Cold War national security planning, implementation, and resource methods and procedures. Perhaps the concept is almost too obvious and too surprisingly profound, and at the same time too threatening to existing institutions and constituencies, to be readily adopted. Of course, the purpose of this writing is to further influence the acceptance process.

### National Stability Factors

Returning to the seven critical national stability factors, it is important to understand the first and dominant factor, legitimacy, on several levels. At the grand or global strategy level, the full expansion of legitimate governance worldwide is the end state for global peace. Legitimate governance at the national level is the state that must be achieved and maintained in order to sustain stability and secure respect for human rights. During times of crises, political transition, internal instability, or external war, the relative legitimacy of competing forces and their actions bear strongly on the ultimate outcome.

Thus, nations with stability problems, especially those in transition from authoritarian political systems to democracy, should strive toward culturally appropriate legitimate governance as the primary national security objective and end state. Transitioning nations should clearly define their holistic end state in terms of the political, social/legal, economic, and security/military dimensions discussed earlier. Unfortunately, history shows that most countries in crisis do not even know that clear objectives are absolutely essential to successful societal transformation. They quickly doom themselves by hoping they can go step by step to "somewhere" and be successful, only to find themselves overcome by adversity. Clearly, many nations need help in the intellectual and practical processes of determining their desired transformation legitimate governance end states. In almost all cases transition nation leaders must have vision and help.

The second factor, unity of effort or congruence, speaks to the fact that even with visionary leaders, nations often fail because of the polarity of political agendas, corruption, and power struggles. Again, nations may need help in determining where they currently are, examining alternative actions, planning, and negotiating the difficult processes of achieving the necessary congruence or unity of effort which is essential for success.

If current plans and programs are insufficient for achieving success in all dimensions, nations invariably fail because they don't deliver or are overcome by adversaries. Most nations need assistance in determining which programs are good, what new ones are needed, and what priorities are appropriate for achieving their objectives. They also may need help in managing some or all of their ongoing programs.

Competence, the third critical factor, confirms that countries will not succeed on their own if they lack the capacity or expertise associated with developing proper objectives, achieving unity of effort, and planning and implementing essential programs. Here again, help is often needed.

The fifth, sixth, and seventh factors involve support and assistance. When appropriate and consistent outside support is needed but not provided, the country is doomed. When a country itself is unwilling to provide its share of the needed energy and resources, success is not possible. Also, if external support to internal adversaries of stability objectives is not thwarted, objectives will not be achieved.

Using the above national stability factors to assess the status of the legitimate governance dimensions of a country in crisis or potentially in crisis is not difficult. Knowing that the factors are quite reliable indicators of national stability, the results can be used for strategic planning, program development, and policy decisions. The assessment should provide the wisdom that will help avoid option-limiting decisions that lead to courses of action which are destined to be infeasible for achieving desired objectives or are only capable of producing suboptimal solutions.

## PART III: WHAT IS TO BE DONE?

First, in discussing what to do, some perspectives on past and present milieus are appropriate in order to set the stage for presenting the concept for a principled grand strategy for national security and crisis prevention. The short perspectives presented are not intended to be comprehensive but are to illuminate strategic perceptions from a national stability strategy view. Then, a critique of what is being done will be provided, followed by what is to be done and how to get it done.

## Cold War Milieu

It can be posited that the U.S. strategy during the Cold War was not really "containment" as espoused by Kennan. It was actually "deterrence," which is a balance of power strategy. Understanding the difference between Kennan's containment theory and deterrence strategy is important to appreciating the impact of the Cold War on the current national security strategy. Kennan's containment theory postulated that democracy and freedom "must eventually find their outlet in either the breakup or gradual mellowing of Soviet power."[5] In essence, the lack of legitimacy would bring the Soviet Union down.

If a proper strategy were implemented from Kennan's postulate, the United States would have, of course, deterred. But while deterring, other things would have been pursued in earnest to hasten the Soviet Union's demise. The principal objective would have been to attack the Soviet center of gravity, the illegitimacy of its political system. The United States would have turned the Cold War into a war between totalitarianism and democracy, rather than communism versus capitalism. While subverting the Soviet system, the United States would have offered to help them from their mess while concurrently surrounding them by making concerted efforts to strengthen democracy around the world. Even though the United States did some of the things mentioned, those efforts were far down the priority list from conventional and nuclear deterrence. The United States did not really believe Kennan. There was no concerted legitimacy strategy to defeat the USSR.

Instead, the United States went the balance of power route, building a massive military machine and promoting its interests around the world through diplomatic, economic, and military assistance means. Rogues of all stripes were befriended if they leaned West. There was plotting, spying, and sometimes fighting to maintain the status quo. But for the most part, promotion of democracy was played down or even avoided because of the possibility of destabilizing not so noble friends. Over time, U.S. national security bureaucracies lost flexibility in shaping the programs that constituted the deterrence strategy. They became heavily influenced by both powerful inside constituencies with favored programs and outside constituencies that provided military hardware, economic assistance, agriculture products, and other types of aid.

For decades the United States busily and blindly deterred with little attention to the ongoing deterioration of the Union of Soviet Socialist Republics. Internally, the USSR could not sustain its illegitimate political, social, economic, and military systems in the face of U.S. and Western world successes. Suddenly, and to the surprise of most, the USSR cracked and then collapsed. Kennan's thesis proved to be more sage than almost anyone believed possible.

Along the way, there were other concerns and shocks including Greece, Korea, Cuba, the USSR's Arab surrogates, Vietnam, Dominican Republic, Nicaragua, El Salvador, Iran, Grenada, Lebanon, and Panama. For the most part, except for Iran, they were viewed as communist containment problems with little emphasis given to legitimacy issues. Especially after the Vietnam debacle, the United States tried to forget low-intensity conflict and such things as nation building and legitimacy considerations. This attitude, which still pervades today, meant that there was little pursuit of the wisdom to be gained from the Cold War experiences. When the Cold War ended and the whole world became a cauldron of low-intensity conflicts and instability situations, the United States was not, and still is not, prepared. As was the case during Vietnam, the few who understood legitimacy issues and saw the "new world disorder" coming were generally ignored, as they continue to be now.

## Post–Cold War Milieu—A Legitimacy Crisis

In the decade following the Cold War, the United States has failed to consolidate the triumph of legitimate governance over competing authoritarian forms, including centrally imposed socialism. The United States did not implement a grand strategy for actively promoting democracy and legitimate governance by assisting and bolstering fragile countries attempting to establish culturally appropriate legitimate institutions.

Most of the decade has seen the United States abrogate world security and moral leadership responsibility to inept multinational entities, provide inadequate assistance to struggling democracies, make ad hoc confrontational diplomatic and military blunders, and form unprincipled economic alliances. The result is that U.S. political, economic, and moral legitimacy in global affairs is weakened, as is its superpower influence in military areas including nuclear.

Into the legitimacy void left by declining and self-emasculating former superpowers, unsavory nations and groups, unconstrained by effective legal, moral, ecological, and economic norms, are pursuing nefarious agendas and forging pseudopragmatic and criminal economic and security arrangements, which are consolidating an amoral framework of a New World Order.

The ubiquitous scope and depth of the legitimacy crisis belies the notion that the world will muddle through with stable democracy triumphant over authoritarianism, extremism, corruption, international crime, and narcotics. From Russia to Haiti, even the word "democracy" is denounced as an evil charade promulgated by the powerful to deceive and rob citizens of the minimal security and well-being they once possessed.

At best, the tragic denouement of the U.S. abdication will be the squandering of the most propitious moment for human progress in history and surrender to an epoch of grinding devolution of civilization: an amoral era of greed, corruption, terror, crime, fear, cowardice, and recrimination . . . a technological Middle Ages. Not at all inconceivable, the world could slide into the abyss as uncontrollable criminality reigns and rogues commit nuclear terror and genocide with cataclysmic consequences . . . "Wormwood."[6]

## What to Do

But the damning scenario is precludable. The ill-fated course is not fully set, and the future is not written. Alternative futures exist that may be grasped, but only through wise, decisive, moral leadership and action by the United States.

The first step is recognition that the lack of moral leadership and the passiveness of the current U.S. approach to foreign policy: "ad hoc, react to events as they unfold—keep options open—promote multilateralism," is responsible for the world's slide toward catastrophe. Rather than preside and dabble, the United States must provide strong, moral leadership and practical, direct assistance in order to promote legitimate governance and a democratic world order. The United States is not doing this.

Second, a change to proactive engagement should be based upon philosophical and practical wisdom that is acceptable to the American people and the world. The United States must embrace the premise that individual freedom, protected by representative democracy, is a proven concept for governance applicable for all nations regardless of culture. The proof includes the U.S. 200-year-plus experiment, successes of other democracies, the existence of democracy-based institutions in almost all cultures, almost universal acceptance that individual freedom is compatible with innate human aspirations, and democracy's demonstrated resilience, inherent stability, and prosperity.

The third step involves morality and vision. The United States must discard its relativistic view of national sovereignty that tacitly accepts the tyrannical suppression of citizens in other countries. The United States must stand for and extend to the world its own vision of the inalienable rights of all persons.

Given the move from passive to proactive promotion of democracy and legitimate governance as a major pillar of U.S. foreign policy, many phenomenal things are possible at little cost that would quickly reverse current negative trends and pave the way for a democratic and prosperous world. Foremost among things to be done is for the United States to offer comprehensive multi-year assistance to fragile governments around the world that wish to achieve legitimate governance.

## Legitimate Governance Program Concept

Initially, an external assessment is conducted of all countries to determine legitimate governance/stability status. Country Reports on Human Rights, Freedom House, and other existing sources are starting points. Priorities are established, and political-military implementation plans (or "pol-mil plans") are developed in coordination with and tailored to support ambassadors in all countries with stability problems.

Ambassadors implement strategies to promote legitimate governance, including, when appropriate, offering legitimate governance transition assistance to their countries. For countries with illegitimate governance that are resistant to reform, incentives and sanctions may be in order depending upon the circumstances. The ambassador would be supported in implementing a long-term strategy.

For priority countries that agree to transition assistance, the assistance would take the form of bolstering indigenous planners in on-the-ground assessing, planning, and implementing holistic democratic transitions. The United States, along with other participating donor nations, would make available highly qualified experts to design and implement the development of culturally appropriate government institutions from village to national level. The program would take three to five years. Appropriate incentives would be provided to ease the process. The cost for the whole world would be less than one Haiti. Because the program focuses on legitimate governance and crisis prevention, it would address situations such as Bosnia and Kosovo early.

Nonpriority countries would not be denied should they request assistance without it actually having been offered by the ambassador. The world is finite. The sooner more countries have legitimate governance, the better for all.

At the same time, in order to provide the principled grand strategy itself with internal and external consistency and legitimacy, the United States should establish a distinguished nonpartisan group to assess U.S. shortcomings and opportunities for enhancing the achievement of American ideals both at home and abroad. The group would make periodic recommendations to Congress and the president.

From a grand strategy perspective, proactive promotion of democracy and legitimate governance reestablishes the United States as the moral leader in the world (the high road). It provides a firm basis for other foreign policy decisions by making them relevant to U.S. values and principles and provides the American people with a sense of purpose and vision for the next century. More important, the principled grand strategy fills the strategic void in the post–Cold War world and changes the global trend from despair and chaos to hope, freedom, stability, peace, and prosperity.

### What Is the United States Actually Doing?

Support of democracies around the world has been a long-standing written and unwritten interest of U.S. national security policy. In 1986 the Goldwater-Nichols legislation required the U.S. government to produce a written national security strategy with annual updates. Since then, support or promotion of democracy has been a stated national interest, with the State Department as the lead agency. The current State Department goal is to increase foreign government adherence to democratic practices and respect for human rights.

According to the State Department,

State provides leadership and coordination for U.S. policy related to the advancement of democracy and the promotion of human rights. State conducts relations with foreign governments and multilateral organizations to promote democratization and human rights. It coordinates implementation of activities of U.S. agencies that provide assistance toward that objective, including activities related to conflict prevention and resolution. State publishes analyses of human rights conditions in foreign countries. State allocates Economic Support Funds (ESF) for building democracy in countries in transition to democracy and manages such funds as may be appropriated under the Foreign Assistance Act for the Democracy and Human Rights Fund and for other programs. State consults extensively with non-government organizations on democracy promotion.[7]

State Department strategies for achieving the goal are:

1. Support democratic transitions, especially in regions and countries of importance to the United States. Lead Agencies: State Department, Agency for International Development (AID), Department of Defense (DOD), and Department of Justice. The State Department provides overall policy direction and coordination for U.S. government support to countries in transition to democracy, and for democratic forces in non-democratic countries of concern. State sets the diplomatic framework for efforts to promote democracy and directs Economic Support Funds (ESF) to countries and regions of emphasis.

2. Build, strengthen, and employ international forums to secure democratic transitions, prevent conflict, promote human rights, including labor rights, and support multilateral sanctions. Promote development of national and multilateral institutions for the promotion of human rights and the rule of law. Lead Agency: State. State provides policy leadership and representation in international organizations to support human rights and democracy activities. State conducts outreach with key non-governmental organizations working to strengthen human rights and democracy.

3. Support respect for human rights globally and intervene in selected human rights cases. Lead Agencies: State, AID, DOD. State leads activities to advance human rights and democracy through bilateral and multilateral diplomacy, the foundation of broad new initiatives, and publishing the annual Human Rights Report.

4. Support democratic transitions through bilateral and multilateral assistance and exchanges, broadcasts, and informational programs to establish and consolidate; competitive political processes, including free and fair elections; politically active societies, enhanced women's political participation, free media, representative labor movements, the rule of law, including neutral and professional law enforcement; and commitment to human rights. Lead Agencies: AID, State, U. S. Information Agency. State is a decision-making partner at key points in the assistance process. State leads in development of requests for and allocation of Economic Support Funds to countries where assistance policies are politically sensitive and/or closely tied to bilateral and regional short-term foreign policy requirements.[8]

Obviously the State Department has—at least in writing—an appreciation for the importance of democracy and legitimate governance to national stability. But it is also true that even with new democracy-related offices in the State Department and NSC, the resources devoted to democracy have been drastically reduced since the Cold War. In reality, there is considerable rhetoric but no shift in priority toward a proactive promotion of democracy program. At the operational level, this can be substantiated by the lack of success by non-government organizations in promoting to the State Department many proposals for more extensive democracy programs worldwide and the actual discouragement by the State Department of private industry efforts to promote democracy. In general, the democracy efforts worldwide from Russia to Haiti are disasters, and little consideration is given to the prospect of using legitimate governance programs as a method for crisis prevention.

The May 1997 Presidential Decision Directive on Managing Complex Contingency Operations (PDD 56) responded to major coordination problems experienced in Somalia, Haiti, and Bosnia. PDD 56 requires a political-military implementation plan (or ''pol-mil plan'') be developed as an integrated tool for coordinating U.S. government actions in a complex contingency operation. Theoretically PDD 56 could be a tool for a democratization program and, were it being used that way now, there could be scores of plans for needy countries around the world. But, in fact, there have been very few pol-mil plans developed and none designed to directly promote legitimate governance.

It is Congress that requires the State Department to annually produce the Country Reports on Human Rights, and the requirement for Security Assistance to be dependent upon the human rights record of recipient countries. Unfortunately, the promise of the human rights reports to influence policy and democracy programs significantly is not being realized, and the human rights requirement for security assistance is easily sidestepped.

There is no doubt that the State Department has the potential for mounting an impressive and principled grand strategy for the promotion of legitimate governance and crisis prevention worldwide. Unfortunately, important ingredients are lacking. The national stability factors provide appropriate criteria for discussing the impotence of the U.S. strategy.

In terms of the first factor, ''legitimacy,'' there is no vision from the president or mandate from Congress to implement a principled grand strategy for promotion of legitimate governance worldwide.

Unity of effort and consensus for a proper strategy do not presently exist. There are numerous institutional and commercial constituencies that would consider such a strategy to be a threat to many decades of dependence on tens of billions of dollars of business as usual. But there are other important groups that would support the strategy. These include industry, with the desire for freer, more secure trade, the military, and the American people—if the strategy were properly presented as America's vision and legacy and as a method for securing peace and prosperity for the future.

As far as plans and programs are concerned, existing ones are generally inadequate. They are, for the most part, piecemeal and short-term rather than holistic parts of a comprehensive integrated, multi-year transition assistance program. New programs would be required, and existing ones would require considerable modification. The organization of the State Department would require revamping to accommodate the new emphasis, and there would be organizational changes in other departments.

The competence issue is not a problem. The United States could implement the strategy quickly. Support is a critical issue. Currently, the State Department, and to a lesser extent other contributing agencies, do not have the organization and resources at national, regional, country team levels, and at educational institutions required to implement the strategy. External support of other nations is not essential to initiate the strategy, but should be welcomed and solicited. Stopping external support to internal detractors may or may not be an issue, depending on the country and its previous geopolitical orientation, including dependence on corruption or external advocates of internal instability and terrorism.

Regardless of the propriety and need for a grand and principled national security strategy for the promotion of legitimate governance and crisis prevention, the Max Factors say that it will not happen under the prevailing conditions. The foremost problem is found in the "Legitimacy Factor." The vision of a global legitimate governance end state and the mandate required do not exist. If they did, all else could fall into place.

### How to Get It Done

Crises are both times of danger and opportunity. Without palpable or impending crises, it is understandably difficult for politicians in a democracy to initiate major change, especially in times of unprecedented prosperity. However, it is possible if the cause is right and the forces with vision across party lines are mobilized. Prohibition, Women's Suffrage, Great Society, Civil Rights, anti-Vietnam, and anti-apartheid are some of the more notable recent examples that resulted in legislation that changed the course of history. Others involving the U.S. military include the 1947 separation of the air force from the army, the military intelligence reform legislation in 1969, the Boland amendment restricting support to the Contras, and the 1986 Goldwater-Nichols legislation that strengthened the authority of the chairman of the Joint Chiefs of Staff over the military services and gave priority to deployed unified commands with war missions.

The Goldwater-Nichols legislation along with components of other major legislation provides good reference for accomplishing great things. In the early 1980s, still in the heat of the Cold War, the American people were not aware of any particular crisis in the military, but a few visionary people found that the existing military structure was inadequate for both conducting and preparing for war. Several years later, after considerable internal and external debate, the case was made and legislation was passed. History, including the Gulf War, has proven Goldwater-Nichols to be good legislation.

In 1999, there was growing political interest in the inadequacies of U.S. foreign policy during the NATO war on Serbia in support of Kosovo autonomy. U.S. foreign policy and the NATO strategy were in crisis with potentially far-reaching consequences to security interests around the world. This, as in Vietnam, promised to be a foreign policy debacle. A decade of faulty crisis prevention had failed in the region because it had been characterized by piecemeal, short-term efforts without strategic, stable end states. There had never been a proper strategy for legitimate governance for Serbia or for the region. Instead, the United States led its allies into suboptimal and option-limiting collaboration with the morally illegitimate Serbian government, a course of action that was doomed to fail.

Despite the failure of an already inadequate strategy, the error was compounded by the bombing of Serbia to achieve the end state of Kosovo autonomy within Serbia. Not only was the objective of this course of action not feasible, practical, or suitable, from either political or military perspectives, many people were being killed, and a country was being destroyed. There was little appreciation by U.S. political leaders that the strategy must have legitimate, stable end states for Serbia—the prime illegitimate instigator of the crisis—and for the region. The predictable short-term result of the NATO strategy was a protectorate for Kosovo, leaving unresolved the illegitimate Serbian regime. With this outcome, the refugees will not return, the region will remain unstable, and there will be serious global repercussions. This is not just a failed strategy; it demonstrates an unacceptable lack of strategic understanding and planning capability at the highest levels of the U.S. government.

Had the denouement of the Cold War been wisdom, the United States would have grasped the historical opportunity for the consolidation of democracy worldwide. The U.S. would have led and moved rapidly to realign its priorities and programs to assist nations during this difficult time. Yugoslavia was a predictable problem, as were Russia and scores of other countries. The history of the last decade of the century would have been far different had the United States acted in accord with its own values. Instead, the United States walked on the other side.

The Kosovo crisis dramatically illuminates the ineptitude of U.S. strategic planning and implementation, and demands the examination of the post–Cold War United States national security strategy for crisis prevention. As with Goldwater-Nichols, the United States finds itself unable to achieve its national security strategy goals. This time it is not the military but the political dimension where crisis prevention has failed. Moreover, there is no viable political-military strategy, and there is no appropriate implementing mechanism.

If you don't pursue peace, you surely will not achieve it. Without question, legislation is required to bolster State Department capabilities and provide an organization which is appropriate for U.S. leadership in the post–Cold War milieu. The legislation, which might be called the "International Stability Act of 1999," should accomplish the following objectives:

- Provide a Deputy Secretary of State for International Affairs answering directly to the Secretary of State.

- Provide legislative impetus to change the charters of international grant and lending organizations, such as the World Bank, International Development Bank, and International Monetary Fund, so that they can directly support governments in their efforts to make transitions from illegitimate to legitimate governance.

- Provide a strategic planning and programs office responsible for planning crisis prevention and coordinating strategic planning with other departments and countries. This office will implement and manage the legitimate governance and crisis prevention program at the State Department.

- Enhance regional and desk office capabilities to manage preparation and review of plans to promote legitimate governance in all countries with stability problems.

- Provide ambassadors in applicable countries with enhanced State Department manning for managing, assessing, planning, and implementing legitimate governance transition programs.

- Realign State regional offices so they better correspond geographically with military unified and joint commands.

- Provide immediate reaction transition assistance capability for dispatch to assist ambassadors when opportunities occur due to changes in governments, coups, and crises.

- Provide the State Department a reserve corps (using retired personnel) that can be mobilized to support ambassadors during assessment, planning, and implementation of transition programs (three- to five-year programs).

- Provide the ambassador access to all intelligence reports to higher headquarters from his country.

- Provide enhanced capabilities in other departments and unified commands to support the additional planning and implementing requirements of legitimate governance transition programs.

- Make the Central Intelligence Agency (CIA) the senior intelligence agency in the United States for foreign affairs.

- Enhance grand and global strategy education and training at the Foreign Service Institute, National Defense University, Senior Service Colleges, etc.

- Establish a nonpartisan group of distinguished individuals to examine and advise the president and Congress of legitimate governance issues within the United States and relationships with other governments. This is to enhance foreign and domestic policy consistency with American values and principles.

- Provide congressional oversight of progress in achieving world stability and legitimate governance including out-of-budget-cycle reporting to Congress.

## END COMMENTS

The Grand and Principled National Security Strategy for Legitimate Governance and Crises Prevention has the "end" of world peace, achieved through the "way" of assisting nations in their quests for legitimate governance and by the "means" of enhanced capabilities of the U.S. Department of State and ambassadors. The strategy meets the tests of feasibility, suitability, and practicality as it consolidates the Cold War victory of democracy over authoritarianism.

This is a crucial time for the world and the United States of America. The window of opportunity is still open for achieving an increasingly more stable, peaceful, and prosperous world through expansion of legitimate governance. Only the United States can lead. The world is praying that the United States sees its duty and fulfills its obligation to humanity and the legacy of those who have sacrificed for freedom everywhere. The recommended legislation provides for a powerful diplomatic and crisis prevention capability that will promote peace and change the course of human history.

## NOTES

1. Sun Tzu, *The Art of War*, Samuel B. Griffith, trans. (London: Oxford University Press, 1971), p. 88.

2. Several SWORD papers were derived from statistical tests based on interviews with more than 300 civilian and military officials and scholars with direct experience in 69 cases. The effort was mandated by Vice Chief of Staff of the U.S. Army General Maxwell Thurman during 1984–1986. The model predicts at an impressive 88.37 percent of the cases examined and is statistically significant at the .001 level. The model, originally called SSI 1 and SSI 2, has also been called the SWORD Model. The *SWORD Papers*, although long out of print, are archived in their entirety by a private research organization, the National Security Archives, in Washington, DC. The 43 cases that pertain specifically to terrorism/insurgency are discussed in some detail in Max G. Manwaring and John T. Fishel, "Insurgency and Counterinsurgency: Toward a New Analytical Approach," *Small Wars and Insurgencies* (Winter 1992), pp. 272–310.

3. Ibid.

4. Richard Halloran, "U.S. Studies Rebels in Latin America," *New York Times*, March 8, 1987, p. 6; "Factores do Max," *Diario de Noticias*, April 10, 1987, exclusivo.

5. George F. Kennan, "The Sources of Soviet Conduct," *Foreign Affairs* (July 1947), p. 582.

6. The Revelation of St. John the Divine, 8:11.

7. *United States Strategic Plan for International Affairs* (Washington, DC: U.S. Department of State, n.d.), p. 6.

8. Ibid., pp. 7–40.

Chapter 9

# Legitimate Civil Society and Conflict Prevention: Let's Get Serious

### Dayton L. Maxwell

Peace interventions are not resulting in a sustainable peace, at least not in the time period desired. One reason is the overly optimistic assumptions surrounding negotiated peace among hostile factions. Achieving a governance which can manage the root cause issues requires a much more effective approach. A greater engagement of civil society in post-conflict recovery, even if it requires greater assertiveness on the part of the intervenors, needs to be explored.[1] Bringing civil society representatives into peace negotiations and crafting a role for legitimate civil society as part of the peace process will be immensely inconvenient to diplomats and military commanders. This concept will be initially rejected as unfeasible. Yet it would send a clear message to leaders of hostile factions that they will have to begin to demonstrate accountability and responsibility to their populations to retain their power, that they do not have an implicit ''right'' to remain in power, that participative management styles is what is expected of them. Exploring this option will elevate the attention during peace negotiations which needs to be placed on the welfare of the population, the role of the youth in breaking cycles of violence, and in general ways to address the root causes of the conflict. It will mean a much more serious effort than is now practiced. This will also likely lead to the need for a greater delegation of authority to field operations, a level of magnitude increase in cooperation at all levels among international organizations (IO), non-governmental organizations (NGOs), the military, and diplomats, and a much improved and comprehensive strategic planning process. Finally, the responsibilities of global civil society (i.e., multinational corporations, arms dealers, those who finance conflicts in various ways, and world citizens interested in promoting peace) also need much greater attention than they currently receive.

## FORMULATING SOLUTIONS FOR TODAY'S CONFLICTS

The irony of the day may be that creation of a democracy in conflict countries is considered the principal ingredient of the solution, but it is the leaders of the violence, decidedly non-democratic by nature, who are generally counted on to do that.[2] This formula is not working in most cases. Indeed, there are a significant number of conclusions, rather alarming ones when examined collectively, which we are drawing from our post–Cold war experiences:

- Democracies are not created through elections alone.[3]
- Leaders who have used violent means to achieve their ends but have accepted a peace agreement in lieu of victory do not necessarily intend to respect the terms of the agreements (e.g., Liberian peace came after thirteen sequential agreements).
- Even leaders who have achieved victory do not necessarily have the skills to bring lasting peace to their country.
- Short donor attention span and donor fatigue are thus counterproductive to lasting solutions.
- Peacekeeping interventions are costly, and the length of these interventions is magnifying the cost.
- Delaying decisions on peacekeeping interventions results in significant costs which, had they been known at the outset, might have mitigated the delay (e.g., Bosnia cost $53.7 billion in peacekeeping, humanitarian assistance, and reconstruction activities from 1992–1998[4]—see also Note 28).
- The number and intensity of intra-state conflicts is not decreasing as hoped, and indications are the number of inter-state conflicts in the developing world is rising (e.g., Democratic Republic of the Congo and its neighbors, Iraq and its neighbors, Ethiopia-Eritrea, the Liberia/Sierra Leone/Guinea/Guinea-Bissau area of West Africa).
- Establishing rule of law and a justice system accountable to the population in post-conflict countries is proving formidable.
- The value of War Crimes Tribunals has yet to be proven, given the difficulties of bringing to these courts the high-profile persons indicted and the constraints on proper investigations (e.g., access to Kosovo).
- The desire to strengthen civil society as a necessary ingredient of creating a healthy democracy and legitimate governance has considerable impediments, including lack of commitment by conflict faction leadership, very little experience base in participative leadership management styles to build on, a historical ethnic atrocity record, and a lack of commitment by international donors to support the long-term programs necessary to overcome the impediments.
- A short-term, compartmentalized political, economic, military, and social approach to work toward resolution of conflict has fallen far short of providing the ingredients necessary to establish a sustainable peace—the whole has not been greater than the sum of the parts.
- Domestic political concerns of donor nations drive international political decisions to

the detriment of the appropriate strategic, long-range thinking efforts needed to more properly address these conflicts.

Of course, the focus of studies like this one does tend to dwell on the unresolved conflicts and this diverts from the lessons which have been learned. South Africa and Mozambique remain the symbols of success stories. Liberia may yet be a success. Nigeria and Nicaragua seem to be evolving into democracies successfully. India and Pakistan seem on the path to avoid further conflict. Yet it is difficult to draw definitive lessons from the few unique experiences. The successes have been more a result of lengthy processes simply wearing down the obstacles rather than of intentional, charted strategies.

The fact remains that troops are now being deployed in Kosovo in addition to Bosnia. In the Economic Community/Military Operations Group[5] (ECOMOG), the Nigerian leadership's attempt to bring peace to West African conflict countries is uncertain as it tries to rebuild its democracy in the face of domestic economic weakness, and ECOMOG's presence in Liberia, Sierra Leone, and Guinea-Bissau seems necessary to keep peace in these countries. Several African nations are involved in the Democratic Republic of the Congo, and their mission can't be described as peacekeeping. At the time of this writing, conflict within Indonesia has not yet attracted external intervention, but it is on the verge of serious internal conflict which, given a highly urbanized marginal population, would lead to significant humanitarian consequences.

An easily implementable formula to achieve sustainable peace hasn't been found and remains elusive. This lends credibility to "do nothing" views being expressed, such as the recent "Just Stay Out of Africa" article by a Carnegie official.[6] The question which deserves much more attention, however, is whether we've yet *seriously* attempted to determine how to assist conflict country officials successfully achieve a sustainable peace. One of the speculations falling out of reading the list above, already widely discussed in some circles, is that finding ways to strengthen civil society to hold governments accountable is necessary to achieve a stable peace. *Let's get serious in our efforts to examine what can be done to do this.*

## THE CASE FOR A PROMINENT CIVIL SOCIETY ROLE IN ACHIEVING SUSTAINABLE PEACE

The central point raised in this chapter is that legitimate civil society representatives need to be represented in peace negotiations. This step is huge. It challenges all of today's conventional wisdom (next section below), including a long-term commitment, accepting the costs of a sustainable peace process, and the need for a more strategic planning process. Yet the critical role civil society plays in a democracy, and the historical evidence that true democracies generally do not start wars, leads to a conclusion that it is imperative to strengthen civil society in a post-conflict peace process much more assertively. Projecting this logic to where the evolution of current experiences will lead us in the future, it is *not difficult* to envision that some day it will become standard operating procedure to bring civil society represcntation into peace negotiations. If it is feasible, even likely, that someday this will happen, then the question of whether employing such a practice can be accelerated merits exploration.

The obstacles are innumerable. The following are illustrative:

- civil society representatives will be subject to immense manipulation by the conflicting powers;
- selection of legitimate representatives of civil society will be onerous;
- civil society representatives who have views opposing the authorities will need some form of protection;
- civil society groups will be formed by the authorities in power in order to control or strongly influence the process;
- some civil society groups will be representing ethnocentric or specific group interests which may be contrary to the interests of the country as a whole;
- a process to engage legitimate civil society representatives will cause very costly delays in being able to reach expedient conclusions to peace agreements;
- the complexity of negotiations will be increased to such an extent they will become intractable;
- determining the responsibility for selection of civil society representatives will itself require negotiation, thus complicating the normal pre-negotiation process leading to peace agreement negotiations.

These obstacles can be balanced by numerous advantages:

- an end state can be more easily and clearly defined in terms of the role of civil society in balancing the role of an elected government;
- strategic planning toward achieving a sustainable peace becomes possible, including developing measures to achieve the end state;
- the message passed to the conflict authorities is clear—that they must accept and develop a governance system which is accountable to their people;
- the number of failed peace agreements should sharply reduce, given the increased level of detail required in peace agreements involving civil society representatives;
- not all elements normally required in a peace agreement need to be nailed down in the first agreement; given multiple host country entity responsibility for implementing a peace agreement, some elements can be left to subsequent negotiations after more detailed considerations are complete (e.g., "Dayton IIs" become possible);
- establishing the rule of law, one of the most difficult aspects of a stable peace, requiring police services accountable to the population and an independent judiciary, can now be planned in a more realistic manner rather than treating it hypothetically as is done in current peace agreements;
- the level of responsibility of civil society groups must grow to meet the challenges

much more rapidly than currently happens; the effort to create responsible groups in a much more time-sensitive manner on the part of outside assistance programs will have very specific, measurable indicators; and

- in general, achieving sustainable peace becomes a much more visible, objective, definable process and results in a more rapid conclusion.

The advantages and the disadvantages are equally weighty. The perplexity seems too overwhelming to even contemplate action. That needn't be.

## CONSTRAINTS OF CONVENTIONAL WISDOM

A scientific approach to resolving problems given the list in the first part and the chasm outlined above would be to develop hypotheses and begin testing them, systematically. A wide range of endeavors would be encouraged, and scientists would work on a range of theories, from testing new forms of current practices to some fairly radical solutions. Diplomacy does not easily lend itself to the scientific process, however. A "peace process" conducted by diplomatic means is described as incrementally facilitating hostile factions to achieve peace over time, saying attempts to define the eventual goal immediately would be unacceptable to the parties and thwart all cooperation.

Yet it would be irresponsible not to try new approaches. Former Canadian Deputy Foreign Minister Gordon Smith says, "It won't be the graybeards that lead us into the future!"[7] His context is the possibility of using today's information systems technology, hardly tapped in diplomatic practice other than for reporting, which seems ripe for applied research in addressing conflict issues.[8] One name used for today's conflicts within the humanitarian assistance community is "Complex Humanitarian Emergencies (CHEs).[9] They clearly see the "complexity" they face in working in conflict countries populated with diplomats, negotiators, peacekeepers, reconstruction officials, human rights advocates, hostile factions, conflict perpetrators, beleaguered local officials, and seriously at-risk populations. Often in the already burdensome attempts to manage chaos no clear objectives exist which will lead to a stable peace. The complex situations defy planning to reach solutions without complex tools.

In addition to the above, other examples of conventional wisdom constraints can be summarized as follows:

1. *Current Funding Mandates Are Adequate.* The nature of post-conflict recovery work has begun to be recognized as distinctly different from either relief or development assistance. This has led the World Bank to establish a Post Conflict Reconstruction Unit, United States Agency for International Development (USAID) to establish its Office of Transition Initiatives, and the United Nations Development Programme (UNDP) to establish the Office of Emergency Response. These offices receive very little funding, however, compared to the needs. Given that the root causes of the conflict must be addressed at the same time as the relief, reconstruction, and initial phases of development assistance

are engaged, a special set of skills are required which are not found in either relief or development assistance personnel. Mrs. Sadako Ogata, the High Commissioner of United Nations Office of the High Commissioner for Refugees (UNHCR), stimulated a meeting to address this "relief to development gap," focusing on funding levels and mandates, a meeting co-hosted by the president of the World Bank, James Wolfensohn. The mixed result:

Complicating the resource mobilization issue was the climate of risk that characterized post-conflict situations. For opportunities to be seized, and a fragile peace strengthened, it was recognized that it was necessary to have resources readily at hand.... The Roundtable considered a number of modalities in relation to funding mechanisms ... global trust fund ... situation/country specific trust funds ... creation of consortia.... Other participants stressed the need to make the existing funding mechanisms work better. It was pointed out that many of the seemingly restrictive conditions to more flexible funding were often of a donors' own making: they were self-inflicted. Most participants agreed there was a funding problem and ... the issue needed some detailed follow-up work to develop options.[10]

2. *Budgetary Constraints Prevent Consideration of Long-Term Strategies.* The post–Cold War conflicts causing some form of intervention began in 1991. Northern Iraq, Somalia, and Bosnia burst upon us in rapid succession. Liberia, Angola, Rwanda, and other countries were also in conflict. Costs escalated at the same time as the U.S. budget deficit and national debt was the highest priority political issue. Those knowledgeable about the requirements for transformation of conflict countries to peaceful democracies, which include long-term strategic planning, tried to raise the issue at the top levels of the administration without success. "They are afraid of the costs."[11] Now that the budget deficit is no longer such an important issue the subject should be raised again, perhaps forcefully. The fatigue factor magnified by the lack of interest in the subject by the new non-internationalist members of the U.S. Congress seems to thwart any renewed effort. Even USAID Administrator Brian Atwood, who talked for a while in 1998 about a "bold new initiative" toward using budget surpluses to prevent future conflict, could not attract support.[12] The Carnegie Commission's revealing study on the *huge* costs of conflict versus the costs of prevention should trigger a much more serious examination of this constraint.[13]

3. *Conflict Resolution Is the Domain of the Diplomats.* The official "Track One" diplomatic community wishes to be in total charge, and it sees other efforts (the "Track Two," or "Multi-Track" diplomacy) as interfering with their efforts. The official diplomatic community certainly has the principal role to facilitate peace agreements and their implementation. It is the distinction between leading a peace process which results in an agreement and a conflict resolution process where the roles begin to blur. The tendency of the diplomatic community is to retain its role through the conflict resolution process.[14] Yet it is generally recognized that the significant increase in conflict, and the com-

plexities of these conflicts, in the post–Cold War period surpasses the official community's resources. Thus "official diplomacy can be greatly strengthened by private sector activity. . . . Track Two diplomacy is increasingly the strategy of choice."[15] A new book to be published later this year is appropriately titled *Herding Cats*, given the recognition of today's complexities, and the catalog entry describing it says, "mediation was a multiparty effort, involving a range of actors . . . working simultaneously or sequentially."[16]

4. *Getting the Economy Functioning Is Sufficient.* "It's the economy, stupid!" said a ranking former military commander in Bosnia, on the requirement for conflict resolution in Bosnia, at a "not for attribution" session recently. Although he would certainly agree that economic "normalization" is not the *only* factor, his statement does represent a common view that it is a *major* factor. The USAID/Bosnia Mission Director indicated that USAID's mandate was to focus on the economy, and in his view that would be sufficient to permit the political process to bring the conflict to an end.[17] This tends to represent a popular viewpoint on many of today's conflicts. One cogent rebuttal can be taken from a recent speech by Dr. Amartya Sen:[18]

democracy has an important instrumental value in enhancing the hearing that people get in expressing and supporting their claims to political attention (including the claims of economic needs). . . . Even the idea of "needs" (including the understanding of "economic needs") requires public discussion and exchange of information, views and analyses. In this sense, democracy has a constructive importance, in addition to its intrinsic value it has in the lives of the citizens and its instrumental role in political decisions. . . . Indeed, the conceptualization—even comprehension—of what are to count as "needs" . . . may itself require the exercise of such rights. It can be argued that a proper understanding of what economic needs are—their content and their force—requires discussion and exchange.

5. *PDD-56[19] Will Resolve Most Inter-agency Coordination Issues.* This is no longer accepted conventional wisdom, given the number of Clinton administration efforts to reexamine it. It is included here because it represents a structural approach toward improving the way responses to conflict are managed within the U.S. government. Far too much attention is being paid to structural solutions and far too little attention to assessing and developing solutions to the problems which cause the conflicts (commonly referred to as the "root cause" issues).[20] Further, much attention is paid to addressing the problems of the intervening community and much less to helping the conflicting parties find the solution to their own problems. Until the focus of attention can be reversed, it will be very difficult to turn the level of attention to the role of civil society in conflict prevention that it merits.

6. *Today's Peace Agreements Aren't Perfect, but They'll Do.* One expression heard in the diplomatic corridors to describe progress on Bosnia is "effective muddling through." This at the same time applauds the efforts achieved by the

Dayton Accords and admits that many problems still remain in achieving a stable peace. Another senior U.S. diplomat repeatedly, in different fora, makes the point that the "peace process" is one which seeks to achieve, in an iterative manner, sometimes over a period of several years (the illustration used is the Israeli-Arab peace process), an eventual agreement of terms which would have been rejected out of hand by both parties at the outset. Both these accepted expressions reflect the consensus that the current manner of achieving peace agreements is the best practical way to do it. Certainly they do represent the most realistic and perhaps effective ways to achieve their purpose in some cases. Unfortunately, in many other cases they do not (Liberia—thirteen broken agreements; Angola, Afghanistan, Sri Lanka, Sudan, Sierra Leone, Congo, and others attest to a record of broken agreements). If peace processes were undertaken with a greater analysis of the root cause issues of the conflict and with a greater attention to the components of the solutions required for a stable peace to be achieved, perhaps they would be conducted differently, and perhaps the nature of the peace agreements would be different from the standard practice today.

## CURRENT ACTIVITIES: CIVIL SOCIETY AND CONFLICT PREVENTION

The Council on Foreign Relations' Center for Preventive Action's Fifth Annual Conference, December 11, 1998, included as one of its four breakout sessions "Aid to Civil Society as a Tool of Conflict Prevention." In its advance concept description for this session it said, "Support for civil society is one of the most common recommendations to prevent civil violence. Yet there is little empirical or analytic work examining two important questions: whether or how a stronger civil society prevents violent conflict; and whether or how foreign assistance can strengthen authentic civil society." Thus examples of current activities which support the concept of accelerating support to civil society in peace negotiations and implementation of agreements are very scarce. The following are indicative of the state of the art in this field:

1. *Tajikistan—Preventing Conflict through Aid to Civil Society.*[21] A "multilevel peace process" (official mediation/negotiation, quasi-official oversight, public dialogue, and civil society relationship building) was begun in March 1993 to sustain dialogue among individuals from different factions of the civil war. This "Tajikistani Dialogue . . . brought together a dozen individuals from different regions, political movements, and nationalities in Tajikistan" who have met 23 times. Over the five years, "the role of civil society in peacebuilding" evolved "into work in five arenas": (1) determining a "dialogue group" role, (2) participating in the "quasi-official National Reconciliation Commission," (3) "promoting collaborative problem-solving skills in . . . Tajikistani society," (4) starting "non-government organizations to contribute to the field of citizenship education and development," and (5) establishing an exchange relationship between the University of Nebraska at Omaha and the Technological

University of Tajikistan. This is a long-term dialogue to contribute to making peace.

2. *USAID/Mozambique—Strengthening Civil Society.* A two year grant was issued to an NGO in late 1997 to assist civil society groups develop policy analysis skills to strengthen their ability to interact effectively with the government. This was based on USAID's analysis that the government was strong and civil society weak, potentially creating conditions for abuse of authority. Mozambique is used as a success story for recovering from conflict, but seeds of renewed conflict remain if government accountability is lax due to a weak civil society.

3. *Former Yugoslavia—Institute for Defense Analyses (IDA) Marketing Economics Simulation.* General Wesley Clark, NATO commander, unable to determine when Stabilization Force (SFOR) troops can depart from Bosnia and concerned that insufficient progress was being made on achieving sustainable peace, has encouraged IDA to develop this simulation, which grows an economy five to ten years into the future. Far too little attention is given by the international assistance community to help the conflict factions develop integrated (political, economic, social, security) plans toward a stable peace. The simulation is intended to bring representatives from the governments, private businesses (including civil society), bankers, donors, and international investors to negotiate economic growth. The game includes over 30,000 equations on very complex data sets on budgets, tax rates, tariffs, social indicators, investment returns, donor assistance—everything included in a modern market economy but in a post-conflict setting. The first field test was conducted in February 1999 for Montenegrans from all sectors and the videotaped results where shown on national TV in Montenegro with very positive public interest. Plans are to continue the development and use of this simulation exercise to bring differing sides together and subsequently use the lessons learned in real management decisions, with a particular focus on Bosnia.

4. *Pearson Peacekeeping Centre—U.S. Institute of Peace—Conflict Resolution Catalysts (CRC)—Neighborhood Facilitator Program (NFP)—Bosnia.* An experiment which combined the interests of the Canadian military SFOR contingent with keeping peace and the civilian interests in encouraging reconciliation for achieving stability in the light of minority refugee repatriation was conducted in 1997–1998. "International forces intervening to support implementation of the Dayton Agreement are confronted with continuing conflict and hostility at the national and regional levels."[22] The NGO CRC trained Bosnian facilitators at the Pearson Centre to work in Banja Luka, Drvar, Prijedor, and Sanski Most. The NFP worked with civil society representatives at the community level to improve their economic and security prospects and assist reintegration of refugees. One example of the activities was the facilitation of a first-of-its-kind meeting with the local police in Banja Luka to promote the accountability of local police to the population. The activities included Human Security, Democratization, Civil Society, Reconstruction and Development, Re-

turn and Resettlement, and Reconciliation efforts.[23] Funding support expired after only a few months, before significant results could be achieved.

5. *Other NGO/UNDP/UNHCR/Other Donor Efforts in Bosnia.* The above effort was unique because it was a joint military-civilian effort. "A variety of independent grassroots peacebuilding projects have made a difference at the local level in the divided municipalities of Banja Luka, Gorazde, Gornji Vakuf, Jajce, Mostar, Sanski Most, Sarajevo, Vitez and elsewhere" is the summary statement in a U.S. Institute of Peace survey.[24]

6. *USAID—Cooperative for Assistance and Relief Everywhere (CARE)— Somalia Umbrella Grant Partnership Project.* This project is *not* a conflict resolution or prevention project by design, but the hope is that it will contribute to building peace in Somalia. An in-depth study of the interim results by the Institute of Development Studies in the UK provides important insights to closely related activities. It is a project designed to build the capacity of local NGOs. The study concludes that "Rebuilding civil society does hold out the promise of giving non military interests a stronger voice and starting the process of changing the aid delivery culture. Achieving these objectives, however, will be a slow and largely indigenous process and there is a need for lowered expectations."[25] This paper also includes an excellent table with comparative examples of other (UNDP, other NGO) civil society rebuilding approaches.

7. *USAID/Bureau of Humanitarian Response (BHR)/Office of Transition Initiatives (OTI)—Sierra Leone.* The elected government of Sierra Leone has deposed its armed forces for abuse of power and is counting heavily on the support of civil society for institutionalizing democracy and preventing further conflict in the long term. USAID's Office of Transition Initiatives is funding activities with World Vision to strengthen civil society contribution from the grass roots. The rebel attacks in late 1998, early 1999, have created serious additional challenges to this initiative. A new peace initiative has begun and civil society representatives are participating in peace negotiations at the Lome Peace Talks. This follows an April 7–9, 1999, "National Consultative Conference on the Peace Process in Sierra Leone," which recommended that civil society representatives at least participate as observers. (Guidelines for civil society participation are included in Appendix 1, and the first request by the Civil Society participants at the Lome talks is in Appendix 2.) Prior to the attacks a conference was held to review with civil society the various national security issues, and the need to develop a credible civil society participation with the government was addressed.[26] That issue will still need to be addressed in the future.

8. *World Bank—Partnership for Capacity Building in Africa: Giving Voice to Civil Society in Africa, A Framework for Capacity Building.*[27] This report lays the groundwork for a more significant contribution by the World Bank to assist in strengthening civil society's contribution to development in Africa. A subsequent report "explores differing concepts, definitions, and perspectives on African civil society in an effort to describe a framework from which to fashion capacity-building strategies."[28] This is an effort which lies ahead for the World

Bank and its African partners. Much of the capacity-building experience for civil society to participate more effectively in development activities will certainly be valid also to prevent or recover from conflict.

9. *Local Capacities for Peace (LCP)*.[29] Mary Anderson has been a leader in assisting several efforts devoted toward finding ways to assist representatives of conflicting parties identify and implement peaceful solutions. These efforts have taken or are taking place in Tajikistan, Lebanon, Burundi, India, Somalia, Southern Sudan, and in other places.

## SOME ASSEMBLY REQUIRED

The obstacles to a greater role for civil society in achieving peace were listed above. They are formidable, very valid, and in no way can they be casually dismissed, overly simplified, or rationalized. The key question is whether the way forward to overcome today's growing propensity for conflict makes it imperative to make more serious efforts.[30] Is the tough road necessary because the alternative is more holocausts? (Did we think keeping the vow of ''never again'' would be easy?) *Can we afford not to try harder?*

Barnett Rubin and Susanna Campbell of the Council on Foreign Relations say that:

An analysis . . . of incipient or developed crisis has shown that *the weakness of civic organizations in processing and absorbing conflict and in holding state leaders and institutions accountable* [emphasis mine] is a chronic condition that leaves societies vulnerable. . . . Although much more evaluation of this experience is needed to determine how and to what extent these networks strengthen the capacity of various societies to prevent violent conflict, all of our work leads us to suspect that international networks of mutual support can play an important role in sustaining institutions that enhance civic peace.[31]

For the thesis of this chapter (i.e., the need for increasingly assertive and responsible peace-building measures), this is an understatement. But it provides an academically rigorous platform upon which to hypothesize. It also indicates that we need to build something new in countries already in conflict. Since strengthening civil society to balance the authority of powerful governments is already recognized as contentious, how much more contentiousness is added by bringing legitimate civil society representatives to the peace negotiation table? We're addressing situations where some form of contentious external pressures are already being applied to reach peace agreements, thus the leap of logic does not need to be seen as that formidable.

Within this context not much is being tried. And certainly that which is being tried is not yet ready for an evaluation of the long-term effects of these efforts. Conflict resolution requires a serious time period, and the examples above are either too recent or too short to help determine what works and what does not.

Moreover, there is a major need to "ratchet up the rigor," according to a USAID official working with World Vision on Sierra Leone. Mary Anderson, in her book *Do No Harm*, raised "two additional concerns that deserve and require additional learning"; that is, "how the micro level of warfare . . . relates to the macro level," and "the appropriate relationship between outsiders and insiders in conflict areas."[32] Much of our learning remains ahead of us.

A scientific approach to building into the peace process an engagement of legitimate civil society representatives will require systematic applied research. The obstacles listed above can be taken as the "givens" for the design of applied research activities. The following might be considered for the design of these activities, based on that list:

1. *Manipulation of Civil Society Representatives.* Civil society participation in peace negotiations would be a disaster if it were manipulated or if it were not capable of contributing in a substantial and constructive manner. On the latter point, the Sierra Leone civil society illustrates one effort to contribute to the peace process (see above), and its progress in achieving credible results is the subject of a paper presented at a Freetown seminar, November 6, 1998 (see Note 24). An example of the need for civil society to work more effectively to produce credible results in this seminar was the recommendation to participate with parliamentarians on drafting new language for the constitution on the role of the new army.[33] On the question of manipulation, applied research activities will be needed to determine how the structure of peace negotiations would change if civil society representatives were included. The contents of peace agreements would also include subjects of vital interest to civil society, which will merit applied research attention. This done, signs and measures for detecting manipulation will need to be developed, along with the responses. A complete new process would need to be built to encompass a greater inclusion of sustainable security (i.e., order with justice) objectives. Given a conducive atmosphere, civil society groups themselves can identify and recommend solutions for the types of manipulation in use.

2. *Selection of Civil Society Representatives.* This poses the greatest challenge, and is related to most other points in this section. Attention is needed on the criteria to be established (qualifications, competencies needed, who is being represented, etc.) as well as numbers, the role of political parties, and participation of the hostile factions in the selection process. The objectives to be achieved in any peace process must be the guiding factor on how these decisions are made. Clearly, the participation of civil society representatives must be done in such a way to add value to how the objectives will be achieved and implemented. Much can be gleaned from the development literature on selection of legitimate civil society leaders.

3. *Protection of Civil Society Representatives.* An extremely comprehensive examination of the security aspects of peace operations has been done by the U.S. National Defense University, complete with recommendations for further work. It concludes:

In the long run, the objective of sustainable security will be assured only when impunity is no longer the norm and justice is perceived to be available to all. . . . Achieving this aim entails mobilization and development of civil society. This is the only way that institutions of public security will reliably be held accountable for their conduct. . . . There should be planning for coordinated action by both military and civilian elements of the peace mission to strengthen civil society as well as to promote good communication with local authorities. . . . At the end of the day, civil society is the constituency that stands to gain if order *with* justice becomes the norm.[34]

This work focuses on the activities of the intervention community but is weak on protection of civil society. It also recognizes that "the outcome of any peace operation will remain hostage to the political will of the parties enmeshed in the internal dispute.[35] But it also contains a plethora of specific recommendations which can form the basis for applied research activities on the "planning for coordinated action by both military and civilian elements" (above). One example is the development of a mechanism to promote transparency of public security institutions (see the Canadian military activity above).[36]

4. *Formation of Proxy Groups Supported by Factions in Power.* This is clearly not desirable and needs to be prohibited or clearly identified. Similar to the "manipulation" point above, means of obtaining information which indicates compromise needs careful examination as part of the environment established around the peace process. Transparency mechanisms are the key. Proxy group representatives would be most problematic in the civil society sessions held external to the peace negotiations with their constituencies.

5. *Primordial Tendencies of Civil Society Groups.* This fear is well justified when representatives of civil society come from ethnic or religious groups that are the participants in the conflict. The potential for a mini-version of the conflict to erupt during the negotiations would create another disaster. It would be preferable, of course, to have civil society represented by integrated groups, such as professional associations (e.g., bar, teachers, university students). The selection criteria might require some participation from those groups, but the ethnocentric groups would also have to be represented. Applied research in the civic education programs which would be necessary to train participants in their duties and responsibilities (e.g., how to contribute effectively, what type of participation would lead to failure and how to communicate back to their constituencies) would be needed for this.

6. *Delays Caused by Including Legitimate Civil Society Representatives.* Diplomats will be horrified by this prospect. Much of their aversion will be related to the unknowns for such a process. The reason for listing the illustrative applied research activities in this section is to chart a path that develops answers to meet most of those concerns. In principle, if the mechanism becomes clear through applied research activities and positive results are achieved, this concern would drop away. Standard Operating Procedures could be developed. This would address Michael Lund's finding:

Though preventive diplomacy is becoming more widely used and discussed—at least within many policy making and academic circles . . . only limited progress has been made in translating this emerging approach into workable operating strategies and ongoing practice. . . . Standard operating procedures for early warning and preventive response have yet to be widely instituted and regularly applied by the United Nations, the U.S. government, and regional organizations, and preventive diplomacy has yet to be elevated to the status of accepted official government or international policy.[37]

7. *Increased Complexity of Negotiations.* Another very important set of applied research activities is needed in the use of management information systems and simulations used directly or indirectly in the peace process. Complex problems require complex tools, such as the use of information systems in negotiating the Law of the Sea Treaty. This would mitigate, possibly eliminate, and possibly even convert the hostile forces to become constructive contributors.[38]

8. *Negotiating Conditions for Including Civil Society Representatives.* Given that the nature of the peace process changes if civil society representatives are included, the negotiations with the hostile factions to include them requires that the desired end-state objectives be put right up front. If this is too cumbersome in certain cases, two stages of peace negotiations might be necessary: (1) the standard cease fire and peacekeeping issues in stage one, which wouldn't have to include civil society representatives but would include establishing the conditions for a second stage of negotiations, and (2) the complex issues to be addressed with respect to establishing and implementing end-state objectives in stage two. The principal point here is that peace negotiations should not be seen by the diplomatic community as finished only when the stage one conditions are agreed to. It would require recognition in stage one that very serious issues remain to be addressed and resolved. This recognition might also lead to seeing the need for more than one event in stage two. (How often has the question of holding a "Dayton II" for Bosnia surfaced? It would certainly have been easier to do had the need been recognized during the Dayton Accords negotiations.) Monitoring and maintenance mechanisms need to be identified and tested to ensure that new ways of using traditional vehicles are developed which can effectively drive the peace process forward.

## OTHER FACTORS

The designers of new processes must constantly be aware of and account for various "extraneous factors." The barrel stave theory is applicable here (i.e., a barrel only holds water up to the level of its weakest stave). Neglecting civil society in peace negotiations is certainly one of the weakest staves in the peace process. There certainly may be others. Here are three:

1. *Cost Effectiveness.* The list in the first part of this chapter included the cost to the international community of $53.7 billion from 1992–1998 in Bosnia. The author raised the question of how the cost-effectiveness factor would be con-

sidered at the first inter-agency meeting in 1993 at the National Security Council on PRD 13 (to become PDD 25, see Note 18), multilateral peacekeeping operations. It was met with a moment of silence, broken only by the Pentagon Admiral saying, "The most cost-effective intervention is to nuke 'em." It was a facetious comment, yet it served to highlight the unwillingness to consider more assertive and responsible action. The price of this unwillingness (for many reasons) to take forthright, strategically thought-through, timely action is high. Evaluation of intervention effectiveness is certain to come. Even the Haiti intervention, defined as a success in restoring a democratically elected government and stopping the refugee flows, is back in question. General Wilhelm testified at a House Appropriations Committee on February 25, 1999, that the U.S. should "end its five-year military presence in Haiti, arguing that American forces have not been able to create stability in the volatile nation and are now at risk."[39] With the budget deficit issues behind us, it is seriously time to examine cost-effectiveness. We expect the answer to be that more significant attention to strategic planning and a greater commitment of "preventive" funding at the early stages of intervention planning will be needed. The cost of a continued ad hoc approach is summarized in a recent interview with the UNHCR High Commissioner, Mrs. Sadako Ogata, commenting on Kosovo but applicable globally: "The crisis is not over, but the humanitarian tragedy continues. International interests have not gelled, and the saddest part of it is that the longer it takes, the worse it gets."[40]

2. *Global Civil Society.* (a) Corporate representatives: Given global prosperity and the continued growth of the private sector and the multinational corporations, the question is increasingly raised about the social responsibility of the commercial sector. John Keane says that "some scholars are presently reflecting upon the possible emergence of a 'global' or 'international' civil society."[41] It is universally recognized that the small arms dealers who provide weapons, the purchasers of looted commodities from rebel groups, and the commercial interests of those who profit from conflict are assisting the conflict makers. The steps to mitigate this are not so clear, as stated by John Tirman:

The flip side of business-and-conflict nexus is the potent role of large corporations operating in zones of conflict. Many of these, mainly extraction firms, have already been stung by their heedless attitudes. . . . But corporations have a stake in stability, peace, the resources and on-the-ground presence to have an impact, and unlimited access to officialdom. What they lack is the vision. Corporations occupy a parallel universe adjacent to civil society. They possess neither nationalistic or universal values. . . . Their goal is to make money, and this imparts a different sort of culture and ethos. But the overlapping interest in peace is nonetheless attractive. How can it be marshaled systematically, creatively? Very few analysts are exploring this question, a glaring oversight.[42]

The purpose of including this factor is not to suggest that global civil society representatives be included in peace negotiations. But certain analysis and applied research is badly needed on the role of these commercial sectors in creating peace. Certainly the civil society representatives which might participate in peace negotiations need to be fully knowledgeable about the commercial interests in peace, and this factor brought to bear in the peace process.

(b) Private international citizens: The Nobel Peace Prize singles out persons who have made substantial contributions to a peace effort. Various individuals and organizations have examined issues and engaged in peace efforts over the years. The rather significant 9,000-plus turnout to "The Hague Appeal for Peace" conference held the third week in May 1999 indicates the potential for an influential "movement" of people around the globe thirsting for peace. The resulting "The Hague Agenda for Peace and Justice for the 21st Century" examined the root causes of war and developed a 50-point agenda for major initiatives and campaigns.[43] It also made a "huge" effort to attract corporate representatives, but it was "one of our failings."[44] Thus also worthy of further examination is the potential for citizens' movements toward peace, and the potential to connect these efforts with the corporate world.

3. *Protectorates.* Trusteeship is a term almost prohibited to be spoken in polite diplomatic conversation. The responsibility and the financial burden implied in today's world makes governments shudder at the prospect. Yet events are conspiring to create today's equivalents—protectorates. Interventions in Grenada, Panama, and Haiti all succeeded in installing new governments more conducive to international peace, but these countries were far from being "protectorates." (An accepted legal definition of a "protectorate" has probably not evolved yet, given that it is a practice evolving with experience.) The decision to maintain international supervision for Brcko in Bosnia, with SFOR providing the teeth, is important in that respect. Karl Bildt, formerly the High Representative for Bosnia, now readily speaks about the validity of the "protectorate" concept. Sadako Ogata and Jacques Klein, former deputy High Representative in Bosnia and in charge of the transition operations in Eastern Slovenia, have both supported the concept of internationally supervised protectorates in order to more effectively achieve the objectives of the international community in interventions.[45]

An indication of changing public moods therefore potentially changing government policies was the U.S. Congress, House of Representatives, approval on March 11, 1999, of the Clinton administration's plans to send U.S. troops to Kosovo. According to Stephen Rosenfeld:

For anyone with even a faint recollection of the impassioned struggle over "war powers" during the Vietnam War, the day-long full-House Kosovo debate was a political landmark. It put a congressional imprimatur on a president's policy dealing with the always tender issue of sending American soldiers on a war mission. . . . Politically, the fallout of any intervention can be uncertain. But it cannot fail to help a president if he has a coherent policy, if he consults Congress as a matter of course and if he goes to the people: if he leads.[46]

This may be what we've been waiting for. Leadership to establish effective long-range strategies to achieve a sustainable peace in conflict countries is sorely needed. If provided, it establishes the conditions under which we can become more serious in resolving today's conflicts.

## CONCLUSION

Consideration of the prospect of bringing civil society to play a more central role in peace building, to accelerate the process, is one which requires anticipating the future. It also requires preparing conceptual approaches whereby such a prospect can be seriously addressed and expediently acted upon when the opportunity arises.

Two significant developments are occurring which are likely to have an important impact on future trends. The first is the decision by the intervening community to institutionalize indefinitely the international supervision of Brcko in Bosnia. Connected with that is the action taken by the intervening authority, Carlos Westendorp, to dismiss President Nikola Poplasen of the Republika Srpska for objecting to the Brcko decision. The second is the peace agreement being worked out for Kosovo (i.e., international supervision of Kosovo for three years). Both represent a greater assertiveness by the international community to take necessary action more conducive toward achievement of a stable peace.

One senior diplomat indicated that "The Brcko decision has demonstrated serious resolve . . . on the part of the international community."[47] The nature of this decision (and the one to come on Kosovo) truly represents a greater "resolve," one which may be more significant than the decision makers realize. This opens the doors to permit strategic thinking and the development of longer-term activities designed to reach a sustainable peace in a more systematic manner.

While these decisions will be fraught with risk and it is clearly too early to know the real significance of these actions, there are no easy choices.[48] Peace-building efforts which are more cost-effective will certainly come with certain undesirable consequences. Yet it can be expected that the vastly increased costs of peace operations, still growing, will drive the international community to seek more cost-effective means of achieving sustainable peace. Until these Brcko and Kosovo decisions, the mode of operation has been to hammer out agreements among the "sovereign authorities" and trust them to implement the agreements. A decision on "international supervision" is *not* trusteeship, but neither is it trusting the "sovereign authorities" to implement the agreement. This is a new category, perhaps the political parallel to Chapter 6 of the U.N. Charter, and one-half military intervention anomaly.

With international supervision comes the enhanced possibility of developing spearhead programs designed to accelerate civil society participation in peace building. Even without it the possibility exists. Much more support is needed for applied research for activities such as some of those described above. The question of whether this is an idea whose time has come is important to ask, and address. Granted, a serious discussion of this requires that several aspects to conflict situations need to come together which to date have not. Institutional inertia causes such a concept to be DOA (dead on arrival) simply because it hasn't been thought of much by those in official decision-making positions. In that case presenting such a concept here may achieve nothing more than planting a seed.

On the other hand, the cost burden of following the current course of action (i.e., costs in terms of human lives, political blame for inaction or ineffective action, actual dollar costs, etc.) may trigger a *search for more effective action*. As in today's conflicts, the Early Warning of what will trigger this search may not be too effective. Nevertheless, it would be to our advantage to *seriously* get ready.

## APPENDIX 1: GUIDELINES TO CIVIL SOCIETY OBSERVATION GROUP PARTICIPATION—LOME PEACE TALKS

1. Your primary objective is to advance the Peace Process.
2. Remember this is group participation as representatives of Civil Society.
3. Note the difference between Negotiators and Observers. You are the latter. You are not lobbyists. In this capacity, you try to convey your fears and expectations to other stakeholders but not in opposition to the process.
4. Accordingly, individual opinions and views of individual organizations shall be scrupulously avoided.
5. Avoid press statements and public pronouncements.
6. Appoint spokespersons and always meet to agree beforehand on the pronouncements.
7. Always be guided by the progress of the negotiations and consciously avoid any word, action, attitude or gesture obstructive to the Peace Process.
8. Your flexibility as Civil Society representative should be visible.
9. Be good listeners and restrained talkers.
10. Take note of issues raised, agreements reached and arguments advanced in support of such agreements. You need to trust the good faith of negotiators.

Prepare for reporting back to civil society on return about the peace process, the concluded agreement and the justification, and recommend civil society support for what your group brings back.

General:

1. Be sensitive to security arrangements in Lome and respect necessary restrictions.
2. Group will be organized and activities coordinated by Dr. J. D. Alie of National Commission for Democracy and Human Rights (NCDHR).

3. United Nations Observer Mission to Sierra Leone (UNOMSIL) has been requested to facilitate contacts and your participation generally.

## APPENDIX 2: STATEMENT FROM SIERRA LEONE CIVIL SOCIETY REPRESENTATIVES TO THE CURRENT LOME PEACE TALKS BETWEEN THE GOVERNMENT OF SIERRA LEONE (GOSL) AND THE REVOLUTIONARY UNITED FRONT OF SIERRA LEONE (RUF/SL)

We, representatives of the civil society groups in Sierra Leone attending the peace talks in Lome, Togo, wish to thank the Government of the Republic of Sierra Leone and the Revolutionary United Front/Sierra Leone for the progress made at the peace talks including the cease-fire agreement, statements by both parties on the release of war prisoners and noncombatants, the delivery of humanitarian assistance in Sierra Leone, and the successful conclusion of the work of the Socio-Humanitarian Committee. We also wish to thank the Military and the Political Committees for the work done so far. We are aware of their enormous and delicate task, but with sincerity, commitment, and goodwill from both parties, we are confident that a common ground will be reached. We note the demand of the RUF to participate in the governance and administration of the State and appreciate their willingness to transform their movement into a political party and enter the mainstream of the democratic progress. We also note Government's preparedness to accede to the RUF's demand to participate in the governance of the country and to help them facilitate that process.

1. However, we are concerned about:

(a) The apparent slow pace of the talks which is having deep psychological impact on the people of Sierra Leone who are anxious to have sustainable peace in order for them to start rebuilding their shattered lives.

(b) The RUF's insistence on the withdrawal of ECOMOG troops in Sierra Leone shortly after the signing of the Peace Agreement. The people of Sierra Leone have made it abundantly clear that such withdrawal will not augur well for their security and protection. These fears must be strongly countenanced by both parties. Moreover, the early withdrawal of ECOMOG troops will affect regional security and go against the spirit of African hospitality and solidarity.

We appreciate the role of International Observers and Friends of Sierra Leone in facilitating the peace process, and wish to remind Government, the RUF, and the International Community to continue to recognize that this is a Sierra Leonean problem and whatever solutions arrived at must be in the best interests of the people of Sierra Leone.

2. To this end, we wish to urge the Government and RUF that any agreement concluded in Lome must:

(a) Ensure the attainment of lasting peace and security;

(b) Facilitate genuine reconciliation and forgiveness;

(c) Promote investor confidence for rapid socio-economic development;

(d) Protect, promote, and preserve the sovereign rights of the people and strengthen democratic principles, processes, and institutions; and

(e) Lay the foundation for Sierra Leone to once again regain its rightful place among civilized nations of the world.

Finally, we wish to express our profound thanks and appreciation to His Excellency

Gnasingbe Eyadema, President of the Republic of Togo and Chairman of ECOWAS, and the Government and People of Togo for providing an enabling environment for the peace talks. We also warmly thank all the international organizations for their role in facilitating the peace process.

Lome, Togo
Dated 7th Day of June 1999.

## NOTES

1. A broad definition of civil society is the context for this chapter. The World Bank's definition is: *"civil society* is taken to encompass the nongovernmental organizations (NGOs), civic and professional associations, citizen groups, community-based organizations, labor unions, and media groups that are either beneficiaries of, or stakeholders in, development efforts." World Bank, "Partnership for Capacity-Building in Africa: Giving Voice to Civil Society in Africa," draft, September 4, 1998, p. i.

2. The title of this chapter uses the term "conflict prevention," which encompasses preventing conflict from occurring at all and preventing the recurrence of conflict once a peace agreement has been reached following conflict. It is likely that the laboratory for designing and testing conflict prevention models will be in post-conflict environments, given that in these countries the issue of whether conflict is possible is superseded. (One of the most serious constraints to performing conflict prevention activities in countries where conflict has not yet erupted is the view by the authorities that they are in control of the situation.) Thus the context for this chapter will be post-conflict country environments.

3. The U.S. Agency for International Development has conducted an evaluation of election results. See Krishna Kumar and Marina Ottaway, "From Bullets to Ballots: A Summary of Findings from Six Post-Conflict Election Studies," in *After the War Is Over, What Comes Next?*, Proceedings of the October 30–31, 1997 conference, "Promoting Democracy, Human Rights and Reintegration in Postconflict Societies."

4. Andrea Kathryn Talentino, "Failed Prevention—Bosnia," in *The Costs of Conflict*, Michael E. Brown and Richard N. Rosecrance, eds. (New York: Carnegie Commission on Preventing Deadly Conflict, 1999), p. 51. Note that eight other countries were included in this survey, which concluded that preventive action would have cost far less, around 25–30 percent of the cost of reacting to the conflict.

5. ECOMOG is a military operations group working under the auspices of the economic community of West African States (ECOWAS). It was first deployed in Liberia in 1992 and has since deployed to Sierra Leone and Guinea-Bissau.

6. Marina Ottaway, *Financial Times*, February 25, 1999, p. 14. She concludes that "most conflicts are about internal failure," thus the appropriate "option is to do nothing except seek to limit the supply of arms to all combatants in the hope that either one side will prevail sufficiently to reconstruct a state, or that the opponents will reach a stalemate forcing them to seek an accommodation." For a similar view, see Edward N. Luttwak, "Give War a Chance," *Foreign Affairs* (July/August 1999), pp. 36–44.

7. Comment made by Mr. Smith at United States Institute of Peace conference on Virtual Diplomacy, Washington, DC, April 3, 1997.

8. Ibid. Mr. Smith's example was the morning after the Tupac Amarou occupation

of the Japanese ambassador's residence in Lima, Peru, when he asked if the cable traffic had what the demands were. This has been the conventional practice. Nothing was in the cables. He went to his office, accessed the Internet, found them, and passed them to his staff.

9. This term came into use early this decade. The U.S. Agency for International Development's Office of Foreign Disaster Assistance (OFDA), prior to 1990, provided over 80 percent of its emergency assistance for natural disaster response. Today over 80 percent is assistance for those affected by conflict. OFDA began using CHE in its reports in 1991–1992 as a result of its interventions in Northern Iraq and Somalia. (The author was OFDA Deputy Director 1990–1993.)

10. "Roundtable on the Gap Between Humanitarian Assistance and Long-Term Development," Meeting Report, The Brookings Institution, Washington, DC, January 15, 1999, pp. 4–5.

11. The U.S. Institute of Peace held many discussions on Bosnia where this subject was constantly raised. This quote was made by a senior USAID officer during one of these discussions in 1997, before the budget deficit had turned into a surplus.

12. Brian Atwood, USAID Administrator, in comments made in the question and answer period following a speech, "Conflict Prevention in Today's World" at Georgetown University, October 8, 1998.

13. Brown and Rosecrance, *The Costs of Conflict*.

14. A senior USAID/Bosnia official near the end of 1998, when asked if there is any new thinking on the use of USAID funding for conflict resolution, responded, "They [the embassy] won't let us [engage in that]." (See Note 11 for the context of this question.)

15. Brown and Rosecrance, *The Costs of Conflict*, p. xxiii.

16. Chester A. Crocker, Fen Osler Hampson, and Pamela Aall, *Herding Cats*, U.S. Institute of Peace Press Spring Books catalog. This book is described as a sequel to *Managing Global Chaos*, also published by the USIP Press in 1996. We look forward to the next edition, which in the face of continuing deterioration of global conditions might bear the title *Starting Over*.

17. Meeting with Mr. Craig Buck, USAID Mission Director, June 12, 1997, Sarajevo, Bosnia-Herzegovina.

18. Amartya Sen, "Democracy as a Universal Value," Keynote Address at the Global Conference on Democracy, New Delhi, February 14–17, 1999, National Endowment for Democracy, in its *Journal of Democracy*.

19. PDD 56: Presidential Decision Determination No. 56. The PDDs are policy decisions made by the Clinton administration (previous administrations used other names). PDD 56 followed PDD 25 on Multilateral Peacekeeping Operations, which updated U.S. policy on criteria for military intervention, and outlines an inter-agency procedure on coordinating activities and reporting during today's conflict interventions.

20. PDD 25 was developed from a scope of work issued by the National Security Council originally intended to address both the military and the humanitarian assistance aspects of peace interventions. The highly successful intervention into Northern Iraq to establish conditions to repatriate the Kurd refugees in 1991 and withdraw the military within two months was seen as a model at the beginning of the Clinton administration. As a result of the Somalia experience, however, PDD 25 became much more limited in scope. A PDD 50 was designed, but never signed, to complement PDD 25 to cover the humanitarian assistance operations. This proposed to establish a formal inter-agency con-

tingency planning committee which would prepare recommendations on appropriate measures to resolve the crisis causing the conflict as part of the intervention strategy. (The author represented the Agency for International Development in the early interagency efforts leading to PDD 25 and PDD 50.)

21. This paragraph summarizes a paper by Harold H. Saunders, Kettering Foundation, and Randa M. Slim, Slim & Associates, "Preventing Conflict through Aid to Civil Society: The Case of Tajikistan," presented by the authors at the Council on Foreign Relations annual conference in New York City, December 11, 1998.

22. David Last, "Soldiers and Civilians in Peacebuilding: Reliable Partners?" a paper presented for the International Studies Association Annual Meeting, Washington, DC, February 17–20, 1999, p. 4 (draft paper cited with permission of the author).

23. Ibid., pp. 12–16.

24. Julia Demichelis, "NGOs and Peacebuilding in Bosnia's Ethnically Divided Cities," *USIP Special Report* (June 1998).

25. Paul Harvey, "Rehabilitation in Complex Political Emergencies: Is Rebuilding Civil Society the Answer?" Institute of Development Studies, Working Paper 60, 1997, p. 1.

26. Dayton Maxwell, "Civil Society and National Security: Achieving Credible Results," paper presented at the National Seminar on the Military and Democracy in Sierra Leone: The Way Forward, November 6, 1998, Freetown, Sierra Leone.

27. This is the title of a report of the African Governors of the World Bank to Mr. James D. Wolfensohn, September 28, 1996.

28. World Bank, "Partnership for Capacity Building in Africa: Giving Voice to Civil Society in Africa—A Framework for Capacity Building," draft, September 4, 1998, p. i.

29. Mary B. Anderson, *Do No Harm: How Aid Can Support Peace—or War* (Boulder, CO: Lynne Rienner, 1999). This book is the current culmination of years of effort developing the concept of Local Capacities for Peace.

30. The National Intelligence Council is currently projecting a new upsurge in conflict following the first upsurge in the early 1990s, which leveled off in the late 1990s. For a very interesting U.S. military technical analysis of its increasingly frequent engagement in "Small Scale Contingencies," see Lieutenant Colonel Patrick J. DuBois and Major Thomas Kastner, "Stochastic Analysis of U.S. Military Deployments and Excursions Since the End of the Cold War," in *Analysis for Peace Operations*, Alexander Woodcock and David Davis, eds. (Clementsport, NS: The Canadian Peacekeeping Press of the Lester B. Pearson Canadian International Peacekeeping Training Centre, 1998), pp. 253–267.

31. Barnett R. Rubin with Susanna Campbell, "Introduction—Experiences in Prevention," in *Cases and Strategies for Preventive Action*, Center for Preventive Action, Sponsored by the Council on Foreign Relations and the Twentieth Century Fund (New York: The Century Foundation Press, 1998), p. 15.

32. Anderson, *Do No Harm*, pp. 145–146.

33. Dayton Maxwell, "Civil Society and National Security: Achieving Credible Results," paper presented at the National Seminar on the Military and Democracy in Sierra Leone: The Way Forward, November 6, 1998, p. 15.

34. Robert B. Oakley, Michael J. Dziedzic, and Eliot M. Goldberg, *Policing the New World Disorder: Peace Operations and Public Security* (Washington, DC: National Defense University Press, 1998), p. 530.

35. Ibid., p. 535.

36. A specific case, not reported in any literature, occurred in Operation Provide Com-

fort, the 1991 Northern Iraq intervention to repatriate the Kurd refugees. The author was the leader of the USAID/OFDA DART team, which included the late Fred Cuny. Two days after the secure zone was established, the author was conducting a tour for journalists to a sparsely populated downtown Zakho (many of the refugees were from Zakho), where we met over 200 of Saddam Hussein's newly arrived police force parading down the main street in a show of central government authority. This represented a severe setback to our repatriation plans, given the Kurd leaders' stated fears of Saddam's authority. Fred Cuny devised a transparency plan, carried out by the British contingent of the Joint Task Force (JTF), which required the names of all the newly arrived police to be posted in public view, plus total access to the police stations and prisons by the JTF. Within a few days, these police disappeared, unable to work under conditions of total transparency.

37. Michael S. Lund, *Preventing Violent Conflicts: A Strategy for Preventive Diplomacy* (Washington, DC: United States Institute of Peace Press, 1996), pp. 26–27.

38. An example of the possibilities for the more effective use of management information systems in conflict countries comes from the author's experience working with George Mason University's Program on Peacekeeping Policy (GMU) in Liberia. In early 1997, after international diplomats had negotiated an agreement to hold elections on May 30, 1997 several months earlier, no in-country plans were still being made in-country to implement the agreement. The World Vision/GMU team facilitated a four day workshop (January 14–18) for hostile faction, political party, interim government, and civil society representatives to develop an election schedule. Gloria Scott, the head of the election commission, which the population suspected of being highly biased, said to us on January 13, "The suspicions of the population about the election commission are high and are growing higher daily." It had no credibility. After four days of workshops using Microsoft Project Critical Path Method, the participants forged a schedule and everyone took home a hard copy. A few days later the commission printed a very similar schedule in the newspaper and tensions were dissipated.

39. Douglas Farah, "General Calls for Pullout from Haiti," *Washington Post*, March 3, 1999, p. A13.

40. Nora Boustany, Diplomatic Dispatches column of the *Washington Post*, March 19, 1999, p. A19.

41. John Keane, *Civil Society: Old Images, New Visions* (Washington, DC: Polity Press, 1998), p. 23.

42. John Tirman, "Forces of Civility: The NGO Revolution and the Search for Peace," *Boston Review* (December/January 1998–1999), reprint copy, p. 5.

43. The Internet site for The Hague Appeal for Peace is http://www.haguepeace.org.

44. Cora Weiss, President of The Hague Appeal for Peace, at a U.S. Institute of Peace session, May 25, 1999.

45. Comments contained in a 1997 BBC World television documentary of conflict countries, narrated by former British foreign minister Douglas Hurd.

46. Stephen S. Rosenfeld, "Surprise Win on Kosovo," *Washington Post*, March 19, 1999, p. A29.

47. R. Jeffrey Smith, "Bosnia Ruling Rekindles Old Antipathy Anew," *Washington Post*, March 9, 1999.

48. For a discussion on "tough choices," see Dayton Maxwell, "Facing the Choice Among Bad Options in Complex Humanitarian Emergencies," in *Toward Responsibility in the New World Disorder: Challenges and Lessons of Peace Operations*, Max Manwaring and John Fishel, eds. (London: Frank Cass Publishers, 1998).

# Part IV

# Coping with Chaos in the Post–Cold War High Operational and Strategic Security Environments

The enormity and the logic of the need to establish a durable and just peace demand serious political, economic, and social institution reform—and concomitant institution building. To deny this as ''too hard'' or ''too expensive'' is to deny the lessons of history.

The difficult political problem of creating a foundation of a legitimate civil society upon which to build security, stability, and sustainable peace is a problem that ultimately must be resolved internally by indigenous leaders. Nevertheless, that effort will require some outside help. If that were not the case, the state in question would not be failing or failed. Unless international and national leaderships recognize what is happening at the macro (i.e., strategic) level and reorient their thinking and actions to deal with the ''essential elements'' that lead to sustainable peace, the micro problem of security and stability in troubled states will resolve themselves—there will not be any. Thus, when U.S. or international interests are threatened by an event or series of events in a weak and failing state, the main element of policy and strategy must go beyond promising simple ''democracy'' (i.e., the election of civilian leaders) to facilitating and guiding supported indigenous leaders in a long-term, patient, but firm and vigilant pursuit of a legitimate civil society.

Within the global security structure, the United States remains the only superpower. No other state currently possesses the attributes necessary for effective international and regional leverage—political clout, economic impact, cultural appeal, and military reach. Still, the United States cannot do everything alone. There are those allies that can and will assist the United States at the high operational (Dziedzic) and strategic levels (McBride and Dorff) in creating a more stable and peaceable security environment—given fully committed leadership. The special status of the United States allows it the opportunity to facilitate positive change. By accepting this challenge, the United States can help replace conflict with cooperation and to harvest the hope and fulfill the promise that peace and stability operations offer.

Jacques Maritain puts the issue in clear perspective:

> For democracies today the most urgent endeavor is to develop social justice (and legitimate civil societies). . . . Then only will the highest functions of the State—to ensure the law and facilitate the free development of the body politic—be restored, and the sense of the State be regained by the citizens. Then only will the State achieve its true dignity, which comes not from power and prestige, but from the exercise of justice.
>
> —*Man and the State*

Chapter 10

# The Anarchic State vs. the Community of Nations: The Real Cleavage in International Security

## Michael J. Dziedzic

The most ominous international cleavage that future soldiers and statesmen may confront is not likely to be a replica of the ideological divide between East and West. Nor are differences in economic development likely to drive a wedge between North and South, given that the South aspires to join the North, and there is nearly universal agreement that open markets represent the proper formula for doing so. While some might conclude from this that history has ended or that civilizations will somehow clash, the schism that is apt to matter most is the divide between states where governmental institutions function and where they do not. Indeed, the history of the post–Cold War has certainly had as its leitmotif the dysfunction or collapse of governmental institutions. These troubled and potentially anarchic states are distinguished by their chronic incapacity to meet the basic needs of their people or by the savage repression of a major element of society. In either case, grave doubt is cast on the legitimacy of the regime in charge. The institutions of government are apt to be tested to the fullest whether they are used to repress or respond to the demands of the populace.[1] Recent examples include the total collapse of governmental institutions (Somalia), economic bankruptcy coupled with brutal repression (Haiti, North Korea), and genocidal assault by the state on an element of its own citizenry (Rwanda, Bosnia, Kosovo). Developing the means to avoid a collapse in governance or to repair the damage when it occurs, therefore, will be one of the central security challenges of the coming era at the high operational level.

Troubled states are not new, but their geostrategic salience has changed fundamentally. In the past, they were significant because of their potential to alter the balance of power, especially if turmoil in one state could be exploited to destabilize an entire region. During the Cold War, they often were the preferred terrain for the superpower rivalry (e.g., Southeast Asia, post-colonial Africa,

Central America, Afghanistan). The Soviets prosecuted "wars of national liberation," and the United States responded with countervailing policies. The common denominator was a vulnerable or troubled state in the other superpower's sphere of influence. Now that the U.S.-Soviet rivalry has ended, troubled states are no longer valued as a means of enhancing (or reducing) great power spheres of influence. If power politics were the only consideration, today, they might have ceased to be a factor on the global stage.

It has been the weakness of states rather than their strength that has often been the source of instability in the post–Cold War period. As the process of state disintegration unfolds, humanitarian catastrophes inevitably ensue that disrupt the internal social or political balance of surrounding states (e.g., Haiti, Rwanda, Bosnia, Kosovo). The failure of institutions of law and order, moreover, can convert the failed state into an incubator of transnational threats, such as organized crime, terrorism, arms trafficking, and even weapons of mass destruction. Troubled states are strategically significant today, therefore, because they lie at the heart of many contemporary security challenges. Accordingly, the strategic focus has shifted to devising strategies to remedy rather than exploit vulnerable and failed states.

Converting an anarchic state into a contributing member of the international community is a task that requires considerable retooling of various instruments of national security policy. Previously, these instruments were designed to respond to the anarchic nature of the international system. Ironically, we are living in an era when anarchy within the state has become at least as great a source of disruption as armed conflict between states. Even more ironic, therefore, that it is the anarchical society of states that must fashion the means of reestablishing order for the anarchic state. The military must become adroit at nurturing peace while simultaneously maintaining its combat edge. Institutions constructed for collective defense against aggression, such as the United Nations and NATO, are being used today to orchestrate multilateral interventions to rescue states in distress. Adequate mechanisms still remain to be devised for effectively integrating the contributions of military actors with their civilian counterparts from international and non-governmental organizations. At a systemic (i.e., operational) level, in sum, the contest is between the sources of disorder that render states ungovernable and the institutions of multilateral and civil-military cooperation that are required to remedy them.

## TRENDS

### Weak States Have Become a Chronic Source of Global Instability

Ironically, it is often the weakest states that are the source of disruption in global affairs today (e.g., Somalia, Haiti, Rwanda, Albania, Zaire, and the former Yugoslavia), not merely the strongest. In an era of permeable borders, free trade,

and an omnipresent media, a state in chaos anywhere is apt to send reverberations across the globe. This is likely to continue to be the case, moreover, owing
to the enduring consequences of nationalism and globalism.

*Nationalism*, taken to excess, contributes to the collapse of multiethnic states.
The notion that every nation or culturally distinct group deserves its own sovereign state has a visceral appeal. This sentiment is especially prone to trigger
separatist movements when the minority involved suffers economic, political,
and social deprivation. Additionally, autocratic rulers may opt to exploit societal
divisions as a means of maintaining power by inciting popular passions against
ethnic minorities (e.g., Slobodan Milosevic in Yugoslavia). Although nationalism was a factor in the Cold War struggle between East and West, its impact
was muted. The Soviet Union's disintegration has exposed the nationalism latent
there, as well as among other members of the Second World and in former
colonial areas of Africa and Asia. The ledger since 1989 has included brutal but
futile repression in Chechnya, genocide in Rwanda, and "ethnic cleansing" in
Bosnia and Kosovo. Rather than performing its most basic function—protecting
its citizens—the state thus becomes a predatory threat to an entire segment of
society. The scenarios associated with this can include wanton brutality, genocide, wholesale migration of internally displaced persons (IDPs), a massive flight
of refugees, and destabilization of surrounding states.

*Globalism* is another enduring phenomenon that will inexorably contribute to
the incidence of troubled states. The outcome of the Cold War demonstrated
that command economies are less rational and efficient at organizing resources
than competitive markets. To maximize the economic capacity of the state, in-
terference with the invisible hand of the marketplace must be kept to a minimum.
Not only commodities but investments and information must flow across international boundaries largely unimpeded if the benefits of this economic model
are to be achieved. For states that either refuse or are unable to compete, however, globalism will likely cause grave difficulties.

Even states that reject free trade will still be governed by the logic of the
marketplace, since their capacity to meet the needs of their citizens will in many
cases decline. In particular, this will be the case where birth rates are high,
which is often characteristic of the poorest countries.[2] For many states, the incapacity to satisfy basic human needs for their burgeoning populations (e.g.,
jobs, food, shelter, health care, education) is the real and present danger.

To retain power, rulers in such regimes typically opt to suppress demands
levied against them. This may set in motion a downward spiral that ultimately
concludes with the masses being driven to a subsistence level, or below. The
international community may unintentionally abet this process by imposing economic sanctions aimed at pressuring repressive regimes. As seen in Haiti, those
who have the means will flee to neighboring states. If this is not possible, mass
starvation may occur, as in North Korea, unless the regime collapses or is over-
thrown.

Globalism will also generate strains in states that are unsuccessful in their attempt to adapt to market economics. Former communist states and other authoritarian regimes will be particularly vulnerable. They confront the dual challenges of privatizing their economies while pluralizing their political systems.[3] The pervasive internal security organizations that once ensured state control and public order tend to metastasize as these societies become exposed to global competition. The result has often been a bonanza for the criminal underworld as gangster elements insinuate themselves into emerging corporate and political power structures. The outcome has ranged from "cowboy capitalism" in Russia to "gangster communism" in the remnants of Yugoslavia. Once transnational criminal networks gain a foothold, they are extremely difficult to dislodge, undermining prospects for democratic consolidation and long-term economic vitality.

Transnational threats such as terrorism, organized crime, arms smuggling, and financial scams have become a severe challenge because the combination of permeable borders and fragile institutions makes many weak states dangerously vulnerable. While the basic aim of criminal enterprises is not the overthrow of governments, they nevertheless neutralize such core institutions as the courts, police, and even the military to facilitate their illicit operations. Control over entire regions of countries has been forfeited to drug lords as a result, and the tenacity of guerrilla movements has been accentuated by linkages with organized crime (Colombia).[4]

Illicit contributions from the criminal underworld can pervert and delegitimize the electoral process, especially in newly democratizing states.[5] Ultimately, the apparatus of the state may be suborned by international outlaws, converting national territory into a sanctuary for transnational crime, as was the case with Panama under Noriega and Bolivia under General Garcia Meza. North Korea provides a variation on this theme, as the government has resorted to trafficking in drugs as a means of generating revenue. Michael Ignatieff captures this trend in the following passage from *The Warrior's Honor*:

Tokyo, Singapore, Taipei, London, Rome, New York, Los Angeles are being wired together in a twenty-four-hour global trading economy. But vast sections of the world—central Africa, parts of Latin America, central Asia—are simply drifting out of the global economy altogether into a subrational zone of semi-permanent violence.[6]

Another destabilizing consequence of globalism is the volatility of capital flows. For emerging economies, external investment is crucial if they are to become competive globally. Without it, the process of opening protected internal markets can simply result in the loss of domestic sales to foreigners with no compensatory gains in penetration of external markets. International investors can be fickle, however, and the magnitude of daily international financial transactions dwarfs the annual gross national products (GNP) of most states.[7] The vulnerability this generates was demonstrated by the Mexican peso's collapse in 1994 and more recently in Asia's financial crisis. These events precipitated

severe economic downturns in the surrounding region with damaging consequences for political stability (e.g., Indonesia, Malaysia), and the reverberations
were felt in emerging markets worldwide.

The troubled state phenomenon is persistent because the underlying dynamics
of nationalism and globalism are enduring. Nationalism will continue to disrupt
multiethnic states, especially those governed in a repressive and exclusionary
manner. In such cases, the state is liable to be thrown into a crisis over its basic
identity. Thus, nationalism is a threat from within the state that is conducive to
disintegration and anarchy. Globalism, on the other hand, is the threat from
outside the state that can lead to a crisis of governability. Economic survival
and the resources available to the state have become increasingly dependent on
vibrant trading relationships. This places immense strains on authoritarian regimes that refuse to open their economies to outside competition and also on
nascent democracies that mismanage the economic transition. States that are
subjected to both the disruptive implications of *both* nationalism and the failure
to adapt to globalism will be particularly vulnerable to disintegration and collapse.

### International Capacity to Respond to Anarchic States Cannot
### Match Demand

Peacekeeping was a United Nations innovation during the Cold War that was
intended to keep inter-state conflict from spiraling out of control and sparking
a superpower conflagration. During its first four decades, the United Nations
was called upon to conduct eighteen peacekeeping missions (an average of one
new mission every other year), almost all of which resulted from conflict between states.[8] Between 1990 and 1999, the United Nations has conducted 31
peace operations, or an average of three per year. Almost all have responded to
*internal* conflicts in troubled states. The United Nations has been unable to deal
adequately with this surge of new missions. Factors contributing to this include
the high cost in terms of financial assessments to member states as well as
peacekeeping troops, a lack of perceived national interests, a limited understanding of how to rehabilitate a failed state, and embarrassment in Somalia and
Bosnia. One consequence is that some failing states have been neglected, with
dire consequences (Rwanda, Zaire).

Another serious limiting factor is the incapacity of the United Nations to
conduct the type of large-scale military operations that have often been required.[9] The United Nations is well suited for peacekeeping activities such as
monitoring and verification that are premised upon strategic consent among the
disputants about the role of the intervening force. These conditions characterized
the traditional peacekeeping of inter-state disputes during the Cold War. When
consent was lost, U.N. forces withdrew, as occurred prior to the 1967 Arab-
Israeli War.

Troubled states have been the focus of post–Cold War peace operations, and

consent has been more conditional and fragile. In successful cases like El Salvador and Mozambique, the conflict had been stimulated in part by the superpower rivalry. Once this ceased to be a factor, local consent became obtainable.
The United Nations has foundered when consent has been marginal and the
need to wield force credibly has been high. Since the United Nations lacks a
standing force, a viable command-and-control system, and consensus among
U.N. Security Council (UNSC) members regarding use of coercive force in
internal conflicts, it cannot manage the robust enforcement operations often required, at least initially, to deal with troubled states.

These deficiencies are unlikely to change. Many countries, including the
United States, oppose an autonomous military capability for the United Nations.
Even administrative initiatives such as a Rapidly Deployable Mission Headquarters have been resisted. Measures to enhance the capabilities of the U.N.
Department of Peacekeeping Operations (DPKO) have probably reached their
high-water mark. The establishment of a 24-hour command post was an essential
improvement, as was the development of a mechanism for mobilizing stand-by
military forces from member states. Another crucial practice, the use of ''gratis''
military officers from willing member states, has been abolished within DPKO,
however, at the behest of developing nations, who insist that all positions be
filled by paid U.N. personnel. Thus, DPKO's capacity to conduct even its current
missions is likely to diminish in the near term.

The United Nations has recognized its limitations in dealing with troubled
states since the setbacks in Somalia and Bosnia. The Security Council has been
willing, to approve peace enforcement operations conducted by coalitions of the
willing rather than the United Nations (e.g., the Multinational Force in Haiti),
and by competent regional security organizations (e.g., NATO in Bosnia). As a
practical matter, this has meant that only troubled states of importance to the
members of the Security Council can be managed. There has been little enthusiasm for large, expensive operations in regions of marginal strategic consequence, such as sub-Saharan Africa. U.S. arrears from previous peacekeeping
activities and a tendency to use the United Nations as a scapegoat for failed
peacekeeping activities serve as further disincentives to undertake new operations.[10] Even when the United States is willing to support new missions financially, other countries may be reluctant to participate unless the United States
also takes the lead militarily.[11]

When a troubled state impacts U.S. strategic interests, other UNSC members
may be reluctant to provide an unambiguous mandate for intervention. This is
especially true in cases where a brutal despot is suppressing his people (e.g.,
Slobodan Milosevic and Kosovo), since some Security Council members find it
vital to preserve sovereign prerogatives in this regard. Thus, there are regions,
such as sub-Saharan Africa, where the UNSC has been unwilling to act. There
are also circumstances, such as genocide, where the Security Council is likely
to be paralyzed. The greatest constraint, however, is the incapacity of the United
Nations to manage the use of force credibly. Hence, future U.N.-led peace mis-

sions will likely be confined to relatively benign circumstances where the consent of the disputants is reasonably assured.

In spite of these limitations, the United Nations performs several essential functions in managing troubled states. No other international body possesses the same degree of legitimacy to issue a mandate for intervening in a sovereign but dysfunctional state. Various U.N. agencies, such as the High Commissioner for Refugees and the High Commissioner for Human Rights, make vital contributions to mitigating the consequences of state failure. The United Nations has also developed extensive expertise in electoral monitoring and civilian policing, and it has an established mechanism to fund peacekeeping activities through assessments on member states. Owing to these competencies, the United Nations is well suited for the later phases of a peace operation, when the emphasis is on long-term institution building (e.g., Haiti).[12] The United Nations also has the potential to prevent the regionalization of internal conflicts by mounting preventive deployments in areas bordering a troubled state (e.g., UNPREDEP in Macedonia).

The greatest deficiency, therefore, arises during the initial phases of an intervention when a credible coercive capability may be essential for peace making or peace enforcement. The United Nations cannot be relied upon for this. Thus, this is another area where demand exceeds capacity, at least until other mechanisms are adapted for this purpose.

## Additional Instruments Must Be Adapted to Manage Anarchic States

Although the United States cannot be the world's policeman, this proposition provides little insight into who should, especially for dealing with troubled states. No amount of reform at the United Nations is likely to fully address this source of global instability. Two other alternatives remain: regional security organizations and ad hoc coalitions of the willing.

Regional security organizations have made limited contributions to management of troubled states in Africa and Latin America. The most significant operations in Africa have been carried out under the aegis of the Economic Organization of West African States (ECOWAS). Dominated by Nigeria, which has supplied the bulk of the troops and material support, it has been involved in bringing an end to the civil war in Liberia and is presently enmeshed as a protagonist in the civil war in Sierra Leone. The Organization of American States has also contributed to resolving regional security concerns in Nicaragua and Haiti.

In general, however, few regional security organizations have much potential to address the more demanding tasks of peace making and peace enforcement. Since they operate on consensus, they will often be paralyzed when faced with situations that might require using coercive force. Unlike the United Nations, where only five states wield a veto, any member can thwart action. Even if a mandate is forthcoming, member states are likely to have competing national interests in the troubled state that will militate against a coherent and constructive role. Thus, most regional organizations suffer from the same defects as the United Nations in dealing with the use of force. In more benign situations where the disputants provide their consent for an external intervention, the United Nations would normally be the preferred option, on the basis of its greater legitimacy, extensive experience, and established procedures for cost sharing.

NATO is qualitatively different. This is due, in large part, to U.S. leadership and the alliance's demonstrated capacity to conduct multilateral operations. NATO allies also share a set of values and interests that can be put at risk by a troubled state on their periphery, such as the former Yugoslavia. Indeed, this "non-Article 5" mission has provoked the alliance's first operational use in Bosnia and first use of force in Kosovo. This issue will also be a major component of the alliance's forthcoming "strategic concept." In addition, NATO continues to incorporate partner states into its operations in Bosnia and to develop civil affairs capabilities in many allied military establishments to facilitate collaboration with international and non-governmental organizations.

Despite NATO's considerable advantages, its freedom to act will continue to be constrained by concerns about a mandate. In spite of the precedent set by bombing Kosovo without an explicit mandate from the Security Council, many allies will be reluctant to undertake an intervention in the absence of a specific U.N. mandate. It remains possible for a regional body, such as the Organization for Security Cooperation in Europe (OSCE), to provide an alternative mechanism for legitimizing collective action.

Another potential response to the troubled state phenomenon would be for European states to develop the capacity to act alone when the United States opts to remain on the sidelines. Although the UNPROFOR experience in Bosnia was unfavorable, the inefficacy of that mission had much to do with the unworkable "dual key" command and control arrangement, with the United Nations one avenue for development of an all-European Security and Defense Initiative. Essentially, this would involve NATO capabilities without active U.S. participation. The other alternative would entail collaboration between the Western European Union and the EU.

As a regional organization, NATO cannot address troubled states everywhere. Nevertheless, it has given itself a measure of flexibility because it has refrained from defining its "out of area" interests in geographic terms. This would theoretically allow the alliance to mount operations anywhere, if there is a consensus that its security interests are sufficiently threatened. Realistically, however, this is likely to be confined to Europe's periphery, and the long-term consequences of intervention in Kosovo are likely to leave the alliance with little surplus capacity or appetite for similar ventures for a considerable period. NATO is also limited in its ability to address the non-military aspects of rehabilitating a dysfunctional state. The United Nations remains the leading potential partner for this; however, the OSCE was called upon to conduct the Kosovo Verification

Mission, and it would likely be a major participant in any future peace implementation mission in Kosovo involving such activities as restructuring the public security apparatus and organizing elections.

To cope with troubled states beyond the penumbra of NATO's security umbrella, "coalitions-of-the-willing" may be the only other alternative. For situations with a potential for high-intensity combat, or at least forcible entry, the United States will undoubtedly be indispensable, as it was for the Multinational Force in Haiti. If the scenario is more permissive, such as the lawless conditions encountered after a nationwide financial scam produced anarchy in Albania, then an operation might be built around another lead nation, as Italy demonstrated in that case. Use of ad hoc coalitions will be contingent on the availability of capable coalition partners and the availability of a mandate from the United Nations or an appropriate regional security organization.

Since Africa has the greatest concentration of fragile states, the United States (via the African Crisis Response Initiative), France, and the United Kingdom have all undertaken programs to train and equip chosen African military forces to enhance their peacekeeping capabilities. The operational use of this capability, however, is liable to be confined to the more benign peacekeeping activities under the U.N. banner or a U.N.-mandated ad hoc coalition.

Asia is the other major region with a potential to experience serious instability from future troubled states. To date, the only major post–Cold War peace operation in the region occurred in Cambodia. Consequently, Asian nations have been involved primarily as troop contributors for missions in other regions. Future developments in North Korea, or deterioration in fragile regimes like Indonesia or Malaysia, could provide an incentive to develop a collective regional capacity to respond to failing states.

### Anarchic States May Require Intervention Before There Is a Peace to Keep

While the international community continues to search for the proper set of tools to manage troubled and anarchic states, the task has simultaneously become more demanding because the threshold for intervention has been lowered. Until recently, there was a sense that a peace mission should only occur after a dispute had become "ripe" for resolution. That is, the parties should have first exhausted themselves, moderated their war aims, and demonstrated a willingness to adhere to a peace accord. By following this prescription, the international community can avoid prolonged entanglements in violent conflicts; however, it also means that instances of genocide would be allowed to unfold and surrounding regions might be destabilized before effective action is taken. By the time such situations become "ripe" for intervention on the ground, the cost in terms of lives and resources can burgeon. Having learned the price of delay in Bosnia and Rwanda, the United States and its European allies sought to avoid a repetition in Kosovo. Consequently, the OSCE fielded the unarmed Kosovo Verification Mission in late 1998 with merely the promise of a final agreement between the government of Yugoslavia and representatives of the Kosovar community. When this effort failed, NATO became enmeshed in a war with Yugoslavia to stanch their assault on the ethnic Albanian population.

Two factors contribute to this trend. First, the vast majority of wars are now internal to the state, and it is these conflicts that have increasingly become the focus of international interventions. Second, many of these internal conflicts involve wanton use of force by armed elements against civilian masses. As in Iraq, Somalia, Bosnia, Rwanda, and Kosovo, humanitarian catastrophes are a likely result. Indicative of this trend, civilians today suffer the preponderance of casualties from armed conflict, whereas at the turn of the century 85 to 90 percent of casualties were military combatants.[13]

When a humanitarian calamity looms, immense pressure will be brought to bear from the media and concerned interest groups to "do something." Aware of this, secessionist forces such as the Kosovo Liberation Army are as likely to pursue a media "war of attention" as they are to conduct a guerrilla war of attrition. As a result, sovereignty no longer confers an absolute right on autocratic rulers to wield unbridled violence against their own people. By the action that has been taken on behalf of the Kurds in Iraq and ethnic Albanians in Kosovo, the international community has begun to establish a tenuous, countervailing right to intervene to prevent wholesale slaughter and displacement of civilian populations. By thus lowering the threshold for intervention, it has become easier to get involved, but more difficult to get out, and riskier to remain. Owing to the high cost and escalating stakes that became involved in the situation in Kosovo, this trend may not be enduring. Nevertheless, the policy dilemmas associated with management of this aspect of the troubled state will not simply disappear, making the outcome of the action in Kosovo a watershed event for this and many other reasons.

## U.S. INTERESTS

As a global power, the United States has a very real stake in avoiding or alleviating the chaos caused by troubled states. Owing to the increasing permeability of national borders, moreover, the pathologies that contribute to their demise could affect American society, as well. As the October 1998 version of *A National Security Strategy for a New Century* states:

Globalization—the process of accelerating economic, technological, cultural and political integration—means that more and more we as a nation are affected by events beyond our borders. Outlaw states and ethnic conflicts threaten regional stability and economic progress in many important areas of the world. Weapons of mass destruction (WMD), terrorism, drug trafficking and organized crime are global concerns that transcend national borders.[14]

To shape the international environment in a manner that is conducive to democratic polities and free market economies, moreover, it will be necessary to mitigate the consequences of chaotic states. Specific interests that may be jeopardized by troubled and dysfunctional states are discussed below.

## Vital Interests

If a troubled state were to collapse in an area of strategic consequence, vital interests could be engaged in various ways.

- If the state's collapse could precipitate the use of, or loss of control over, weapons of mass destruction or intercontinental delivery systems, (e.g., North Korea, Russia, or China).
- If access to strategic minerals might be denied or severely restricted as a result (e.g., a major oil-producing nation).
- If domestic turmoil were to stimulate a massive exodus of refugees to the United States (e.g., Haiti or Cuba).

Even when vital U.S. interests are not involved, the rationale for intervention can still be compelling because other strategic concerns are at risk, as discussed below.

## Regional Instability

When an oppressed domestic group becomes the target of systematic violence, this inevitably spawns a mass migration in search of a safe haven, either internally or in a foreign land. If the turmoil persists, the prospect of a destabilizing exodus of refugees will increase. Regional stability will be especially precarious if rebel groups become mingled with the flood of refugees. This often happens because refugee camps offer sanctuary and a ready source of recruits. To retaliate, opposing government forces will be tempted to conduct operations across international boundaries. The state receiving these refugee flows may be further destabilized because of cultural linkages between the refugees and a restive population of its own, and other regional powers will predictably act to protect their interests as this chain of events unfolds. As a global power, the United States clearly has a substantial stake in preserving regional stability. It is not in the national interest to permit this escalatory cycle to unfold to the point that an entire region is in turmoil.

## Transnational Threats

Transnational security threats are a major factor in the institutional deterioration that produces dysfunctional states. The relationship cuts the other way as well, because the failure of a state creates an institutional void that may be exploited by transnational actors of various sorts. Osama bin Laden's terrorist network, for example, exploited turbulent conditions in Afghanistan to establish a base of operations. The absence of law enforcement in Albania, moreover, was used to project his operation throughout Western Europe and to support operations against U.S. embassies in Kenya and Tanzania. Drug traffickers have also exploited anarchy in the Balkans, expanding their smuggling networks across Europe to Scandinavia, where half the heroin traffickers are presently in Swedish jails and 80 percent of the traffickers in Norway originated in Kosovo and Albania.[15] The well-being and social order of the U.S. homeland are similarly vulnerable to troubled states, even those in remote and obscure locations. In an era when continued prosperity depends on the international movement of products, money, and information, sealing U.S. borders is not a realistic option. While economic globalism is a boon for U.S. consumers, its corollary will be domestic insecurity unless transnational threats emanating from troubled states can be contained.

## Humanitarian Concerns

An enduring feature of the American character is a desire to assist victims of major international calamities. When natural disasters strike, the United States contributes its fair share and more. Man-made disasters, however, are more complex, since there can be a considerable risk that U.S. lives will be lost, especially if the United States becomes enmeshed in an internal conflict. As Somalia demonstrated, the public will not permit the shedding of American blood unless substantial national interests are at stake. Humanitarian impulses alone, therefore, will not justify U.S. intervention when the costs are likely to be denominated in lost U.S. lives.

The most intractable situations entail *internally displaced persons* (IDPs). In this case, the victims remain under the sovereign jurisdiction of the same regime that has caused their displacement. IDPs may assert a right to independence and seek recognition for a sovereign state of their own, and their cause will invariably be supported by international human rights organizations. Intervention will be opposed by governments interested in preserving the primacy of national sovereignty, and by those opposed to the alteration of national borders through force. As a result, a clear international mandate for intervention is not likely. Resistance can also be expected from the state involved, especially if they view the displaced masses as the center of gravity for eradicating an opposition movement. Unless other strategic interests are also at stake, therefore, it would normally not be prudent to use U.S. forces to protect the delivery of humanitarian assistance to internally displaced persons.

Most of these impediments do not arise when dealing with *refugees* who, in contrast to IDPs, have fled their native land. The crucial difference is that international assistance is likely to be sought by states that are the recipients of refugee migrations. If decisive action is taken at the earliest stages, it should also be possible to maximize prospects for preventing the spread of instability throughout the surrounding region. This would involve developing a capability to provide a secure environment for refugees and relief activities. This will necessarily entail controlling the same rogue elements—guerrillas, local gangs, arms smugglers, and criminal syndicates—that would spread disorder transnationally, as well. Since protecting humanitarian assistance for refugees would typically serve both U.S. humanitarian values *and* identifiable national security interests (i.e., regional stability), it provides a more prudent basis for action by the United States.

## CONSEQUENCES FOR U.S. POLICIES

The demands on the United States and the international community will vary as a troubled state degenerates toward chaos, becomes the subject of multilateral intervention and, under favorable circumstances, is nurtured back to responsible membership in the community of nations. At the earliest stage, statesmen may be able to avert a crisis or, if they fail, they may be able to prevent the internationalization of the domestic conflict. If a major intervention is warranted, there will be the complex task of laying the foundation for stable governance. The response to a dysfunctional state, therefore, involves a broad spectrum of overlapping security challenges associated with conflict prevention and mitigation, full-scale peace operations, and peace building.

### Averting the Collapse of Troubled States

The fundamental challenge is not early warning, nor is it simply a matter of early response. The most vital requirement is to identify cases where preventive action can make a difference and where it is in our interest to try. The criteria suggested below would limit the number of potential cases as follows:

- Democratic regimes under extreme duress (e.g., Colombia).
- Countries aspiring to a democratic transition that falter, in part, because of external or transnational sources of instability (e.g., Macedonia, Indonesia).

Preventive action normally begins with a traditional package of diplomatic, military, and economic assistance programs. If one source of instability is the spillover of conflict from a neighboring state, then the international community could mount a preventive peace operation similar to UNPREDEP in Macedonia. If these efforts fail, and a general climate of lawlessness develops; there will not be time to await the results of typical training and assistance programs. To reverse this downward spiral, the performance and legitimacy of state institutions must be reinforced quickly, especially those dedicated to providing law, order, and justice.

The option of using an unarmed international civilian police (CIVPOL) organization would probably be inappropriate because it would be incapable of self defense. An international constabulary or armed police organization, however, could be mobilized to monitor, train, and operationally assist local police and judicial authorities. The guiding principle would be to inculcate in the local public security establishment principles of democratic policing and equality before the law. In extreme cases, a constabulary force might also require reinforcement by an international military contingent. Mounting an effective border patrol could also be extremely important in such situations. Over the long term, public security assistance offered by international organizations, individual governments, and non-governmental organizations would play a valuable role in the evolution of stable governance.

## Mitigating the Humanitarian Consequences of State Anarchy

Relief workers have traditionally depended on an unarmed, nonthreatening posture and neutrality as their primary means of defense. These principles lose their protective value, however, when the relief community is seeking to assist a population that has itself become a primary target in the domestic conflict (e.g., the ethnic cleansing of Albanians in Kosovo). The risks will be compounded if refugee camps become safe havens for rebel forces. Under such circumstances humanitarian workers may be targeted for kidnapping or assassination (e.g., The International Committee of the Red Cross, in particular, has suffered deadly consequences in recent years in Rwanda and the Chechen Republic). Rival groups may commandeer relief supplies, and order at warehouses and distribution centers may also be precarious owing to food riots and the activities of armed gangs. Unless security can be provided, relief activities may need to be suspended, or they may even be too perilous to mount in the first place.

Protecting the delivery of humanitarian assistance could entail a range of tasks, including:

• Security for convoys, warehouses, and living quarters of humanitarian workers.
• Protection of refugees and safe areas.
• Demilitarization and disarmament of combatants.
• Public security within refugee camps.

Each of these tasks may require a different combination of the capabilities described below since none of these protection options is without significant liabilities.

Standard *military combat units* are not well suited for the task of protecting humanitarian assistance. Lacking nonlethal force options, when they are thrust into a situation where petty crime and gang activity are rampant, the danger of excessive use of force can be high (as befell the elite Canadian airborne brigade during UNITAF in Somalia). They can perform a crucial function, however, by ensuring that legitimate law enforcement agencies are able to establish their writ over throngs of refugees.

One way to address the public security void in refugee camps might be to deploy units of *constabulary or armed police* to work with the international relief community. Operating in concert with local security forces to the maximum extent possible, they could keep armed elements (gangs or guerrillas) away from refugee camps and help to maintain order at food distribution points. The mere presence of a capable international security force of this sort would tend to encourage local civilian and military security forces to perform their duties more responsibly. A constabulary force might help local authorities curtail the activities of armed gangs inside refugee camps using investigative techniques, expertise at community policing, and, when confronted, nonlethal control measures. This would improve the security climate within the camps and increase the likelihood that humanitarian assistance would arrive in the hands of the neediest rather than the most heavily armed.

*Civilian police* (CIVPOL) units are typically comprised of individual volunteers from various countries. Thus, they do not have an organized capability to conduct operations, such as demilitarizing refugee camps, and traditionally are unarmed. Once a secure environment has been established, however, they can cull abusive personnel from existing police forces, recruit trainees, establish training programs, and monitor the performance of the entire public security apparatus. Bilateral assistance programs, coordinated with or managed by CIVPOL, provide the bulk of financial and technical support for retraining of domestic police forces.

One common alternative, especially for humanitarian organizations dealing with internally displaced persons, has been to hire *local security guards*. This can be risky, however, since these personnel may be aligned with one of the warring factions, which could invite retaliation from their rivals. Private international security firms are another alternative. They may be cheaper than a military intervention force, but quality control and adherence to human rights standards could end up being compromised.

Governments hosting refugees have the greatest obligation to provide for their security. In reality, however, they often lack the capability to do so. One attractive option, therefore, is to provide international assistance, through CIVPOL and bilateral assistance programs, to *local security forces* so they can perform this mission more competently. Local governments will be more likely to cooperate with the relief effort, moreover, if they receive something in the bargain. Monitoring would also be required to prevent further victimization of refugees by a police force that would be alien to them.

Another promising option would be to *train cadres from the refugee community* itself to maintain law and order inside the camps. Known as ''encadrement,'' this would provide employment for military age males who might otherwise cause problems and also create a security force familiar with the refugees' distinctive legal traditions. This option would require international training assistance and monitoring and would probably work best if implemented in concert with local police, judicial, and penal systems.

In general, humanitarian protection missions that are the least reliant on military resources are the most likely to receive an international mandate. Nevertheless, there remains a need to develop concepts and coordination mechanisms that integrate military Quick Reaction Forces effectively with constabulary units, international civilian police monitors, and local authorities. One way to promote this sort of collaborative effort would be to establish a Protection Coordinator for every situation requiring protection of humanitarian relief.

### Peace Enforcement in Anarchic States Requires Nonlethal Capabilities

Normally, an international mandate directs a peace mission to establish a safe and secure internal environment. During the initial phase of an intervention, the military contingent will often be the only source of order, and it is apt to be tested by civil disturbances, violent clashes between antagonistic local factions, and theft of its own resources. The military can be a blunt instrument, however, and if even a single incident is mishandled through the use of excessive force, the entire mission can suffer because local consent will be squandered. Inaction, on the other hand, can risk the loss of credibility (e.g., the disorders that accompanied transfer of the Sarajevo suburbs under NATO implementation forces [IFOR]). The media spotlight will be unavoidable, and the consequences for the success of the peace mission can be enduring.

To limit loss of life and destruction of property in the anarchic circumstances often encountered at the outset of a peace mission, nonlethal capabilities should be included in the initial force mix. Constabulary or armed police organizations have training and expertise in crowd control, nonlethal force options, and general experience in policing and could be deployed simultaneously with the military contingent. Until the CIVPOL contingent becomes operational, the constabulary could also begin organizing an interim local security cadre and monitoring their performance.[16] In this manner, a constabulary presence could help to accelerate the process of reconstituting the local police force.

In addition to reestablishing order, a multilateral peace operation must also shape the political context in a manner favorable to the peace process. Unless this is done successfully and peace becomes self-sustaining, other reconstruction and peace-building activities will be stillborn.[17] Since disgruntled political elites or "spoilers" may attempt to disrupt the peace process, military peacekeepers may be required to respond to various forms of violent resistance, including civil disturbances.

Military forces are reluctant to engage in confrontations with civilians because they are generally not trained in the measured use of force, riot control, negotiating techniques, or de-escalation of conflict. Unarmed CIVPOL personnel are not capable of handling such violent challenges, either. Constabulary forces can counter this vulnerability to stage-managed civil unrest, as demonstrated by the deployment of the Multinational Specialized Unit (MSU) as a part of the Stabilization Force (SFOR) in Bosnia in mid-1998.[18] Comprised initially of Italian carabinieri and Argentine gendarmes, the MSU has given SFOR the information-gathering capability to detect incipient unrest and to deter it by concentrating MSU patrols in restive areas. The MSU has also successfully defused potentially violent confrontations through negotiation. Only very rarely has the MSU actually had to use force, suggesting that by eliminating this gap in SFOR's capabilities, the likelihood that the peace force will be challenged in this manner has been greatly diminished.[19]

## Building Sustainable Peace Requires a Capacity for Long-Term Management

For peace to be sustainable, core institutions of government such as the courts, prisons, and police require more than training and restructuring; their fundamental mode of operation must be transformed. Indigenous institutions must be coaxed into functioning in rough accordance with internationally acceptable standards. This will usually entail a radical transformation of the culture of law enforcement. The public security system will often have operated as an instrument of state repression; it must begin to serve the public interest instead and function in a manner that respects the political and human rights of members of all groups, whether they wield political power or not. This requires time.

Training a new police force is regarded as a multi-year project. Subsequently, the conduct of police, judges, and jailers must be effectively monitored and supervised. Without such oversight, the training and assistance that the international community provides could merely result in making these forces more competent at repressing their own people. Reconciliation will never happen under such conditions.

Innovative approaches to this challenge have been attempted in Bosnia by the International Police Task Force (IPTF). The concept developed there, termed "colocation," entails placing seasoned IPTF police officers alongside local police chiefs and senior Interior Ministry officials. Similar programs would also be warranted for the courts and penal systems. One of the primary constraints on implementing such a transitional phase is that there is not an adequate international mechanism to mobilize and field an adequate number of such highly qualified personnel.

### The Impact on Military Readiness

The post–Cold War "peace dividend" has now been collected, and the defense establishment is scarcely two-thirds the size it was at the end of the 1980s. Operational deployments, however, have tripled. Not all this increase is attributable to the exigencies of troubled states, of course, since natural disasters and more conventional security challenges, such as Iraq and North Korea, account for much of this. Nevertheless, there are serious concerns whether the armed forces can retain their fighting edge while engaged in continuous operations aimed at managing troubled states.

The experiences of the 25th Infantry Division in Haiti (as part of the Multinational Force) and the 1st Armored Division in Bosnia (as part of the Implementation Force) provide invaluable insights. In both cases, a minor but temporary degradation of some perishable combat skills (e.g., gunnery) occurred. However, these skills were quickly restored, and within a couple months were at pre-deployment levels. The impact on leadership skills and organizational proficiency with complex war-fighting tasks, in contrast, was significant and enduring. Daily patrolling in the challenging and unpredictable environments of Haiti and Bosnia placed a premium on decentralized decision making and small-unit leadership. Such maturation could not have been achieved in artificial training environments. These are capabilities that will be central, moreover, to the decentralized and digitized battlefields envisioned in the future. After refreshing perishable skill sets, therefore, both units were more combat capable after the peace operation than before.

To achieve this outcome, certain essential steps had to be taken. Unit integrity was maintained,[20] and commanders conducted an active training program throughout the deployment. Finally, they went in with overwhelming force to be prepared for a worst-case scenario. Under the more benign circumstances actually encountered, it was possible to satisfy requirements both of the mission and an active training program.[21]

While the direct impact of peace missions on readiness is not necessarily negative, the cumulative impact along with numerous other smaller-scale contingencies and continuing exercise commitments has been an unacceptably high tempo of operations and level of personnel turbulence. This is having a major impact on quality of life and contributes to a severe retention problem. In sum, the recent tempo of operations cannot be sustained with the present force posture and is having a particularly harsh impact on specialized career fields, such as military police and civil affairs, that have uniquely valuable skills for managing troubled states.

### The Need to Integrate Civil and Military Contributions

Troubled and anarchic states are distinguished by their failure to perform such essential functions as sustaining life, resolving political conflict, maintaining public order, and generating employment.[22] Mounting an effective response to such abysmal political, social, and economic conditions requires the integration of a wide array of both military and civilian specialties.[23] The need for the international community to act, however, is more apparent than the proper formula for response. The key is to be found in recognizing the interdependent relationship between military and civil components of contemporary peace missions and constructing effective regimes for their collaboration.

Integration of effort will always be imperfect because the array of states, international organizations, and NGOs involved will each have their own interests in a given troubled state. Nevertheless, U.S. leadership is often essential to mounting an international response, and, thus, it may be possible to leverage this to ensure that mechanisms are established that are conducive to an integrated effort. Among these would be to designate a single political manager (such as a Special Representative of the Secretary General when it is a U.N.-led operation) to oversee implementation of the peace process and a common operations center for key international agencies involved. More fully exploiting the integrative potential of information technology (e.g., Geographic Information Systems) could greatly facilitate information sharing, which is the first step toward task sharing and coordinated planning. Additionally, military civil affairs officers (also known as Civil-Military Cooperation or CIMIC in NATO) perform an invaluable integrative function during interventions of this sort, and proper account needs to be made for this in military force.

The other key to unity of effort is to take steps to rectify the many ''missing links'' in global capacity for addressing troubled states. Several of these have been suggested above (e.g., availability of constabulary forces and senior police administrators). Various other areas require attention if a cost-effective transition from the military phase of an intervention is to be made to one where international civilian efforts predominate, and ultimately returning control to indigenous authorities. Improvement is needed, for example, in the capacity to mobilize CIVPOL personnel, to address the judicial reform issue, and to disperse funds for reconstruction activities during the early stage of an intervention.

## CONCLUSION

There is no interest in the Balkans, Bismarck once observed, ''worth the bones of a single healthy Pomeranian grenadier.''[24] By the calculus of his day, there was little utility in seeking to ''manage'' a troubled state such as the former Yugoslavia. The costs, measured in units of national power such as Pomeranian grenadiers, would have been substantial, yet the gain would have been nil. Nothing has happened since Bismarck's time to make the Balkans more attractive as a strategic asset; however, the strategic implications of troubled and anarchic states have changed.

In Bismarck's day, inter-state relations were governed by the logic of power politics. One state's gain in terms of national security represented a corresponding loss for its competitors. By this logic, a nation's security would generally stand to benefit from the weakness of neighboring states. Today, in contrast, a ''positive-sum'' logic has emerged, at least where stable democracies and liberal trading regimes predominate.[25]

How do troubled states figure into this calculation? The national security of the United States is buttressed by the continued expansion of the realm of free market democracies. Accordingly, U.S. policy seeks to promote the consolidation of fledgling democracies. Since regimes are at their weakest when they are in their infancy, it is at this stage that emerging democracies will be most prone to failure. In our dealings with tyrannical regimes, on the other hand, the policy aim is to promote a transition to legitimate governance. Autocratic rulers, however, are prone to use draconian measures to prevent power from slipping from their grasp. As Slobodan Milosevic has demonstrated in Kosovo, the internal humanitarian consequences of this process can be horrendous and the impact on surrounding states can gravely imperil prominent U.S. interests. In contrast to Bismarck's world, therefore, weak and troubled states today can present serious national security challenges.

## NOTES

1. These manifestations of a seriously challenged state have in common the failure of mechanisms to resolve disputes in a peaceful manner, maintain public order, generate employment/income, and the incapacity to allocate the scarce resources of society in a way that avoids massive suffering and mortality. Thus, the conflicts that arise are internal to the state and driven by the failure of political or economic institutions, as opposed to natural disasters. Until such elemental activities have been regenerated, the affected state and society will be unlikely to sustain peace autonomously. Consequently, the surrounding region will be at continued risk of destabilization.

2. One path-breaking study of the incidence of state failure found that among nondemocratic states, in particular, the factors most closely linked to breakdown are a low level of trade and a demographic bulge in the number of youths between the ages of 15 and 29.

3. In general, new regimes are at a considerably higher risk of failure than those with greater longevity.

4. The government of Colombia has effectively lost control of a vast portion of its interior bordering on Brazil, Peru, and Ecuador.

5. The Samper government in Colombia (1993–1998) was irreparably tainted by well-founded allegations that his campaign accepted a $6 million contribution from a local drug trafficker.

6. Michael Ignatieff, *The Warrior's Honor: Ethnic War and the Modern Conscience* (New York: Metropolitan Books, 1998), p. 98.

7. Some $800 billion worth of transactions take place each day.

8. The Congo operation was the major exception.

9. See John Hillen, *The Blue Helmets: The Strategy of UN Military Operations* (New York: Brassey's, 1998).

10. The United States is presently responsible for funding 30.7 percent of each peace operation, and the costs associated with intervening in an internal conflict vastly exceed those involved in a simple monitoring mission between two rival states.

11. For example, none of the nineteen states that had designated stand-by forces was willing to make them available to the United Nations when a mission was proposed for Rwanda.

12. The Haiti mission transitioned from a coalition of the willing, the Multinational Force, to the U.N. Mission in Haiti.

13. Dan Smith, *The State of War and Peace Atlas* (Oslo: International Peace Research Institute, 1997), p. 14.

14. The White House, *A National Security Strategy for a New Century* (October 1998), p. 1.

15. Swedish Foreign Minister Jan Eliasson pointed this out in a conversation with Ambassador Robert Oakley and Colonel Michael Dziedzic, U.S. Air Force, on March 6, 1998, in the Swedish Foreign Ministry.

16. The Rules of Engagement would be identical to those of the military force, most likely authorizing use of force to prevent loss of life or serious injury to members of the international community and, if indigenous authorities are unresponsive, for innocent local civilians as well.

17. If the peace process falters, refugees will be extremely reluctant to return to their homes, private investors will assuredly calculate that the risk to their venture capital outweighs any potential gain, the outcome of future elections could easily be determined more by bullets than ballots, and resources spent on relief and reconstruction could merely result in a prolongation of the conflict. Transnational criminal organizations, moreover, are prone to seize upon such openings to intimidate or suborn even the most senior government officials and insinuate themselves into positions of influence.

18. This does not negate the overarching objective of placing the burden of policing on local authorities. Until the dominant sources of political resistance have been quashed, however, it would be unwise to rely totally on a politically motivated police establishment to maintain order.

19. The controversial decision regarding the status of Brcko was announced in March 1999, and in spite of Serb verbal protests about the outcome, there was no orchestrated campaign of public disturbances.

20. If units had been formed from individuals drawn from across the army, the impact on readiness would have been decidedly negative.

21. The 1st Armored Division in Bosnia had an advantage in this regard since ranges were available in-theater for periodic use by their units.

22. *"Essential functions"* are defined as clusters of related activities (political, social, or economic) that must be performed at least at some minimal level to preclude a return to conditions that originally provoked the international intervention.

23. In cases where a peace operation is undertaken, the extent to which these "essential functions" are regenerated will vary. Some may not be addressed at all (with likely implications for achieving a stable outcome). However, all peace operations will address at least some of the areas.

24. Edward Crankshaw, *Bismarck* (Middlesex, England: Penguin Books, Ltd., 1981), p. 348.

25. The fundamental economic law of comparative advantage that provides the rationale for free market economics is clearly a "positive-sum" concept. The notion that democracies are not prone to wage war on each other also is conducive to a "positive-sum" conclusion that the United States will be more secure in a global environment populated by increasing numbers of stable, consolidated democracies.

Chapter 11

# America Coping with Chaos at the Strategic Level: Facilitator for Democratic Stability in the Post-Counterinsurgency Era

## Joseph N. McBride

> The ruling of distant peoples is not our dish . . . there are many things Americans should beware of, and among them is the acceptance of any sort of paternalistic responsibility to anyone.
>
> —George Kennan

Regional crises with a humanitarian twist will become a major focus of national security policy in the post–Cold War era. Many less developed countries (LDCs) threaten to become ungovernable, overwhelmed by population growth, economic decline, and breakdown of social order. Intervention in one form or another may be forced on a world community unwilling to endure the anguished faces of cyclical tragedies. Neither Cable News Network (CNN) nor pressure group politics will permit national leaders to claim, "We didn't know," to excuse inaction.

For the longer term, the $4 billion to $5 billion required increase in international community contributions to family planning services in the less developed countries (LDCs)[1] will be "minuscule compared to the benefits."[2] In the medium run, reinforcing regional security organizations to assume greater responsibility is probably our best hope. Regional leaders like Nigeria, India, Brazil, and Mexico should be encouraged to assume leadership in subglobal security groupings and share the burden of maintaining civilized order among their neighbors that "go critical." Bosnia, Kosovo, Liberia and Sierra Leone show that this will take time, however, and may not always work.

United Nations peacekeeping or peacemaking and unilateral U.S. intervention all have serious drawbacks, although each may be suitable from time to time. Cold War–style counterinsurgency is now "dead on arrival" and does not warrant resuscitation: as practiced by the United States, it was largely a failure in its time, is clearly out of step with the times, and could bust the budget to no purpose.

The question remains whether U.S. bilateral policy toward the LDCs can be reinvented and our instruments retooled to support a concept of "democratic security"—one focused on governments that are willing to be held to international norms, open to rethinking their survival strategies, and able to meet their challenges relying primarily on their own resources. (Any such effort would have to be a sub-theme in an overall U.S. policy to support democracy, human rights, and peaceful conflict resolution as our primary thrust within the LDCs.)

Should we embark on such a course, much of the old thinking and most of the old ways of security assistance should be thrown overboard. The entire purpose behind our effort should be to help the host countries do better with what they already have—and to do so at lower levels of violence. This means focusing assistance primarily on the police and local court systems in a democracy stabilization program tightly constrained by overarching U.S. support for democracy and human rights.

Residual U.S. military aid should focus our friends on fixing their strategic shortcomings and look beyond mere tactical improvements. Above all, we should drum home the need to build political consensus, underwriting the host government's "unity of effort," and maintaining its moral legitimacy at home and abroad.

Earlier in the decade, the Shining Path (*Sendero Luminoso*) challenged the survival of Peru. The Bush administration defended assistance to Peru completely on anti-narcotics and humanitarian rationales—anything other than "the c word," counterinsurgency.[3] Something similar is happening in Colombia right now, although the guerrillas have no chance of seizing power. Put simply, following Vietnam and El Salvador, the adage seems: "We don't do mountains, we don't do jungles—and we don't do counterinsurgency." With the end of the Cold War, this prevailing popular prohibition merits rigorous rethinking.

Instability, domestic disintegration, and insurrection, however, threaten to become more pervasive. Many ruling elites from the ex–Soviet Union to Africa and South America may prove incapable of coping with the challenges of a more crowded, competitive, and interdependent world. Global population pressures will be immense as the planet struggles to feed 3.1 billion more people—a 57 percent increase by 2025, almost all of them in the LDCs. "The worst case scenario? Human population could almost quadruple to 20 billion by the year 2100."[4] Even under the best assumptions, the world population will double by the end of the next century.

Somalia is the clearest example of a vicious downward cycle, but similar deterioration is manifest elsewhere. The majority of the population in the ex-Soviet republics of Central Asia is under the age of 20, and in several states it is under 15. In the 1980s, Latin America and the Caribbean suffered a 1.1 percent real annual decline in gross national product (GNP), a "savage reversal of 20 years of progress" during which annual real growth averaged almost 3 percent.[5] Trends in Haiti, Peru, Panama, Argentina, and Venezuela "bear witness" to the range of problems threatening to overwhelm the "capacity to govern" in many Latin American countries.[6]

The United States has been involved in some 60 low-intensity conflicts over the past century. This includes eleven insurgencies, two of them (El Salvador and the Philippines) in the last decade.[7] Will the United States be able to stand apart totally from the turmoil and internal disruption that is likely to wrack many LDCs in the coming decades? If history is a predictor, the answer is, "probably not." If that is the case, what interests would likely impel our involvement and what form would U.S. intervention best take?

## INTERVENTION AND U.S. NATIONAL INTERESTS

The end of the Cold War has completely undercut our traditional "national security" rationale for countering communist insurgencies in the LDCs. Similarly, jeremiads against the "widespread political and economic collapse with potentially grave consequences for the international economy"[8] are not convincing. If one LDC collapses, others will gladly step in to absorb its market share in providing most raw materials we need. (Petroleum is arguably the one exception. And Operation Desert Storm proved that we were ready to take decisive military action to protect our interests on that score.) Intervention to protect "stable markets" in the LDCs would have little appeal.

If standard national security and economic rationales for intervening in the LDCs fall flat with the demise of the Soviet Union, what would compel us to intervene in these countries? Three other challenges to our interests could trigger us to act:

*Humanitarian revulsion* to barbarity visited on our homes daily by CNN: Some would term this an "ideological interest." However characterized, it packs the most potent political punch of the three. It is the most likely scenario and the one national security planners should primarily focus on—if they want to get ahead of the power curve on future Somalias, Bosnias, Haitis, and Kosovos.

*Mass population migrations* triggered by a breakdown in order, in Mexico for instance. The North American Free Trade Agreement (NAFTA) should be our first line of defense.[9] But if development falters and violent challenges to the established order break out, we will seek alternatives to turning the Rio Grande into another Maginot Line. The Darien jungle provides some protection against population surges from South America, but it can be passed—especially by sea. (In Europe our NATO allies have no such protection if further disintegration and chaos overwhelm Russia.)

Risk of *regional instability* genuinely affecting our security interests: The best example would be a Muslim extremist takeover in Egypt. It would raise questions about access to the Suez Canal. More important, it would rip apart the Middle East peace process of two decades to bridge the trying gap between our oil interests and our commitment to Israel. Similarly, a repeat of Operation Just

Cause in Panama, for whatever reason, would adversely affect our interests throughout the region and would be better avoided.

## TYPES OF INTERVENTION

There are four general approaches for the United States in intervention in the LDCs, and they are not necessarily mutually exclusive. In time sequencing, they cover the gamut from indirect intervention before violence breaks out to after-the-fact cleanup of a situation that has already gone bad. Similarly, they range from multilateral efforts at the global or regional levels to strictly unilateral undertakings.

### SWAT Team Approach

Operation Just Cause in Panama might be termed the "SWAT team exception"—seldom invoked but quick and decisive. A good case has been made that this model incorporates the "four salient lessons of Vietnam"[10] and provides an operational doctrine for intervention against a regime that has not fully consolidated power. For it to work, however, the intervention force must hand over power rapidly to a successor government (which can gain legitimacy) and withdraw promptly.

### "Peacekeeper" or "International Social Worker"

Unable to get early consensus to act, it appears that by default our "preferred style" of intervention—when we can get it—would be that of "peacekeeper": for example, operating as part of an ex post facto, multilateral peacekeeping force invited in to repair the damage after the contending factions have exhausted themselves. Under this scenario, we would join with others under a multilateral banner in seeking to restore a degree of normalcy and governance where chaos had held sway. The closest example might be a Somalia intervention deferred to 1994, but with the United Nations in on the take off as well as the landing.

The "benefits" of this remedial approach may pall rather fast. Whole populations may die in front of CNN cameras before the contestants stagger to a stalemate as the world gears up. Reconstruction costs mount exponentially when urban infrastructure has been devastated (for example, Phnom Penh).

Above all, leaders at home and abroad who volunteer their forces to participate will pay a growing political bill. Potential "donors" may dry up fast as Fijians-for-hire run out and the United States and Japan tire of passing the hat as the costs grow.

### "Peace Enforcer" or "Universal Umpire"

Popular sentiment seems to be gradually building for multilaterally sanctioned "conflict suppression" operations or the creation of "protected zones." The Economic Community of West African States' (ECOWAS) deployment to Liberia and Operation Provide Comfort for the Kurds in Iraq are cases in point, not to mention the evolving situations in Somalia and Bosnia.

Peace enforcing would appear to suffer from most of the liabilities of peace-keeping—and then some—namely:

• Heightened probability of the Good Samaritans' taking bullets from both sides.

• Peace enforcers' responsibility to dictate political terms, including population resettlements, that may be repugnant.

• Difficulty imposing a settlement that endures beyond the peace enforcers' withdrawal.[11]

### "Tutor to Regional Security Linchpins"

In this alternative, the United States would attempt to reinforce regional security arrangements as the first line of response to LDC crises. The United States could provide ad hoc technical support for specific interventions but rely primarily on regional powers to muster most of the troops, provide most of the funding, and accept most of the political responsibility.

This model is very attractive and *in the long term* may be the paradigm most worthy of our attention and investment. It is, however, far from being realized—as European inaction in Bosnia demonstrates today. Moreover, even where it is put into effect (for example, ECOWAS in Liberia) the way it is done and the results it produces may not be entirely to our liking.

On balance, these four approaches show serious shortcomings. At least in the near to medium term, they appear to have limited applicability. The potential breakdown in internal order posited for much of Africa, some of Latin America, and part of the ex-USSR requires a different approach. If the United States still wants to address these situations (for the reasons earlier identified), we may have to consider the final two approaches: "the world's policeman" and "facilitator/consultants."

### CAMELOT AND COUNTERINSURGENCY: THE "WORLD'S POLICEMAN" DOESN'T WORK

Vietnam permanently prejudiced the policy environment against counterinsurgency—even if U.S. combat forces are not directly involved. In El Salvador, the efforts of the Farabundo Marti National Liberation Front (FMLN) and President Reagan's unique obsession brought a one-time rematch that ended in a tie after twelve years. The exception however, only confirmed the rule: "We can't do that again."

Even without U.S. combat forces, the costs were just too high:

- 60,000 Salvadorans dead (the equivalent of 2.7 million Americans);

- 25 percent of the population becoming refugees, including one million illegal immigrants into the United States;

- Moral repugnance at U.S. failure to control 40,000 death-squad killings by the Salvadoran military with $6 billion in U.S. assistance;

- Massive repudiation of the Republican interventionist position at the polls; and

- Heavy opportunity costs to top U.S. policy makers who had to spend scarce political capital with Congress and commit time that would have been better used elsewhere.

In the end, only the preemptive collapse of the USSR (and with it the Cold War) averted "our defeat."

"Counterinsurgency" is a pariah term, hurled to stigmatize U.S. programs (or be hotly denied) in the two countries where it might most logically apply: Peru and Colombia.[12] In both cases, the term "narcoterrorist" had to be coined (with arguable analytical justification) to duck the political paralysis invoked by any taint of counterinsurgency. The end results are dual-purpose security assistance programs, marginal to both *their* insurgency problems and *our* narcotics objectives, certainly earlier in Peru and perhaps currently in Colombia as well.

The objectives of both the United States and Peru could have been better served if we could have differentiated between the narcotics and insurgency problems and focused on the highest payoff response to each. The quid pro quo for our helping to hurt the Shining Path, say with helicopters for the high sierra, would be cutting off narcotics trafficking from airfields in the Upper Huallaga Valley (UHV) already under government control. The U.S. sine qua non for continuing this kind of cooperation to maximum mutual advantage could be tangible reduction in Peruvian human rights abuses—the Achilles' heel of our bilateral cooperation. But it was not to be. Cold War–style counterinsurgency remains too tainted for policy makers to touch—even as a vehicle to verified improvements in human rights.[13]

### Well-Intentioned But Futile Web Spinning at SO/LIC

DOD doctrine for "low-intensity conflict" (LIC) is a bewildering potpourri covering insurgency, counterinsurgency, counterterrorism, peace contingency operations, and peacekeeping. The Harvard Symposium on Small Wars in 1988 concluded that:

The National Security Decision Directive on low intensity conflict signed by President Reagan has all but dropped out of sight. . . . There appears to be limited interest in creating functional experts in LIC with experience in many different small wars.[14]

An experienced observer concurred:

People problems at the top predominate. . . . State should be a primary player, but . . . top State officials, with rare exceptions, couldn't care less. . . . The problems would quickly disappear . . . if the President, his Secretary of State, and Secretary of Defense assigned SO/LIC a high priority. [But they don't.] Meanwhile marginal improvements are the best we can expect.[15]

An NSC-chaired "Deputies Meeting" in June 1990 refused to institute an inter-agency LIC backstop mechanism. And DOD's *1990 Doctrine for Joint Operations in Low-Intensity Conflict* remains in limbo, a "draft publication" lacking official imprimatur.

Most recent SO/LIC brainstorming, however, is a quantum step forward in sophistication. *Peacetime Engagement: A Policy for the Environment Short of War* is an impressive new framework for approaching post–Cold War regional security.[16] This draft policy proposal does not, however, pin down "the devil in the details." How the new administration treats this legacy remains to be seen.

## Outdated Security Assistance Programs

Foreign military assistance in the Cold War essentially paid for base rights to maintain the structure of containment and the tempo of operations. Reforming host country capabilities to deal with domestic instability was an ancillary benefit, but far from essential. What was important was to keep the aid flowing. For that we relied on big ticket hardware transfers and basic skill training in soldiering—things we could readily take off the shelf and plug in anywhere.

This "cookie cutter"[17] approach to stamping out security assistance packages applicable anytime, anywhere, by all accounts produced "not very impressive" results.[18] Former Ambassador to El Salvador Thomas Pickering summed it up:

We had neither the doctrine, nor the support nor the coordination in the United States government that would really be required to deal effectively with that kind of operation. I don't think we ever developed it; we are still kind of *ad hoc* in our way of viewing the problems. That is really quite a critical comment.[19]

Finally, we will not have the funding to support security assistance programs that can pay for high-priced equipment and training as in the old days. Former SOUTHCOM commander General Wallace Nutting lamented several years ago:

For the cost of steaming a carrier group up and down the coast (of Central America) for a week, we could fund most of the training programs and most of the material assistance needed (for all of Latin America) for a year.[20]

Subsequently, security assistance funding cuts have only gotten worse,[21] as did the size of the potential problems to be dealt with. Colombia has roughly seven times the population, and is 57 times the size of El Salvador—yet its army has less than one-fourth the number of helicopters as the country which Ronald Reagan marked as the ramparts of freedom. Obviously, the old formula just will not work, nor should it be attempted.

In sum, attempts to rehabilitate Vietnam-style counterinsurgency—minus U.S. combat troops—failed in El Salvador and have never had a chance to get off the ground in the Andes. As a paradigm it is dead on arrival, costing more in blood, dollars, and domestic political turmoil than we are willing to commit against foreseeable threats. The lack of strategic vision, coherent doctrine, effective coordination mechanisms, and appropriate personnel policies that plagued us in El Salvador should not be repeated. Were they to be tried again on a country more difficult than five million people right on our doorstep, their failings would be more obvious and more costly.

## ADVOCATES FOR "DEMOCRATIC SECURITY": CONSULTANTS AND FACILITATORS

Multilateral humanitarian intervention is gaining new cachet,[22] but often comes "too little, too late" as in Somalia, Bosnia, and Kosovo. The United States may find that multilateral handholders are often unavailable. But we may have another option—aggressive advocacy of "democratic security" to prevent a breakdown of civilized governance *before* it occurs.

A proactive policy of supporting "democratic security" should entail a three-tiered approach:

• Low cost–high value support for democratic programs and human rights *before* trouble strikes;

• Conciliation service should violent breakdowns begin; and

• Finally, in limited circumstances, indirect intervention through the provision of security assistance cast from a brand new mold (for example, geared to the recipient's "center of gravity" rather than U.S. surplus capabilities) when a reasonably democratic, human rights–abiding, and reform-oriented regime is imperiled with ominous implications for important U.S. interests.

The elements of this three-tiered approach are not mutually exclusive (for example, the final phases of El Salvador.) As a general matter, however:

- Democratization and human rights assistance should be available largely for the asking;
- Conflict resolution assistance might be extended where both sides were ready for it; and
- "Reinvented security assistance" should be extended only in special cases.

## Democracy and Human Rights as Rallying Points

Democracy and human rights must be pillars of U.S. policy in strife-torn LDCs for three reasons:

- They are intrinsically "good" in American eyes.
- They should contribute to conflict resolution through politics instead of violent upheaval.
- A reasonable track record of adherence to democracy and human rights is a sine qua non for extending U.S. security assistance to LDCs threatened by internal turmoil.

Support for democracy and human rights must replace containment as the central, unifying theme in American foreign policy. "Only by uniting our national interests with Americans' basic values can we mobilize and sustain broad, bipartisan support for U.S. global leadership in the new era."[23] Wherever we have diplomatic relations we should be prepared to offer a range of "democratization services," including:

Programs which develop political parties; assist in administration and monitoring of fair elections; train parliamentarians, lawyers and judges; enhance the rule of law; build free trade unions; support independent media; cultivate open markets; aid private sector institutions supporting human rights; and encourage political participation by all groups in society.[24]

In Latin America at least, our policy should include a number of specific elements to support democracy and human rights, some of which have already proven reasonably effective, such as:

- Public fair warning that we will freeze all government-to-government assistance and vote "No" on international financial institution (IFI) loans wherever democratic regimes are toppled.
- Renewed efforts to get the Organization of American States (OAS) to amend its charter to "suspend" participation by any state that has had a coup.
- Conversion of all international military education and training (IMET) to the IMET-E (expanded) format which includes civilians for management of military establishments, budgets, and codes of justice, including human rights.
- Requiring that all U.S. military assistance and sales agreements be signed by host-country presidents to reinforce civilian control over the military.

- Making human rights enhancement programs central pillars of the "annual country plans," a fact instead of lip service.[25]

## Facilitating a Negotiated Settlement

Now that the tide of communist-controlled insurgencies has receded, we should prefer peace negotiations over military victory as the way to end the "uncomfortable wars" in the LDCs. At least three mechanisms commend themselves for consideration, and others may be possible.

- Restructure significant aid programs, around presidential certifications designed to reward (or punish) both government and insurgents, depending on their behavior. (The insurgents get "punished" if their abuses or recalcitrance to negotiate in good faith, etc., trigger a legally mandated presidential certification providing an automatic increase in U.S. assistance to the government.) We have a real-world precedent: The Dodd-Leahy amendment on El Salvador, which infuriated the administration but had the effect of pushing all sides toward a negotiated solution.[26]
- The same approach could be adopted as a matter of declared administration policy with regard to our generally decisive vote on IFI loans.
- Finally, the United States could provide facilitative encouragement for negotiations to be mediated by third parties, as in the case of Guatemala.[27]

## INDIRECT INTERVENTION

After perusing the above efforts to enhance democracy, human rights, and peaceful conflict resolution, we come to the issue of developing a new approach to security assistance—to help stave off the "breakdown of governance" in LDCs where local conditions and U.S. interests permit. Perhaps a radical redesign of counterinsurgency assistance could restore its policy utility under certain limited conditions. If so, what would those conditions be, and how would this new approach look?

The United States should consider giving reconfigured counterinsurgency assistance only when the following criteria are met:

- The U.S. national interest is sufficiently compelling to outweigh allegations of getting our hands dirty by association.
- The host government's popular support can be solidified.
- The host government is truly capable of implementing wrenching internal reforms that address relevant grievances.
- U.S. global "credibility" will not become hostage to "victory," and we retain the ability to walk away if things go sour.
- U.S. combat forces will not be required.[28]

If any of the first three criteria cannot be met, indirect intervention via security assistance won't work, and we should keep our hands off. If the last two criteria cannot be met, let's not fool ourselves: once we are involved, it will soon become a matter of U.S. direct, unilateral intervention. Still, in selective cases, it ought to be possible to "do security assistance right"—if we pick our clients as well as our fights and greatly revise how we go about it.

## MAKING SECURITY ASSISTANCE WORK: A CONCEPT-INTENSIVE APPROACH

The United States generally approaches client states gingerly, lest we appear colonialistic—and properly so. But as a consequence, field advisors in Vietnam and El Salvador soon learned the lament: "a house leaks from the roof"—and it doesn't get fixed by working at the rice roots.

A successful strategy begins at the top, but U.S. policy makers seldom embrace the responsibility that simple insight implies. It is futile to beef up marginal operational capabilities (simply because we know how to do so) and ignore the strategic vulnerabilities of the country we presume to help.

This has been generally our pattern in the past. Once launched into the swamp, we tend to rely on "more bailers with deeper hip boots and bigger buckets"—instead of calling for hydraulic engineers to attack the source instead of the symptoms. What is needed is a few hard-eyed policy analysts with seats at the tables of power, not a plethora of hard-charging field men from the "can do" school of counterinsurgency.

Above all, this takes leadership in the country team and backstopping in Washington—people who are focused on systemic issues and openly determined to walk away if our efforts are marginalized and our resources are squandered.

### Six Keys to Their Victory—and Ours

Reflecting on frustrating years in El Salvador, one American observer concluded that "the ultimate outcome of any counter-insurgency effort is not primarily determined by the skillful manipulation of violence"[29] in battle. Instead victory goes to the side that achieves more: (1) legitimacy, (2) unity of effort, (3) intelligence, (4) effective external support, (5) military discipline and capability, and (6) impact in reducing the opposition's external support. To the extent that the government has the upper hand in all six factors, it has a decided advantage. If, however, the government fails completely in any one of the six, or is weak in most of them, its prospects are poor.[30]

Legitimacy,[31] unity of effort, and intelligence[32] are the three most important factors for success—but U.S. programs focused most heavily on issues of external support (for example, the Ho Chi Minh Trail and "passing the supplemental appropriations bill") and military capability. And for good, but self-defeating, reasons: these were issues we could easily attack with what we had on hand—money, weaponry, and military expertise.

Legitimacy, unity of effort, and intelligence were key to our client's success—but all depended primarily on the host government's reforms. Getting these reforms required the creation and exercise of U.S. leverage with the host government. However, while we had plenty of resources to bestow on our clients during the Cold War, the more aid we gave, the more leverage we surrendered. Recipients from Saigon to San Salvador "knew" that we were inextricably bound to their survival. Only when it became clear that we were pulling out (after Tet 1968 and the November 1989 Jesuits' murder) did calls for internal reform and political settlement acquire compelling force.

In the "new world," the United States does not have to defeat any global rival, nor contend with Soviet "war by proxy" in the LDCs. Our interests do not require the survival of any client regime as the key to a global mosaic. This new-found ability to "walk away" provides us with potentially decisive leverage in dealing with client states—if we dare use it and use it wisely.

## REINVENTING U.S. SECURITY ASSISTANCE

Our military assistance in Peru was tied to an "anti-narcotic" rationale; at the same time, it had to address the Peruvians' top security priority: the Shining Path. Neither the A-37s we ultimately supported nor the originally proposed battalion training center in the Upper Huallaga Valley were very relevant to either drugs or Sendero—but they were something that we were institutionally comfortable doing. Ultimately, that determined what we did, but it could have been different.

In Peru earlier, Colombia and elsewhere, the United States should adopt a new style of providing security assistance consistent with the new circumstances in which we find ourselves. That new "style" should:

- Help the host government identify and correct its key strategic shortcomings and de-emphasize our traditional assistance focused around "the business end of the gun."
- Accept that the United States does not have "the answers" to mainline into other political systems. But we do have a variety of mechanisms[33] that could help the host country expand its political dialogue in search of a broad consensus on an appropriate strategy that would permit true "unity of effort."[34]
- Key on helping the government reinforce its all-important "legitimacy" at home and abroad.[35]
- Emphasize good police work and intelligence based on motivated local cadre with something worth fighting for.

In short, we should begin to act more like international consultants, helping our LDC clients reconcile what they do with what they have—rather than playing the aging Santa Claus rapidly running out toys for resentful pre-teens with guns. This new role as a "facilitator, rather than as a fireman, would require several changes in how we organize ourselves to do business, namely:

1. Replace U.S. operationally oriented military assistance officers with more Foreign Area Officer (FAO)–type diagnosticians to design and manage security assistance programs.

2. Shift to more country-specific tailoring of assistance and away from vertical "stove pipe" programs pumping out primarily what Washington and Regional CINC backstop offices are geared to provide on short notice. Such horizontal integration between various agency programs can only take place at the country team level and would require full ambassadorial backing.

3. Renew the executive-legislative understanding on the purpose of security assistance by completely updating the Foreign Assistance Act (FAA) which has become "barnacle encrusted" since it was first passed in 1961.[36] Such an effort should clearly specify the standards the United States requires with regard to human rights and democracy for cooperative assistance.

4. Repeal Section 660 of the FAA, the 20-year-old legal prohibition against most U.S. aid to police. This prohibition is no longer appropriate in an era when democracy and human rights have replaced an earlier obsession with anti-communist stability as the lodestars of U.S. policy. Such an effort should be located in the reconstituted Narcotics and Crime Bureau directly under the new Undersecretary of State for Global Issues who is primarily responsible for human rights and democracy.

Along with improving LDC criminal justice systems, smarter police work should replace military aid as the cutting edge of U.S. operational assistance to threatened governments. British counterinsurgency expert Sir Robert Thompson had the right emphasis when he said that the government's (internal) defense generally should rely primarily on the police and not the military. This should be reflected in U.S. assistance programs as well.

Military assistance should adopt a leaf out of AID's book and "subprojectize" some of its programs, each with its own "conditions precedent" attached. The purpose would be to allow us to hold host-country officials responsible for making a reasonable effort to meet agreed targets—without threats of across-the-board assistance cancellation for nonperformance.

Last but most important, we should set priorities for our objectives and not attribute to a given level of assistance more leverage than it is intrinsically worth.

## FACILITATING COLOMBIAN SOLUTIONS TO COLOMBIAN PROBLEMS . . . TEST CASE FOR "HAVE WE FINALLY LEARNED?"

The situation in Colombia in 1999 has reached a turning point. It has become so stark that Colombians can no longer deny it, individually and collectively. But they are only now beginning to confront just how much they have to do to change it.

The presidential election of 1998 was largely resolved on the issue of war/peace. More important, however, was the local/departmental election of October 1997 when 10 million people voted in the face of guerrilla death threats (carried out in many cases) to prevent the elections. People have had enough, and they are ready to put their lives on the line, if necessary, to stop madness before it destroys the country.

In the last several years, many have called for foreign intervention to produce a solution. Colombians seem to feel that they are unable to save themselves. The *illusion* of a foreign deus ex machina is, however, just that, an *illusion*. Colombia is in the throws of a problem of largely Colombian making—and only they can save them from themselves.

But how? Here, international facilitation can be useful—even decisive. Here, international nudging can, perhaps, provoke the Colombian political class to acknowledge and act on three principles:

1. Colombian "political will" is decisive. With it, everything is possible; without it, nothing is. Discrete international intervention can, perhaps, help nurture local political will. But that is something that cannot be imported. In the end, Colombians have to summon it out of the fire in their own bellies.

2. Colombia needs to forge its own national strategy: political, economic, social, and security. The carrots and sticks of a negotiation can only be of Colombian devising because they must come from a broad, popular consensus about how much they are willing to pay for peace—in power adjustments versus the blood of their sons. Moreover, this dynamic consensus must endure beyond any single government because half a century of fighting will not be finally solved in three or four years.

3. Colombia is a rich country. By and large, it is going to have to finance its own salvation. Here, too, others can help, but with only 3.5 percent of their PIB going to national security (including the police), Colombians are ill-advised to hope for others to come in and bail them out. There is no free lunch.

This is where "international friends" come in—as *facilitators* in a Colombian search for a Colombian solution to a Colombian problem using Colombian resources.

Nurturing authentic "political will" in another country, encouraging consensus building over an indigenous "strategy," and sparking a Colombian commitment to mobilize the resources necessary to get the job done—these are the keys to negotiating a peace. It is a tall order to ask one's foreign friends to serve up, much less that they do so without imposing their own political agenda and bureaucratic imperatives on the host nation. This is what the U.S. government set about doing in a series of unclassfied conferences in Houston, Cartagena, Villa de Leyva, and Medellin. These conferences were all a transparent attempt at positive political intervention to prod the process of civic dialogue starting before there was a formal peace process and when there was still no elected government committed to perusing it.

The Cartagena conference in May 1998 on "The Lessons of Peace" in Cen-

tral America followed on an earlier conference in Houston—with the participation of a broad spectrum from the left to the right—on the "Lessons of War"
in dealing with insurgencies around the world. The U.S. embassy has sponsored
several other conferences, some on the role of the press in covering insurgencies,
some on civil-military relations and defense-congressional relations. The latest
was the April 9–11, 1999, conference in Medellin on human rights with participation from Colombia and around the world, including the Assistant Secretary
for Human Rights as a keynote speaker.

As this "Houston/Cartegena process" of U.S. government engagement started
back in January 1998, many asked then and many ask now: "What do the
gringos really want? What are they really after? What is this all about?" The
answer—although few may believe it—is that they are trying to help Colombians find their own solution to their own problems using their own resources.
It is as simple as that.

The U.S. government provides considerable material and training assistance
to Colombia, but it will never amount to more than a fraction of the $3.5 billion
that Colombians spend on their own national security budget. The Americans
should want to help Colombians figure out how to spend their own resources
smarter. By energizing a vigorous debate between Colombians over what its
national strategy should be—political as well as military—and encouraging a
consensus over a basic framework, the United States is doing what it can to
help Colombians find their own way out of a conundrum largely of their own
making.

Since the formal peace process started with President Pastrana's July 9, 1998,
meeting with the Revolutionary Armed Forces of Colombia (FARC), there have
been many calls for the international community to push the process more ag-
gressively, to one side or the other. These implorations for foreign intervention
are mistaken, like trying to impose unsolicited and unwelcome advice to a man
on how to make love to his wife. It won't work if both sides don't want it, and
the outside therapist probably doesn't know enough about the couple to make
a difference anyway.

It is better for Colombia's friends and well-wishers to confine themselves to
doing what they do best: setting a table where Colombians of good will from
the far left to the far right can meet and talk in open dialogue about how to
cure the problems that plague their benighted land. The guerilla forces may have
11,000–17,000 men permanently under arms and the paramilitaries another
5,000–7,000. This is still less than 10 percent of the 250,000 Colombians in the
military and police. Nobody has ever put the willing and active supporters of
the groups outside of the law at more than 1 percent of Colombia's population,
probably far less. The various guerrilla groups can boast a positive image with
only 4 percent of those polled, and the number is falling fast.

Once the vast majority of the country begins to wake up and cries "halt,
enough of this madness," Colombia has the capacity to solve its own problem
in its own way. True, many of the rich recently have been leaving in unseemly

droves. This is probably as it should be, clearing the decks for action after the summer soldiers have departed from Valley Forge.

It will not be easy, but if Colombians muster the political will, strategy, and resources to do so, they themselves can put their own house straight. This is what the ''Houston Process'' as carried forward to many subsequent conferences in Cartagena, Villa de Leyva, Medellin, and so on is all about. Will Colombia's international friends also play an active role in the formal peace process? Possibly, at some point, quite likely. But that, in the end, is likely to prove less valuable and less decisive than what they are doing through the Houston/Cartagena/ Medellin Process''—helping Colombians figure out what they themselves want so they can put their own house in order, as they set about getting it.[37]

## FORGING CONSENSUS

The Clinton administration has been carving out a new approach to change in the LDCs. The population explosion is coming anyway; we can either cope with it or get bowled over. At the State Department, DOD, and the NSC new structures are evolving to grapple with its implications: the Undersecretary for Global Affairs at State, the Assistant Secretary for Democracy and Human Rights at DOD, and the Global Issues unit at the NSC.

The existence of this interconnected bureaucratic architecture should help all three agencies synchronize on a new concept of ''democratic security''—one that focuses more on what the United States is for than on what we are against. Proactive programs supporting democratic institution building, human rights, and constructive political dialogue must come to the fore in our assistance efforts. We should rapidly phase out most LDC conventional military assistance programs—which we can no longer adequately fund in any case. Advocates for democracy and human rights must help redesign a new U.S. strategy for LDCs— and become central to the domestic constituency supporting it.

If the administration has a proactive program of democracy, human rights, and support for political consensus building in place, it will be more feasible politically to reinvent a security assistance program that works, in place of irrelevant hardware transfers and technical training. This new approach would be focused on programs that do the following:

- reinforce host-government legitimacy at home and abroad;

- stimulate the local political class, including but not limited to the officer corps, to confront the shortcomings of its strategy—political as well as military—and create a consensus for both the carrots and the sticks in a national framework for peace negotiations.

- give primacy to local security, police, and criminal justice issues over tactical military operations.

- provide more ''concept-driven'' assistance focused on our allies' ''center of gravity,'' rather than what we have coveniently on the shelf to offer.
- Relentlessly pit the government's strengths against the guerrillas' weaknesses.

The United States can be neither the world's policeman nor its universal social worker. With concentrated effort, however, we might become be a good ''diagnostic consultant'' and ''facilitator'' to countries that dare to profit from our principles and seek help in putting them into practice.

By innovative redesign of security assistance programs, the key action agencies (particularly DOD and the intelligence community) can either drive policy or be left behind by it. To ride the wave, however, they must revise radically how they do business. On the military side, this means the Defense Security Assistance Groups (MAAGs), and Defense Attache Offices (DAOs) should be rethought from the ground up, and the yawning gap between security assistance and ''global issues'' in State needs to bridged.

The policy planners need to wicker all of this into a new strategy for ''democratic security.'' Congress, too, must be drawn into a compact for constructive engagement. But above all, DOD's operational program has to come up with a new vintage, rather than rebottling aged stocks already gone bad. Perhaps policy on low-intensity conflicts never got a fair testing; but by now it has gone sour in the cask and cannot be rehabilitated. That holds true in spades for Cold War–style counterinsurgency assistance.

One cannot be too sanguine about early results, despite the best of intentions. The mindsets of too many players are deeply scarred by previous ideological battles, and overcoming institutional resistance will be formidable. Moreover, the ''bad neighborhoods'' of the LDCs will limit the success of even the best policy. Many situations cannot be resolved, and we need the wisdom and courage to let them pass us by. In the end, tough cases where U.S. policy equities contend (like Peru and Colombia) may well be decided by the power of clashing advocacy groups, rather than by the merits of the issues.

Coming to grips with instability and disorder in the LDCs will be an uncomfortable process. U.S. Cold War strategy had its false starts (Alliance for Progress) and failures (Vietnam) and required a number of mid-course corrections (the Nixon doctrine replacing Southeast Asian Treaty Organization and CENTO) before proving ultimately successful. Constructing a consensus to cope with chaos in the LDCs—preemptively—will be even more confusing and conflict-ridden. One way or the other, we will have to do so. It is long past time that we start to do so—with our eyes open.

## NOTES

1. Less developed country (LDC) is used throughout to cover all non–First World states—including the former Soviet Union. In the context of this paper, it is more accurate, if less fashionable, than the euphemism ''developing countries.''

2. Carnegie Endowment National Commission, *Changing Our Ways: America and the New World* (Washington, DC, 1993), p. 42.

3. Peru references come from my 1988–1992 tour as Embassy Lima Political Counselor. The Colombia references come from my 1996–1999 tour as Political and Economic Counselor in Bogota. In neither case do they necessarily reflect the official position of the Department of State, nor of the U.S. government.

4. Carnegie Endowment National Commission, *Changing Our Ways*, p. 41.

5. "Rethinking Security in the Americas," in *North-South Issues: Democratization* (Coral Gables, FL: University of Miami, September 1992), p. 3.

6. William J. Olson, "Low-Intensity Conflict: The Challenge to the National Interest," *Terrorism*, Vol. 12, No. 2 (1989), p. 76.

7. John M. Collins, *U.S. Low-Intensity Conflicts 1899–1990*, a Congressional Research Service Study for the House Armed Services Committee (September 1990), pp. 23, 43. Collins' definition of low-intensity conflicts is a bit different from the four-part typology used in standard DOD doctrine (viz., he includes U.S.-stimulated coups d'état).

8. Olson, "Low-Intensity Conflict," p. 76.

9. OMB Director and former Joint Budget Committee Chairman Leon Panetta, *Washington Post*, April 1 and 27, 1993.

10. William S. Lind, "An Operational Doctrine for Intervention," *Parameters* (December 1987), pp. 30–36, lists the four lessons of Vietnam as: "First, we cannot sustain the long-term commitment counterinsurgency usually requires. . . . Second, we have not been very good at training and equipping foreign armies. . . . Third, it is not possible to go into another country and change its culture to conform with our ideas of human rights, good governmental military efficiency, or anything else. Fourth, war is not won on the tactical level . . . but on the operational level" (p. 30).

11. Marshall Hoyler and John Tilson, *Conflict Suppression/Peace Zone Operations* (Alexandria, VA: Institute for Defense Analysis, November 10, 1992).

12. To illustrate with some Peruvian examples: The aborted proposal for a U.S.-provided training base for three Peruvian infantry battalions in the Upper Huallaga Valley and the substituted support for A-37 attack aircraft in Peru in FY-1991 are cases in point. The training of conventional infantry battalions (made up of draftees who rotate out after two years) would have had little impact on either the Shining Path or the narcos. In the end, it proved too hard to sell in Congress. With regard to the A-37s, Peruvian fighter aircraft have downed narcotics traffickers. The traffickers, however, soon shifted to night flights, against which Peru had no intercept capability. Nor are these A-37s likely to be much good against Shining Path terrorists, who are either hidden in jungle bases or intermixed with urban populations.

13. The potential for achieving real synergy through tacit quid pro quo bargaining was demonstrated in the summer of 1991 when Congress forced the suspension of all non-humanitarian aid disbursements to Peru—primarily over human rights, although the narcotics lobby tried for its pound of flesh as well. Through tacit bargaining, we got a major human rights breakthrough: (1) total access for unannounced and private International Committee of the Red Cross (ICRC) inspection visits with prisoners in all military and police facilities throughout the country; (2) ICRC access to a new national registry of all prisoners, which was updated daily; and, (3) a 4 percent drop in the rate of human rights fatalities attributable to the government over the following ten months. Similar progress has been evident in Colombia following the adoption of the Leahy Amendment in 1996. Under this provision, the USG is precluded worldwide from pro-

viding State Department assistance under the Foreign Assistance Act to units of security forces against whom there are credible allegations of gross human rights violations— unless the Secretary of State certifies to the Congress that the country in question is taking "effective measures" to bring the culprits to justice. A similar provision applies to DOD-funded assistance, except that it calls for "all necessary corrective steps" to be taken, a somewhat more vague standard.

In return for this (and some marginal narcotics improvements), we released AID Economic Support Fund (ESF) disbursements to keep Peru's rehabilitation program with the International Monetary Fund (IMF) and World Bank on track toward reintegration in the international financial system.

14. JFK School National Security Program, Harvard University, *Small Wars Symposium: The Case of El Salvador*, a Conference Report, March 29, 1988, p. 18.14.

15. John M. Collins, Senior Specialist in National Defense, Congressional Research Service, unpublished text of remarks at unspecified SO/LIC symposium, December 11, 1990.

16. DOD/OASD(SO/LIC), *Peacetime Engagement: A Policy for the Environment Short of War*, Working Draft Paper 5, April 14, 1993.

17. Colonel John D. Waghlestein, USA, "Post-Vietnam Counterinsurgency Doctrine," *Military Review* (May 1985), p. 44.

18. Douglas S. Blaufarb, "Security/Economic Assistance and Special Operations," in *Special Operations in U.S. Strategy*, Frank R. Barnett et al., eds. (Washington, DC: NDU Press, 1984), p. 217.

19. Max C. Manwaring and Court Prisk, *A Strategic View of Insurgencies: Insight from El Salvador*, McNair Paper No. 8 (Washington, DC: NDU Institute for National Strategic Studies, May 1990), p. 13.

20. Ibid., p. 22.

21. Susan B. Clark, *The U.S. Army in a Civil-Military Support Role in Latin America*, Institute for Defense Analysis Paper P-2703, June 1992, A-3 and State Department data/ contacts.

22. Carnegie Endowment National Commission, *Changing Ways*, p. 51.

23. Will Marshall and Martin Schram, eds., *Mandate for Change* (New York: The Progressive Policy Institute; New York: Berkeley Books, 1993), p. 297.

24. Carnegie Endowment National Commission, *Changing Ways*, p. 83.

25. This should include: (a) establishing unofficial human rights performance baselines (drawn from the local human rights groups' data) to monitor trends for "extrajudicial killings"/assassinations or "disappearances;" (b) making it clear to all concerned that specific elements of our bilateral/multilateral assistance would be adversely affected by deterioration in human rights performance; (c) coordinating with the ICRC and other transactional human rights players the use of U.S. funding leverage to reinforce their access to prisons and lists of detainees, etc.; and (d) presenting specific military human rights improvement programs for funding as part of the annual budget cycle, including such things as: (1) Judge Advocate General (JAG-to-JAG) and Inspector General (IG-to-IG) exchanges on human rights; (2) support to military human rights training and monitoring systems; (3) human rights sensitization exposure on the Hill for key commanders prior to deployment; and (4) doctrinal assistance at armed forces Staff and War Colleges in developing internal defense strategies consistent with human rights. On JAG human rights aid, see: Major Jeffery F. Addicott, USA, and Major Andrew M. Warner,

USA, "JAG Corps Poised for New Defense Missions: Human Rights Training in Peru," *The Army Lawyer* (February 1993), pp. 78–82.

26. The Dodd-Leahy amendment to the El Salvador appropriation in October 1990 "halved" the already appropriated funds for FY-90 if the FMLN: (a) refused good faith negotiations, (b) committed excessive human rights violations, (c) militarily threatened the survival of the government, or (d) accepted external assistance—in which case full funding would be restored. Conversely, Dodd-Leahy would have totally eliminated aid to the government if the president could not certify that it was in compliance with the established conditions—particularly prosecuting the murderers of the six Jesuits. The administration bitterly opposed the amendment at the time, but in the words of one legislative liaison, "somewhat unconsciously in this building [State] we adopted the structure of his amendment—as long as we could keep the certification trigger under presidential control." Mark Kirk, Director of Legislative Affairs, ARA, State Department. Personal interview, December 13, 1992.

27. After decades of killing and 300,000 deaths in Guatemala, both the government and the insurgents have publicly welcomed U.S. behind-the-scenes pressure to reach closure in the current negotiations. "Progress Reported in Guatemala Talks," *Washington Post*, March 17, 1993, p. A-28.

28. Even U.S. advisors or trainers are to be avoided as generally more of a domestic liability than they're worth in the field.

29. Max Manwaring, "Toward an Understanding of Insurgency Wars: The Paradigm," in *Uncomfortable Wars: Toward a New Paradigm of Low Intensity Conflict*, Max Manwaring, ed. (Boulder, CO: Westview Press, 1991), p. 20.

30. Max G. Manwaring and John T. Fishel, "Insurgency and Counter-Insurgency: Toward a New Analytical Approach," *Small Wars and Insurgencies* (Winter 1992), pp. 272–310. Manwaring refers to an unpublished study which found an 88 percent correlation between these factors and the outcome of "a sample of insurgencies that have taken place over the past 40 to 45 years" (pp. 19, 20). There is an alternative typology, however, for getting at these issues from the vantage point of the insurgent instead of the counterinsurgent. See Bard O'Neill, *Insurgency and Terrorism: Inside Modern Revolutionary Warfare* (Washington, DC: Brassey's, 1990).

31. Legitimacy is the accepted "moral right" to govern. It largely conditions a government's ability to attract voluntary support. International legitimacy may be harder to earn than domestic support due to different minimum acceptable standards regarding democracy and human rights, as in the cases of Argentina and Peru.

32. The two most important elements of which are: ferreting out the insurgent leadership and incentive structures to develop local cadre committed to contest for control of their homes.

33. For instance, military Subject Matter Expert Exchanges (SMEEs), USIS, the National Endowment for Democracy (NED), and IMET-Extended, Anti-Terrorism Training (ATT) funded by the State.

34. The introduction of a specially tailored U.S. counterterrorism seminar conducted by ex-Rand analysts, Brian Jenkins and Cesar Sereseres, for top Colombian leaders in the late 1980s is supposed to have greatly helped Bogota rationalize its strategy. The first of two similar efforts in Lima flopped, but the second in 1991 provoked the beginning of some real interest. These are the kinds of high-level, "concept-related" consulting services we should focus on—instead of Detachments for Training (DFTs) and

Mobile Training Teams (MTTs) to teach the troops how to bail water among the alligators.

35. By relatively inexpensive steps such as: instituting proactive human rights programs with the military; beefing up our anemic Administration of Justice (AOJ) and International Criminal Investigation Technical Assistance Program (ICITAP) under AID and the Department of Justice, rescuing them from the backwaters of U.S. security assistance and making an effective criminal justice system a central focus of our bilateral country strategy; increasing host country tax collection capability; introducing IGs to help control corruption; and assistance through third party intermediaries (for example, the OAS) to the mechanics of local elections where needed and appropriate.

36. The International Cooperation Act of 1991, H.R. 25605, was a House Foreign Affairs Committee–inspired effort to do just that. It passed conference but fell short of administration desires on three counts and was vetoed. With a Democratic administration and a Democratic Congress, the time may be ripe to try again, this time leaving the executive with some more room for policy flexibility. Conversation with State Department Assistant Legal Advisor for Politico-Military Affairs Edward Cummings, March 19, 1993.

37. A seminal piece on this line is Alberto R. Coll, ''America as the Grand Facilitator,'' *Foreign Policy*, No. 87 (Summer 1992).

Chapter 12

# Responding to the Failed
State: Strategic Triage

## Robert H. Dorff

The challenges to international security posed by failed and failing states are significant and growing. Numerous authors, analysts, and policy makers have identified the phenomenon as one of the central problems of security in the post–Cold War world.[1] Brian Atwood, head of the Agency for International Development (AID), concluded that "disintegrating societies and failed states ... have emerged as the greatest menace to global stability," and he considers them a "strategic threat."[2] Leslie Gelb calls the "wars of national debilitation" that occur in these failed states "the new core problem in post–Cold War politics that a new strategy must address."[3] However, the failed and failing state is hardly a new phenomenon. Indeed, it is part of the larger historical problem of "weak states."[4] The fact that the problem has taken on some new and different dimensions in the post–Cold War security environment should not mask the fact that it has important historical antecedents in international affairs.

Elsewhere I have argued that the failed or failing state is a security threat, and I have identified several reasons why.[5] I have also argued that the United States and others will find it difficult, if not impossible, to avoid responding to the crises they engender and that there will likely be more opportunities to respond as we enter the next millennium.[6] If these premises are in fact accurate, then at least one critical question is obvious: How should we respond? My argument is that sound strategy must guide the selection of a proper response and that such a strategy must begin with a reasonably complete and accurate understanding of the nature of the problem confronting us. But we must also have reasonable and realistic expectations of what we can hope to accomplish. For if we set our sights too high, we may in fact do more harm than good in the responses we choose.

I will concentrate on the general concept of the failed state and not on any

specific country or even a specific region. This is not to say that specific countries or regions are inappropriate units of analysis for such an inquiry. To the
contrary, I believe that regional and national factors are crucial not only for
explaining state failure but also for explaining state rejuvenation. This is also
true because not all states that fail do so for the same reasons. While there is a
"generic" class of fragile, failing, or failed states that most of us can agree
upon and while the characteristics of state failure are often quite similar, individual states encounter different trigger mechanisms and travel different paths
on the route toward failure. And in the end, therefore, only specific responses
tailored to meet the exigencies of individual cases of state failure offer much,
if any, hope of success. Yet given the relative infancy of this search for an
effective strategic-level approach to the problem, it seems appropriate to begin
at a general level in an attempt to identify the critical components of such a
strategy. As a matter of convenience and to further narrow the focus of this
analysis, I will also approach the problem from the perspective of U.S. security
policy. Nonetheless I believe that many of the issues and arguments are generally applicable to other state and international institutional actors.

## STATE FAILURE

### The Problem

Different authors use different terminology to describe the problem. Zartman
uses "state collapse" to describe "the breakdown of good governance, law, and
order. The state, as a decisionmaking, executing, and enforcing institution can
no longer take and implement decisions."[7] Moreover, he distinguishes "state
collapse" from "societal collapse" which he defines as

the extended breakdown of social coherence: society, as the generator of institutions of
cohesion and maintenance, can no longer create, aggregate, and articulate the supports
and demands that are the foundations of the state.[8]

In earlier works I have used the simple definition offered by Helman and Ratner,
who describe the failed state as "utterly incapable of sustaining itself as a member of the international community."[9] But no matter what definition one prefers,
the essential characteristics of the failed or failing state seem clear and consistent: the state loses the ability to perform the basic functions of governance, and
it loses legitimacy. The establishment or restoration of the basic functions and
the legitimacy of the state apparatus therefore become the core objectives of any
strategy for salvaging the state from failure.

Other characteristics grow out of the conditions created by state failure, and
they may be present in these countries to varying degrees. Civil and communal
strife, including all-out civil war, is certainly one of the core problems in many
failing and failed states. Humanitarian crises, such as starvation and mass ref-

ugee movements, are common. Increasing criminality and widespread corruption frequently appear in all aspects of society, including political and economic institutions. And the formal economy is often nonexistent, having given way to a burgeoning informal economy characterized by black markets, extortion, and widespread criminal activity. In sum, the country is subject to the entire range of "gray area phenomena."[10] With the steady erosion and at times complete absence of legitimate governance, the challenge becomes one of "governing the ungovernable" and, failing that, managing the consequences of that ungovernability for national, regional, and international security.

A quick and slightly different look at the types of state failure we have witnessed in the post–Cold War world serves to illustrate the point that not all state failure leads to precisely the same mix of political-economic and social conditions. Although this overview is crude and necessarily very general, it provides some necessary foundation for the subsequent discussion of responses. Three general types of state failure come readily to mind. The first is typified by the ongoing situation in the former Yugoslav state. In this case, state failure was as much the result of conscious decisions by political elites to seek territorial gain through the use of force as it was a result of eroding legitimacy and institutional failure. The resulting conflict has many of the traditional trappings of a "classic" civil war. In many ways it resembles inter-state conflict, having identifiable protagonists, leaders and their armed followers, and territorial bases from which they operate and began the conflict. Somalia, on the other hand, represented what we might call the post–Cold War "ungovernability" form of the failed state. Here we saw a number of competing warlords and clan-like organizations consciously seeking to drive the country into a state of chaos from which they could subsequently carve out their own sub-regions or "turfs." Conflict in this kind of failed state looks more like "gang wars," and often the protagonists are more difficult to identify, and leaders have significantly less ability to control their followers than in the more traditional kind of conflict such as in the Yugoslav case.[11] Finally, Haiti provides an example of perhaps yet another kind of state failure. Here one finds less a case of rampant criminality and warlordism than a state in which the institutions and the people were simply exhausted. Military rule by the few was possible not so much because it was forcibly imposed on the people as it was passively accepted by an increasingly large segment of the public who had grown excessively cynical and pessimistic about the chances for effective governance. The state failed as much through apathy as it did through attacks on it from internal or external sources.

We will come back to this attempt to differentiate among the kinds of state failure in a moment. What is worth noting in concluding this section on the failed state is the fact that, in all three kinds of cases, the inability of political institutions to meet the basic functions of legitimate governance is also accompanied by economic collapse. In all of the cases, economic collapse leads to an explosion in the size of the informal economy and its dominance by corrupt, if not criminal, actors and activities. Unraveling the cause and effect puzzle is, at best, difficult and, at worst, impossible. Did the steady erosion of the economy and the increasing inability of people to meet their basic needs lead to the collapse of legitimate governance? Or did the collapse of legitimate governance lead to the steady erosion of the economy? Fortunately, for the purposes of this chapter, it is not necessary to answer such questions. What is important, and what has become increasingly clear to me as I have worked on the problem of the failed state, is that this economic collapse is almost everywhere present in cases of state failure.[12] Although it is a difficult proposition to prove, I am convinced that the path out of state failure must be paved with economic development and economic stability. The reasoning is simple (perhaps simplistic) enough: If individuals are unable to meet their basic economic needs (e.g., food, shelter, clothing), the nature of the political regime will be a distant and, at best, secondary concern. Moreover, they will be willing to use whatever means necessary (legitimate or not, legal or not, moral or not) to meet those needs. This is little more than a basic Maslovian argument, but it seems to be lost in much of the policy debate today about why states fail and importantly how we might best respond to the challenge of the failed and failing state. In my view, this economic dimension of the problem is essential for constructing a strategy for that response, and for informing our assessments about what we can hope to accomplish through such responses.

### The Challenges: Manifestations of State Failure

Before we can discuss possible responses, we must address the manifestations of state failure and the challenges they pose to those who wish to respond. In simple terms, those challenges fall into four broad categories: humanitarian, political, economic, and military. The humanitarian challenges are perhaps the most visible and were a main underpinning of Boutros Boutros-Ghali's assessment that state sovereignty in the post–Cold War world might be less important than the human rights of individuals and groups within those states. Using that line of reasoning, he argued that United Nations (U.N.) intervention in the domestic affairs of member states would be appropriate in the face of a collapse of domestic governing authority, displaced populations or gross violations of human rights, or when developments within the failed state posed a threat to international peace and stability.[13] The kinds of humanitarian challenges we might see include the condition and treatment of refugees, mass starvation and privation, and, of course, the slaughter of innocents. Even natural disasters may exacerbate the weaknesses of failing states and completely overwhelm the capacity of the system to respond. So disaster relief in response to naturally caused suffering may fall into this category.

Military challenges will also occur with alarming frequency, and they may take different forms in different cases. Earlier I alluded to what some of those differences might be in comparing Bosnia to Somalia. In the former, the military conflict closely resembles the "classic" civil war, with intra-state conflict characterized by clearly identifiable groups, leaders and followers, chains of command, and territorial bases. In the latter, the nature of the military conflict is much more ambiguous and amorphous.[14] A state that has collapsed because of challenges to its formal authority from organized criminal groups and competing warlords has a very different set of problems and poses a different set of challenges to our use of political, economic, and military instruments of power than does a state that has more accurately collapsed under the weight of its own incompetence or the people's weariness. A military operation in a country with multiple contending groups only somewhat organized and following no clear chain of command (as we saw in Somalia) poses serious risks of a unique nature to our military. In Haiti there were virtually none of the same risks inherent in the Somali operating environment. Similarly, a state that is "failing" because of a classic civil war being waged between contending parties (what I argue has been the situation in Bosnia virtually since the inception of that conflict) also presents different kinds of risks. But it is also an environment with more predictability because the parties to the conflict are essentially known and identifiable, and they more or less follow the commands of their superiors. While I do not mean to downplay the risks that exist in any of these environments, it seems clear to me that military operations in a Bosnia are much easier to plan and execute than in a Somalia. Neither military operation may contribute ultimately to a successful strategy for resolving the conflict (a point to which we shall return), but getting in and getting out may be a qualitatively different kind of challenge.

The political challenges are perhaps the most obvious, in no small part because they have received the most attention. In general terms, as discussed earlier, we must focus on creating or restoring to the state the basic functions of government and its perceived legitimacy. Too often, however, we have focused on the institutional dimension of the problem (restoring or establishing branches of government, holding elections, creating political parties, and the like) to the detriment of other, perhaps more important and informal dimensions. Much of this falls into the category of "civil society." It is perhaps a typical U.S. view that politics is inherently institutional; in my opinion, this view is, at best, flawed and, at worst, wholly incorrect. While institutions can contribute significantly to the reinforcement of underlying dispositions and inclinations to cooperation or conflict, institutions alone cannot establish or restore legitimate governance.[15] Another tendency that has detracted from the effectiveness of our strategy is the preoccupation with democracy and especially its peculiar American form. Too often we mistakenly attribute the durability of American democracy to its institutions rather than to the attitudes and norms of its people. Then we compound the problem by making "democratization" both an end (objective) and a way (concept) in our national security strategy. We might do better to consider the establishment or restoration of "legitimate governance" as our objective, and thereby grant that there may be many variations on the democracy theme that will allow for government to perform its functions effectively and achieve legitimacy in the eyes of its people.[16] Yet no matter what terminology we use and what the specific institutions and rules are that we seek to implement, we must recognize that in this realm we engage in nation building or state rejuvenation.

The economic dimension is similar to the political dimension in that what is lacking is frequently a combination of institutions and norms. Simply declaring a free market and letting it go provides little guarantee of healthy capitalism. In fact, the simultaneous existence of weak political and weak economic institutions and norms seems almost certain to lead to widespread criminality and corruption, as we have seen over and over again in places like Russia, the former Yugoslavia, Albania, and so on. If my premise stated earlier is correct, then a minimally functioning economy is necessary for any restoration and survival of a healthy system of legitimate governance.

Where does this leave us in our search for answers to the question of how to respond to failed or failing states? We know that states fail for a variety of reasons but that most of them can be boiled down to the loss of legitimate governance. Economic failure and a host of visible problems such as military conflict, human rights violations, humanitarian crises, and increasing criminality and corruption accompany this failure on the political dimension. So what is it that we wish to respond to in this witches' brew of problems? Therein lies the real challenge. For we cannot alleviate many of the problems if we are not willing to address the more fundamental problem of state failure. I have written that "A strategy for dealing with failed states must include a prescription for 'curing what *fails* it'."[17] What I meant is simply that many of the crises to which we feel compelled to respond are the result of state failure and as such are merely symptoms of that failure. If we genuinely wish to solve the problem of state failure, we must address it at its root level. To do less means only that we are providing Band-Aids and not a cure. At the same time, we must understand that not all state failure is curable, and that there may well be situations in which providing a Band-Aid is the best we can do. A proper understanding of each individual case and the challenges it presents should help us decide what our best response is. Responding to state failure by attempting to establish or restore legitimate governance is certainly an ambitious and costly undertaking. But when we consider the fact that lesser responses often require us to intervene again and again and that each cycle of state failure leads to even greater social, economic, and human costs, the more comprehensive response at the outset may indeed be the most effective as well as the least costly overall. But before we turn to a more specific discussion of the response alternatives, we must examine one other aspect of the challenge: the role of national interests.

### A Dilemma: The Interest-Threat Mismatch

A common argument in realist approaches to international relations and security issues is that underlying national interests motivate the behavior of states. The more important the interest, the more likely the state is to respond and to respond with serious intent. The corollary is that states are unlikely to take serious risks when the underlying interest does not warrant it. I do not wish to debate here just how important interests are, nor the serious questions of operationalizing them. Rather, I would like to accept the notion that some configuration of interests do underlie state behavior and that they play a significant role in the decisions to act both unilaterally and multilaterally (as part of an international institution or ad hoc coalition). Even if this is only partly true, the problem I wish to outline here is one that we must consider in our search for a strategy to guide responses to the problems of state failure.

First, where are the cases of state failure most likely to occur? Most if not all will occur in the developing world, or what Singer and Wildavsky called the second tier.[18] The conflicts, crises, and atrocities will therefore tend to be far from the geographic backyard of most of the developed Western world. The military conflicts will not appear to threaten vital interests, and even the threat of spreading conflict will appear distant and remote. Consequently, we can conclude that almost all of the instances of state failure will involve at most some important and generally more peripheral interests of the major state actors. So immediately we face an interest-threat mismatch: Where our vital interests exist, there are very few realistic threats to them; where there are real threats (such as the ones we are discussing here), there are mostly only peripheral interests.

The implications of this interest-threat mismatch are important. Given the fact that not responding to humanitarian crises and atrocities is difficult at best, we face a real dilemma. A public outcry to respond is likely to ensue. But as we will discuss shortly, an attempt to restore a failed state is a long and expensive undertaking, and one for which a public is unlikely to provide the necessary support over the long haul for interests that they cannot see as vital or even important. Especially where the use of military force comes into play, and with it the risk of casualties (both in the failed state and in the military forces sent by outside countries), the tension may be impossible to resolve. If the U.S. public has a low tolerance for using high levels of force against the offending parties and for U.S. casualties but favors some kind of response, we are likely to find ourselves on the horns of a dilemma: We must respond but cannot do so with the appropriate ways and means. The public will want the atrocities stopped, but without killing or injuring others in the process, and especially not American soldiers. Further, they will want all of this accomplished at minimal cost to the taxpayer. To varying degrees, this dilemma will confront most of the countries in the first tier that have the military, political, and economic resources to respond. In this way, it will also affect the ability to act of many major international institutional actors such as the United Nations. Recognizing this dilemma in the interest-threat mismatch is an essential aspect of devising an effective strategy for responding to state failure.

Perhaps we should consider focusing on "pivotal states" as one way in which to address this potential interest-threat mismatch.[19] The identification of specific states as "pivotal" is less important for the argument presented here than the

notion that some states play more critical roles within regions than others. By
focusing our efforts on restoring, promoting, and strengthening legitimate governance in a selected number of critical states in important regions, the United
States could conceivably make the best use of its limited resources and actually
leverage those resources through the continued efforts of those pivotal states.
Chase et al. suggest that the United States "focus its efforts on a small number
of countries whose fate is uncertain and whose future will profoundly affect
their surrounding regions."[20] This may at least provide a more effective basis
for arguing why the United States should be involved in such efforts to promote
or restore legitimate governance in areas where we seem to have no vital interests. And as we will discuss shortly, the concept of a "pivotal state" may also
prove essential in the application of strategic triage for failing states.

### The Choice: How to Respond?

We now come to the central focus of this inquiry, the question of how to
respond. I have tried in the preceding sections to lay out several critical aspects
of the problem that bear directly on the choices we may have. My argument is
that we must ground that choice in three fundamental areas: (1) a proper understanding of the nature of the problem confronting us; (2) a clear idea of what
it is we would like to "fix"; and (3) some modicum of risk assessment to
include the likelihood of the chosen response leading to the successful accom-
plishment of the objectives. While this may sound relatively simple and straightforward, I maintain that we have rarely employed such a framework in our
choices to date about responding to the challenges posed by failed or failing
states.

One of the first questions we must answer is whether we want to respond at
all. This goes to the heart of U.S. grand strategy and revolves around the role
the country will play generally in international affairs. In its simplest form, we
must know whether the United States will choose some variation of engagement
or opt instead for a variation of isolationism.[21] If the grand strategy is largely
one of isolationism or extremely limited engagement, then much of the discussion that follows is irrelevant. For if we see no need to respond and can effectively counter public outcries for such a response, the answer to the question of
choice is obvious: no response. In this writer's opinion, however, such a universal "no response" strategy is very difficult, if not impossible, to sustain in
the United States today. So we now consider the range of possible responses
from the highly limited end of the response continuum to the full engagement
end.

The first issue of strategy in assessing the range of responses is the selection
of objectives. As touched on in the earlier discussion of challenges, we must
decide what it is that confronts us. Is it, in fact, a failed or failing state? For the
purposes of this analysis, we assume that the state in question falls into this
category. Now we must decide what we want to accomplish; in other words,

what is our objective? At the full engagement end of the spectrum, and therefore the most ambitious, is the objective of establishing legitimate governance. At the other end of the spectrum lie more limited objectives, such as responding only to the immediate manifestations or consequences of state failure. This would include efforts to alleviate starvation and other forms of human suffering, but without tackling the root causes of that suffering. Let us consider some examples of possible responses across this spectrum of objectives.

## AMBITIOUS OBJECTIVE: ESTABLISHING LEGITIMATE GOVERNANCE

This is the most ambitious objective at the full engagement end of the response spectrum. The goal here is to address the failed or failing state at its very core by rejuvenating the state. Clearly this is a daunting task of "nation building," and the record suggests that successes are at best elusive.[22] Although we appear to understand much better today the challenges involved in nation building, it is not the same as knowing how to do it. Our earlier discussion suggested that we have focused too much on formal institutions and too little on informal factors such as norms, attitudes, and the development of civil society. Moreover, we have frequently failed to see and address the significant role played by economic performance in state failure and state rejuvenation. There are, of course, reasonable explanations for these shortcomings. For one thing, it is much easier to mandate the creation of political institutions than to instill democratic norms or values. One can impose the former on societies through written agreements, while the latter entails social engineering of the "hearts and minds" variety. The existence of institutions is also much easier to measure than the extent of democratization among the people (elite and mass publics). Similarly, requiring formal elements of economic liberalization and free markets is substantially easier than implementing successful economic performance, to include growth and development. In the end, engineering the formal institutions is simply much easier than tackling the tougher issues of establishing and maintaining successful and enduring political and economic performance.

But there are also real issues of cost and time. Establishing legitimate authority in the failed state involves the widest spectrum possible of policy instruments. It is fair to say that virtually every element of political, economic, informational, and even military power must be mobilized and brought to bear on the problem. Moreover, we are certain that the process will take a long time but are just as uncertain how long "a long time" is. Not surprisingly, democratically elected officials such as the U.S. president and members of Congress are extremely wary of committing the country to such costly undertakings of unspecified duration. The "interest-threat mismatch" discussed earlier only serves to increase the general unwillingness of policy makers to engage in a strategy that has establishing legitimate governance as its objective. While they might openly state that this is the long-term goal of intervention in a failed state, few policy makers today are willing (or perhaps able) to back up the policy rhetoric with the means and ways required for achieving that objective. Haiti is probably the best current example of this strategy gap: Restoring Aristide to power was "doable"; establishing a functioning democracy was not.

The three questions with which we began this section help to clarify the challenge we face in this situation. The problem is one of state failure with all of its attendant ramifications. To "fix" it at its most fundamental level requires establishing legitimate governance and economic viability. Such an objective would require the application of the widest possible range of tools and instruments, and probably a mobilization of national and multinational institutions as well as non-governmental actors (discussed briefly in the last section). We can expect success only if we are willing to stay the course for the long haul, understanding that the establishment of institutions is only the first step in a long-term process of infusing norms and attitudes and reinforcing patterns of behavior conducive to successful democratic politics and market economics. The likelihood of such a comprehensive response leading to the successful establishment of legitimate governance is at best low, given the large number of unknowns in this equation and the fact that sustaining the response over a sufficiently long period of time will be especially difficult given the interest-threat mismatch. Undertaking full-blown nation building as a largely national-level response to state failure remains today a highly costly and risky proposition with a relatively low likelihood of success. At the same time, if we fail to address the root causes of state failure, we may find that we are forced to respond over and over again, with each successive iteration proving more costly and more difficult than the one before. If we are not careful, the total costs of such incremental interventions may vastly exceed the costs of a more comprehensive response at the outset.

Therefore, it is also wrong to conclude that we should *never* engage in attempts to rejuvenate failed or failing states. However, the logic suggests that we use considerable caution before committing to such an ambitious objective. At a minimum, we should assess the degree and kind of state failure on a case-by-case basis, including the likely consequences of that failure for national and regional interests. Then, we must reserve the commitment to state rejuvenation for those cases that either appear to be reasonably likely to succeed, or for which the consequences of state failure are so great that we simply must respond to the failure itself, even if the likelihood of full success is quite low. In any case, we must also recognize that the means and ways necessary to achieve success probably include the whole panoply of actors (states, international institutions, NGOs, PVOs, etc.) and their capabilities (political, economic, and military), applied over a significantly long period of time. Coordinating effective policy across such a range of actors and instruments is a further challenge to success in this area. And finally, we must draw on academic and policy expertise that covers a wide range of disciplines and approaches, not just the institutional engineering so prominent in our earlier attempts to address the problem of state failure.

## LIMITED OBJECTIVE: STOP THE FIGHTING

Among the less ambitious responses we might choose is limiting the objective to halting or substantially reducing the fighting. In some cases, and depending on the nature of the conflict that has caused the fighting, this is a reasonable objective with a reasonable chance of success. But it does depend on the nature of the conflict. In the traditional U.N. peacekeeping operations of the Cold War era, this was the primary objective when the parties to the conflict consented to the peacekeeping. An obvious example is the ongoing operation in Cyprus. But such consent is less often present in the failed state cases we see in the post–Cold War era, and it is precisely the absence of consent that should make us cautious when considering this objective.

In Bosnia the Dayton Accords arguably "extracted" consent from at least one of the warring parties (the Serbs). Nonetheless, the objective of stopping the fighting still appeared "doable" and to date has been substantially accomplished. The NATO uses of implementation forces (IFOR) and stabilization forces (SFOR) have succeeded in creating and maintaining a cease-fire in the primary region where they deployed.[23] There is still another reason why this objective was an appropriate one for this case, and it brings us back to interests. Although much debated, one can argue that the United States and its European allies had important (and perhaps in some cases vital) interests in halting the fighting. First, the possibility of the fighting spilling over posed a genuine threat to regional stability. This was certainly not lost on the closest neighbors of the former Yugoslavia, nor on those countries like Germany that were receiving the largest number of refugees fleeing from the conflict. Second, and arguably the primary reason for the Clinton administration decision to engage the United States in the Dayton process, was the threat to the credibility of NATO. If NATO could not respond effectively in the face of this crisis, then what future was there for the alliance? Whether objectively true or not, both of these arguments illustrated the important role played by interests in such situations. A limited objective such as stopping the fighting is appropriate if the fighting itself poses a threat to vital or perhaps important interests. Risking the lives of military personnel and paying the monetary costs of such operations ("blood and treasure") are justified by those interests, even if the response chosen is unlikely (or not even intended) to fix the failing state. A serious attempt at nation building might be far too complex, carry exorbitant costs, and have little likelihood of success.[24]

The situation in Somalia was more complicated than that of Bosnia, and even the limited objective of stopping the fighting was more ambitious in that case. The reason lay in the important differences between the two cases discussed earlier. Given the nature of the warring parties and the conflict itself, imple-

menting and maintaining an effective cease-fire in Somalia was a more ambitious and risky objective. Moreover, the absence of vital or important interests
for the actors who intervened further complicated the situation. Policy makers
should have considered these factors more carefully than they did prior to the
decision to intervene in the first place, and certainly prior to the decisions to
increase the scope of the military operations.[25] Although the decision to intervene may have occurred just the same, policy makers might have selected more
limited objectives and therefore tailored the response more effectively to that
which could realistically be accomplished given what was available in resources
and ways of using them.[26]

Yet in both of these kinds of cases, we should recognize at the outset that
limiting the objectives to the military dimension alone will hardly get at the root
causes of the conflict. Therefore, we must prepare to keep external military
forces on the ground for a long and perhaps even indefinite period of time (the
reality of the Bosnian case today). Or we must prepare to deal with the reality
that the fighting will most assuredly break out again as soon as those external
forces withdraw. Stating the objective clearly and realistically at the outset may
help sustain the response in the face of public scrutiny and growing impatience
over time.

## LIMITED OBJECTIVE: HUMANITARIAN RELIEF

One can also limit the objectives to addressing the purely humanitarian manifestations of the failed state. If the problem is human suffering in the form of
starvation, we can intervene to alleviate some of that starvation. Limiting the
response to the provision of food is certainly not going to rejuvenate the failed
state, but it still may have merit. Of course there are other serious problems
with this more limited objective. For one thing, the contending factions in the
failed state may view food as a weapon in their struggle and seek to use it as
such (as happened in Somalia). For the international community to provide food
may also require that it deal directly with what masquerades as a government
in that failed state. This can have the negative consequence of indirectly supporting the legitimacy of that government. And finally, the even harsher reality
may be that the provision of food (and other humanitarian items such as water,
medicine, temporary shelter, and so on) has the unintended consequence of
prolonging the process of state collapse and the fighting that leads to the terrible
loss of human life. In other words, through such intervention we inadvertently
prolong the suffering. For this and other reasons, some authors have suggested
that we might do well to let the state proceed quickly down the path to failure
before we choose to intervene.[27] Still, recognizing that such limited objectives
are available and at times appropriate may increase the likelihood that we will
choose effective responses that have significantly greater chances for succeeding,
even if only in a limited way. Too often we unnecessarily raise public expectations (both in the failing state and internationally) for what can be accom-

plished, thereby setting the stage for the overall response to fail and leading to even greater suffering and disillusionment.

## LIMITED OBJECTIVE: ECONOMIC GROWTH AND DEVELOPMENT

The economic challenges posed by state failure are as difficult as the political, in no small measure because it is impossible to achieve economic stability, growth, and development in the face of anarchy and chaos. The very elites who are locked in a struggle to control the failed state will almost certainly be incapable of providing the basis for enhanced economic performance. Relying solely on internal elements to lead a process of economic rejuvenation in a failed state is surely a prescription for further failure. Providing economic aid in any form other than purely humanitarian assistance is likely to accomplish little more than further lining the pockets of corrupt officials in the failed state. In this initial cut at the problem, it appears that economic rejuvenation can occur only in the context of political rejuvenation, and the latter can occur only in conjunction with the former. Stating this brings us back to the realization that nation building, or the establishment of legitimate governance, is an ambitious undertaking of the highest order that goes well beyond the institutional engineering that has largely preoccupied Western policy makers to date. Holding elections, declaring victory, and going home may provide some salve to the wounded souls of the affronted publics who witness the corollary atrocities of state failure, but such actions provide little in the way of an effective response to the manifestations of state failure. And they provide absolutely nothing in the way of an effective response to the reality of that failure.

The discussion of strategy for responding to the failed state has focused to this point primarily on the *objectives*. But there are two other critical components of strategy, *ways* and *means*. The means are the resources, and the ways are the concepts for employing those resources in the pursuit of the objectives. A quick review of these two components is necessary before drawing some preliminary conclusions.

There are three primary categories of means or resources. They are political, economic, and military. In our discussions of the nature of the challenges and the selection of objectives, we have indirectly addressed the use of resources. Not all means are appropriate for accomplishing all of the objectives, and matching the proper means to the objective is one of the many challenges confronting a strategy. In the case of the failing state, we have at times lost sight of this fact, thinking that we can solve the problem of state failure by merely halting the fighting (the military means) or by engaging in simple institutional engineering (the political means). I have suggested here that such means may be appropriate for accomplishing more limited objectives but that they must be used and understood in the context of those limited objectives. If we wish to use limited means, we should be explicit about the limited objectives we realistically expect to accomplish. And of course, means are always limited. But the more serious the perceived threat, the more willing and able one is to elicit the necessary sacrifice and support to divert means from other uses to the ones required. Therefore, in what cases, for what purposes, and in what ways we use those resources comprise the very essence of a strategic response, and they shape the likelihood of its success.

And so we come to the very crux of the problem. Rejuvenating the failed state is indeed an ambitious undertaking. It requires the fullest set of means available, most probably including political, economic, and military instruments. If we are to respond to the failed state with a strategy of state rejuvenation, we are in for a long, expensive commitment that in my view will be almost impossible to sustain in the United States or any other country as long as the perceived interests remain at best important and at worst peripheral. And yet a strategy of piecemeal response to the manifestations of state failure may be even more costly and time-consuming as we find ourselves drawn back into the failed state again and again to address yet another manifestation. Moreover, a strategy that attempts to respond to every case of state failure dooms us to overall strategic failure; what successes we might achieve (and they will be very few) will quickly drown in the face of the failures. We should reserve attempts at full-blown state rejuvenation for those cases where national, regional, and international interests are decisively engaged or where the path to rejuvenation is comparatively clear to see and relatively easy to follow. Such might be the case in countries with preexisting experience with market economies and legitimate governance, but by this very qualification we should expect to encounter few such cases.

Yet I also believe that we cannot sustain a consistent strategy of doing nothing in response to state failure. Despite the fact that these cases will rarely engage vital or even important national interests, the consequences of state failure will continue to press on us and push us in the direction of responding.

### Tough Decisions: Strategic Triage for Failing States

Perhaps the best approach is what we might call *triage* for the failing states. We should work on developing those criteria that will help us sort out the cases where no amount of intervention will reverse the course of state failure from those where some intervention may actually help. We should put the greatest amount of effort into trying to save those states that have some reasonable chance of surviving, and into those whose failure would have the most serious consequences (for example, the so-called ''pivotal states''). For the worst cases, we should be prepared to explain to concerned and outraged publics (and, of course, the media) just why it is that no response (or a very limited one) is the truly humanitarian thing to do. Triage on the battlefield or in the face of an epidemic is never a pretty thing to see or an easy one to explain, but few people question the humanitarian, moral, and practical considerations that underlie it.

If the physicians tried equally to save each and every life without regard for the likelihood of success given their resources and their ways for employing them, surely the suffering and the loss of human life would be much greater. So, too, in the world of the failed state. If we exhaust the means available, which includes the willingness of publics to support the efforts involved, by tackling truly hopeless cases, we will needlessly squander our ability to provide meaningful aid and comfort, and perhaps even to rejuvenate some of the more hopeful cases. And our efforts to rejuvenate the hopeless cases may actually condemn a much larger number of countries and their peoples to even greater levels of suffering over longer periods of time than if we had simply let them alone in the first place. Durch does not use the triage metaphor, but he does employ the medical imagery when he concludes his analysis of Somalia with the following observation about humanitarian interventions:

Here, then, is the dilemma of humanitarian intervention: either the outsiders feed, vaccinate, and stand aside, letting the local parties settle disputes in their own uniquely bloody way while providing some minimal protection to non-combatants; or the outsiders quash local power centers and look for more acceptable local alternatives. The 'local alternatives,' by definition, have not been strong enough to win on their own, which makes them wards of the intervention and prolongs anarchy until the new system grafted on by the outsiders can take hold. This approach obligates the international 'surgeon' to complete the course of treatment, but he rarely has the time or attention span; in fact, he really has only the foggiest idea of how to do the surgery and he fears the sight of blood, especially his own. Given these choices, the long-term prognosis for humanitarian intervention is not good.[28]

I obviously agree with much of Durch's assessment, but I would qualify his prognosis on the basis of the analysis I have offered in this chapter. The prognosis is not good if we fail to prepare the policy makers and the publics for dealing with these tough choices. But I believe we can do precisely that by a systematic, strategic approach to the problem of state failure and its many manifestations. A careful selection of objectives with a strategy tailored to achieve them can provide a rationale for the reality of triage. Knowing that our objective was nothing more than providing some aid and comfort to the noncombatant "casualties" of the Somali collapse might not have silenced all the critics, but it would have set a much more realistic tone for the expectations of many people who only began to pay attention once the intervention started. Preparing the public for the fact that providing food would not stop the fighting and the attendant atrocities might have in turn helped policy makers avoid the escalation of objectives that characterized the different phases of the operation. And importantly, knowing precisely what the military was there to do—ensure that food and other relief items got to the suffering innocents—and the corollary of what it was not there to do—stop the fighting or, even worse, join in it—would have allowed those forces to do everything they needed to do to accomplish that objective at minimal risk to their own security and lives.

One other matter deserves attention, although I cannot address it more than superficially in this chapter. It concerns the planning, implementation, and co-ordination of such a strategy for responding to the failed state and its manifestations. Simply put, it is the organizational challenge. As anyone with any experience in this area knows, even the most limited objectives discussed here require extensive coordination among a host of actors that include national governmental, international institutional, and non-governmental actors. Given the seriousness and the scope of the challenges we face and the desirability of an effective response, we need all of these actors and their capabilities to address the problems and achieve the objectives. But getting all of these actors to follow a coordinated plan and effectively support the strategy is itself a daunting task. The United States has responded to this with the promulgation of Presidential Decision Directive (PDD) 56. This document attempts to spell out the general lead agency and inter-agency responsibilities for complex contingency operations such as those conducted in Somalia and Haiti. While PDD 56 is an attempt to improve what has been a difficult and confusing planning and operational environment, I think the problem runs much deeper than what PDD 56 addresses. Fundamentally, the inter-agency process cannot make up for the fact that the U.S. security apparatus is organized to address Cold War kinds of threats and challenges. The challenges that arise from failed states simply do not fall neatly into the categories along which we have organized our security policy-making community. To believe that the various and frequently competing views and objectives can be effectively sorted out and coordinated in the inter-agency process is to engage in the extreme of self-deception. If we truly wish to address the challenges of failing states more effectively (along with many other of the relatively new security threats and challenges of the contemporary international system), we must consider a complete overhaul and reorganization of the way we do business. But this is a topic for further analysis and consideration.

So in the matter of failed or failing states, the question ultimately is not whether we *can* respond, for surely we can. The questions are rather *how* we can respond and what we can reasonably *expect* to accomplish, and, therefore, whether we *should* respond. Such decisions must rest in a sound understanding of the nature of the problem confronting us and in the setting of proper objectives and the allocation of means employed in effective ways to accomplish those objectives. We simply must set those objectives with a clear set of expectations about what we can reasonably accomplish and balance our strategy accordingly. Setting the objectives too ambitiously may lead to failure when the response cannot be sustained, while setting the objectives too timidly may only insure failure of a different kind. Failing to maximize the appropriate resources in the most effective ways possible will also lead to failure. Balancing the ends, ways, and means in an effective strategy as a guide to those decisions about when and how to respond is a critical step in addressing this kind of challenge in the post–Cold War world.

## NOTES

1. See, for example, Robert H. Dorff, "Democratization and Failed States: The Challenge of Ungovernability," *Parameters*, Vol. 26, No. 2 (Summer 1996), pp. 17–31 (especially pp. 3–7); Gerald B. Helman and Steven R. Ratner, "Saving Failed States," *Foreign Policy*, No. 89 (Winter 1992–1993), pp. 3–20; and Leslie H. Gelb, "Quelling the Teacup Wars," *Foreign Affairs*, Vol. 73, No. 6 (November/December 1994), pp. 2–6.

2. Quoted in Jeremy D. Rosner, "Is Chaos America's Real Enemy?" *Washington Post*, August 14, 1994, p. C-1.

3. Gelb, "Quelling the Teacup Wars," p. 5.

4. It is in fact a classic problem in international affairs, as evidenced in the following observation: "In 1915 Walter Lippmann wrote that 'the chief overwhelming problem of [international] diplomacy seems to be weak state[s], . . . "weak," because they are industrially backward and, at present, politically incompetent' to prevent outbreaks of internal violence. Serious breakdowns of internal order endangered the nationals and trade of the great powers, disposing one or another to intervene." Quoted in David C. Rapoport, "The Role of External Forces in Supporting Ethno-Religious Conflict," in *Ethnic Conflict and Regional Instability: Implications for U.S. Policy and Army Roles and Missions*, Robert L. Pfaltzgraff, Jr., and Richard H. Shultz, Jr., eds. (Carlisle Barracks, PA: Strategic Studies Institute, U.S. Army War College, 1994), p. 59.

5. Dorff, "Democratization and Failed States," pp. 20–21.

6. Robert H. Dorff, "The Future of Peace Support Operations," *Small Wars and Insurgencies*, Vol. 9, No. 1 (Spring 1998), pp. 160–178. Reprinted in Max Manwaring and John Fishel, eds., *Toward Responsibility in the New World Disorder: Challenges and Lessons of Peace Operations* (London: Frank Cass Publishers, 1998), pp. 160–178.

7. I. William Zartman, ed., *Collapsed States: The Disintegration and Restoration of Legitimate Authority* (Boulder, CO: Lynne Rienner, 1995), p. 6.

8. Ibid.

9. Helman and Ratner, "Saving Failed States," p. 3. One advantage of this definition is that it draws our attention to the international and systemic implications of state failure. In other words, state failure is not simply a matter of domestic institutional failure but also of the regional and international implications of that failure for matters of security.

10. See Max G. Manwaring, ed., *Gray Area Phenomena: Confronting the New World Disorder* (Boulder, CO: Westview Press, 1993). In that work, Ambassador Edwin G. Corr defines the gray area phenomenon or GAP as "threats to the stability of nation states by nonstate actors and nongovernmental processes and organizations," involving "immense regions or urban areas where control has shifted from legitimate governments to new half-political, half-criminal powers" (p. xiii). In my own work, I have referred to this problem as "ungovernability." See Dorff, "Democratization and Failed States," especially pp. 23–25.

11. The Somalia case represents most closely the type of anarchy addressed by Kaplan. See Robert D. Kaplan, "The Coming Anarchy," *The Atlantic Monthly* (February 1994), pp. 44–76.

12. Of course in some cases, there was virtually no functioning formal economy at

any time prior to state failure. At a minimum one must wonder whether such a state has any alternative to failure if it cannot effectively promote a modicum of economic productivity and development.

13. See Boutros Boutros-Ghali, *An Agenda for Peace 1995*, 2nd ed. (New York: United Nations, 1995), especially Section VI, "Post-Conflict Peace-Building," pp. 61–62. This publication contains the original 1992 report of the Secretary-General and the supplement to it dated January 3, 1995.

14. In the case of Colombia, Marcella and Schulz even refer to the "three wars" simultaneously occurring in that country and the "strategic dilemma posed by ambiguous warfare" to the United States. See Gabriel Marcella and Donald Schulz, *Colombia's Three Wars: US Strategy at the Crossroads* and Richard Downes, *Landpower and Ambiguous Warfare: The Challenge of Colombia in the 21st Century* (Carlisle Barracks, PA: Strategic Studies Institute, U.S. Army War College, March 1999).

15. See, for example, Francis Fukuyama, "The Primacy of Culture," *Journal of Democracy*, Vol. 6, No. 1 (January 1995), pp. 7–14.

16. This is why I prefer the term "legitimate governance" as used by Manwaring and Corr. See their discussion in Manwaring and Corr, "Confronting the New World Disorder," p. 32, as well as my discussion in Dorff, "The Future of Peace Support Operations," p. 172.

17. Dorff, "Democratization and Failed States," p. 28.

18. Max Singer and Aaron Wildavsky, *The Real World Order: Zones of Peace/Zones of Turmoil*, rev. ed. (Chatham, NJ: Chatham House Publishers, 1996). See also Donald M. Snow, *National Security: Defense Policy for a New International Order*, 3rd ed. (New York: St. Martin's Press, 1995); and Steven Metz, "Strategic Horizons: The Military Implications of Alternative Futures" (Carlisle Barracks, PA: Strategic Studies Institute, U.S. Army War College, 1997). Metz argues that there are, in fact, three tiers, with his third tier including the worst of the second tier in the Singer and Wildavsky world.

19. For a discussion of the concept of pivotal states, see Robert S. Chase, Emily B. Hill, and Paul Kennedy, "Pivotal States and U.S. Strategy," *Foreign Affairs*, Vol. 75, No. 1 (January/February 1996), pp. 33–51.

20. Ibid., p. 33.

21. That engagement could be highly selective or largely indiscriminate. The former is arguably a large part of what the United States is currently pursuing as its grand strategy. The latter would be consistent with a strategy of maintaining U.S. primacy or hegemony. For a good discussion of U.S. grand strategy options, see Barry R. Posen and Andrew L. Ross, "Competing Visions for U.S. Grand Strategy," *International Security*, Vol. 21, No. 3 (Winter 1996–1997), pp. 5–53. Richard N. Haass has a similar review of grand strategic options in his book, *The Reluctant Sheriff: The United States After the Cold War* (New York: Council on Foreign Relations Press, 1997), especially Chapter 2, "A Doctrine of Regulation."

22. Although I will not address the issue in any detail here, I am arguing that there are different degrees and kinds of state failure, and that the objective of state rejuvenation may be more attainable in some cases than in others. In theory, this allows us to make reasoned decisions about when rejuvenation is more likely to succeed and, therefore, when we should select it as an appropriate objective.

23. It is worth noting in this context the use of Implementation Force and Stabilization Force for the phases of these operations. IFOR had as its objective "implementing" the

cease-fire established under the terms of the Dayton Accords. SFOR had as its objective the stabilization of that cease-fire, with the corollary that other objectives could be pursued as the military dimension remained stable. It is in this area of the other objectives, many of which deal with nation building, where progress not surprisingly has been much slower and more difficult to achieve.

24. The case of Kosovo was cause for serious concern using precisely the same line of reasoning. Serbian opposition to a NATO presence on "their soil" (different from Bosnia) and the political sensitivity for Milosovic if he were seen as allowing that presence were key ingredients in the failure of attempts to "extract" consent for a NATO peacekeeping operation prior to the bombing campaign.

25. For this admittedly simplified discussion of the Somalia case, I rely heavily on the treatment by William Durch, "Introduction to Anarchy: Humanitarian Intervention and 'State-Building' in Somalia," in *UN Peacekeeping, American Politics, and the Uncivil Wars of the 1990s*, William J. Durch, ed. (New York: St. Martin's Press, 1997).

26. One obvious military aspect of this problem was the decision not to use "overwhelming force" against the opposition forces. This was most evident in the denial of the field commander's request for armor.

27. Zartman argues, for example, that there may be cases when "the process needs to run its course before a new structure of law and order or legitimate authority can be constructed" (*Collapsed States*, p. 10). Of course, this is easier said than done. Recognizing that the suffering will end quicker in the absence of an intervention is a difficult justification to make in public for not responding.

28. Durch, "Introduction to Anarchy," p. 126.

# Part V

# Where to from Here?

Well over half the countries of our "global village" can easily be categorized as "fragile, failing, or failed" states. Many—if not all—of these troubled states are only one event away from some form of crisis that will bring calls for the United States and for the international community to step into the situation and resolve the instability that makes a given fragile, failing, or failed state a threat to international security. And it is quite likely that the president and Congress will continue to involve the United States in these conflicts.

Again, the United States cannot do everything, everywhere. Logic, as well as good management practices, dictate making pre-crisis grand strategy decisions regarding which pivotal states are important enough to justify involvement or intervention and which are not (Dorff, again); and what is to be done—or not done (Corr and Manwaring). Such an order of thought is not a matter of "putting the cart before the horse." It is a matter of being clear where the horse and cart are going—and how they are going to get there, and what they are going to do once they have arrived.

Ambassador David C. Miller, Jr. warns that

> Success in achieving these measures depends on fundamental strategic conceptual, high-level organizational, and relevant operational means that have been the "pillars of success" in the past. But, there is little evidence that strategic thinking or action have been controlling factors in U.S. foreign policy and military management over the past several years. At its base, the successful application of these means depends on civilian and military leadership that can think, plan, and act strategically.
>
> It is not so much that people need to be taught what to think, but how to think.
>
> —Interview; also see *Managing Contemporary Conflict: Pillars of Success*

# Chapter 13

# Some Final Thoughts

## Edwin G. Corr AND Max G. Manwaring

Since the ending of the Cold War, the international security system has undergone fundamental changes. In place of the relatively orderly and predictable Cold War structure, the "new world disorder" has generated a system in which time-honored concepts of security and the classical military means to achieve it are no longer completely relevant. This is a global security environment in which ambiguous non-traditional, *intranational*, national, transnational, regional, and international "well-being" considerations—as opposed to traditional national territorial, resource, market, and other interests—are paramount.[1]

Well-being tends to be defined as political stability, coupled with an improving quality of life and justice. Stability is defined in terms of the degree to which a society perceives that its government is providing political freedom, socioeconomic development, necessary public services, and personal and group security effectively *and* fairly. That is, the more positive the perception that government is acting legitimately, the more stability. On the other hand, when it is perceived that government is not acting legitimately, the more instability—and the more violence.[2]

Legitimate governance is defined as governance that derives its just powers from the consent of the governed and generates a viable political competence that can and will manage, coordinate, and sustain security, and social, economic, and political development in morally and culturally acceptable ways. Legitimate governance is inherently stable because it has the political competence and societal support to adequately manage internal change and violence affecting collective and individual well-being. Governments that have not been responsive to the importance of the legitimate governance reality find themselves in a "crisis of governance." They face growing social violence, criminal anarchy, and eventual overthrow.[3]

The evidence over time and throughout the world is that instability and violence are the general consequences of unreformed political and economic institutions, and concomitant misguided, insensitive, incompetent, and/or corrupt governance. In these terms, legitimate governance is the basis of stability and well-being, and illegitimate governance is the basis of the instability and violence. Thus, contemporary stability and well-being is essentially an issue of perceived legitimate or illegitimate governance.

## THE PROBLEM OF GOVERNANCE

The clash of civilizations and almost chronic political chaos can be seen propagating their respective forms of instability and violence in large parts of Africa, Eastern Europe, the Middle East, Asia, and elsewhere around the world. In many of these cases, governments are either waging war on their citizens, are fighting to survive assaults from their citizens, or have become a mere faction among competing forces claiming the right to govern all or part of a disputed national territory. These "teacup wars" are "wars of national debilitation, a steady run of uncivil wars sundering fragile but functioning states and gnawing at the well-being of stable nations."[4] In these terms, it is important to understand how and why these *intranational* wars for the right to govern come about, and the results.

### The How and Why of "Teacup Wars"

An attack against an incumbent government centers on its moral right to govern, or on its ability and willingness to govern. The assault can be either direct or indirect. But because of the asymmetry of power, gray area "destabilizers"—such as criminal anarchists, extreme nationalists, irredentists, militant secular and religious reformers, ideologues, demagogues, greedy civil and military bureaucrats, terrorists, illegal drug traffickers, insurgents, warlords, ethnic cleansers, and rogue states—find it disadvantageous to overtly or directly challenge the superior power of a given government. By transforming the emphasis of conflict from the level of direct military confrontation to the level of indirect political-psychological-moral struggle for the proverbial "hearts and minds" of a people, virtually anyone with a cause can strive for the political control necessary to achieve their aims.

The underlying premise of this type of assault on a government is that the ultimate outcome of the confrontation is not primarily determined by the skillful manipulation of violence in the many military battles or police engagements that might take place. Rather, the outcome will be determined by the relative ability of the violent opposition and the government to shift the "hearts and minds"— and support—of a people in their respective favor. Thus, effective political-psychological persuasion coupled with political-psychological-military coercion on the part of the violent internal opposition leads to a general weakening of government. The attack, then, is not against the government directly. It is against the legitimacy of government. Weakening an incumbent regime is achieved in direct proportion to its perceived illegitimacy.

As a consequence, the intent of an attacker—through persuasion and coercion—is to create the perception that a governing regime is not or cannot provide the necessary balance among political freedom, economic and social development, and physical security that results in peace, stability, and well-being for the peoples of a society. Additionally, the intent is to convince a population that the illegal violent internal opposition's proposed alternative political philosophy—even if it is as extreme as militant reformism, ethnicism, warlordism, or tribalism—represents a relatively better well-being than that which has been previously experienced. Finally, the intent might simply be to create and maintain a level of violence, chaos, and regime inadequacy that allows freedom of movement to pursue unconscionable personal and group enrichment.

### Results of *Intranational* Instability and Violence

The consequences of these dynamics is a vicious downward spiral that manifests itself in diminished levels of popular and institutional acceptance and support for the incumbent regime and generates further disorder, violent internal conflicts, and mushrooming demands by various groups for political autonomy. These legitimacy issues further translate themselves into constant subtle and not so subtle struggles for power that dominate life throughout much of the world today. This, in turn, leads to the slow but sure destruction of the state, the government, and the society—and hundreds of thousands of innocents. Finally, results of these dynamics can be seen not so much in the proliferation of a host of new countries, but in an explosion of weak, incompetent, misguided, or corrupt governments throughout the world.

Sooner or later, the spillover effects of *intranational*, national, regional, international, and transnational destabilization place demands on the international community, if not to solve the problems, at least to harbor the victims. In that connection, related threats to international stability are acknowledged by the more than 60 formal declarations regarding destabilizing *intra-state* conflict made by the U.N. Security Council since 1990.[5]

Finding solutions to the problems of legitimate governance and stability takes the international community, or individual intervening powers, beyond providing some form of humanitarian assistance or refugee assistance in cases of human misery and need. It takes international political actors beyond traditional monitoring of bilateral agreements or protecting a people from another group of people, or from a government. It takes these actors beyond compelling one or more parties to a conflict to cease human rights violations and other morally repugnant practices, or repelling conventional military aggression. Solutions to the problems of stability and well-being take us back to where we began— legitimate governance.

The first step in developing an appropriate response to the problem of illegitimate governance is to become aware of the reality of world disequilibrium and popular sovereignty, and begin to deal with the relationship of instability to legitimate governance. The second step is to realize, whether one likes it or not, or whether one is prepared for it or not, a populace-oriented legitimacy model rather than an attrition-oriented military model of conflict appears to provide the most relevant guideline for surviving the "new world disorder."

## THE STRATEGIC OBJECTIVE: A SUSTAINABLE PEACE— WITH JUSTICE

Given the essentially political-psychological-moral nature of the legitimate governance problem, the contemporary security environment requires a new populace-oriented paradigm. It must be remembered that an "enforced" peace is only the beginning step in developing an appropriate response to the instability and violence that "are so hard to prevent, they must now get the attention they so urgently deserve."[6]

### A Populace-Oriented Model

A populace-oriented extension of the Small Wars Operations Research Directorate (SWORD) Model for taking responsibility for intranational interventions and going beyond "declaring victory and coming home" depicts the activities and efforts of the various players involved.[7] It portrays the allegiance of a population as the primary center of gravity. Persuasive and coercive measures will determine success or failure in the achievement of a just civil society and a durable peace. Thus, both the government and its external allies and the internal illegal opposition and its external allies can coerce, persuade, and demonstrate the populace into actions on behalf of either side. Then, in addition, the people can coerce and persuade the government or opposition to change the conditions in society, to meet their demands, and to undertake the types of behavior and actions that the citizenry perceives to be legitimate.

### Unifying and Legitimizing Dimensions That Lead to Sustainable Peace

The SWORD Model also takes into account the major unifying and legitimizing dimensions of the development of stability, a just civil society, and a sustainable peace. Additional steps toward those ends must be built on a foundation of carefully thought out, long-term, phased planning and implementation processes that focus on the "offensive" extension of the seven dimensions of the SWORD Model.[8] Three broadly inclusive elements contribute most directly to the allegiance of the populace and the achievement of that end: establishing security, regenerating and bolstering economic prosperity, and nurturing legitimate governance.

First, probably the most fundamental societal requirement is that of security. It begins with the provision of personal security to individual members of the society and extends to protection from aggressive internal (including criminals) and external enemies—and, perhaps, from repressive internal (i.e., local, regional, and national) governments. Personal security, in turn, is the primary basis upon which any form of societal allegiance to the state is built. Providing security to every member of a society, to include the isolation of belligerent internal forces, also includes (1) establishing order and the rule of law, and freedom from intimidation and violence; (2) isolating warring political and criminal factions from all sources of internal and external support; and (3) sustaining life, relieving suffering, and beginning to regenerate the economy.

Second, continuing the regeneration of the economy and providing meaningful work—and pay—to individuals is also fundamental. This need not and cannot normally lead to immediate prosperity—only a reasonable hope for things to steadily improve, especially for one's children. Providing meaningful work provides another sense of security and gives people a stake in their society and governing institutions. It also gives people hope for a meaningful future. With no stake in society and no hope for the future, experience strongly demonstrates that resort to violence to force some kind of change is the usual option.

The need to provide for the socioeconomic development of a people is generally well understood. In the past, however, it was expected that stimulation of the economy would automatically lead to societal stability and political development over the long term. Somehow, stimulation of the economy was also expected to improve economic disparities, equity, and justice. That has not happened. In order to generate a viable political competence that can and will manage, coordinate, and sustain security and economic and political development, it is necessary to accomplish two additional goals: foster political consent; then establish and maintain peaceful societal conflict-resolution processes. With these additional building blocks in place, a legitimate civil society becomes a real possibility.

Finally, in nurturing a sustainable civil society and a durable internal peace, it is also necessary to develop the aggressive *unified* political-diplomatic, socioeconomic, psychological-moral, and military-police engagement in society that can and will deal effectively with the multidimensional root causes that brought on the internal conflict in the first place. The intent and requirement is to generate the societal acceptance and support that governing institutions need to adequately manage internal change and violence—and to guarantee individual and collective well-being.

### Implications

The primary implications of this analysis are clear. The ability of failed, fragile, and menaced governments to control, protect, and enhance their sovereignty, stability, and well-being is severely threatened in the contemporary global security environment. International organizations—such as the United Nations

252 Where to from Here?

(U.N.), the North Atlantic Treaty Organization (NATO), and the Organization of American States (OAS)—and individual national powers are increasingly called on to respond to real and perceived injustices and instabilities generated by unreformed political and economic institutions, and irresponsible or incompetent political leadership. Furthermore, the international community is increasingly expected to provide the leverage to ensure that legitimate governance—once regained—is given to responsible, incorrupt, and competent leadership that can and will address the political, economic, and social root causes that created the crisis and intervention in the first place.[9]

## THE CHALLENGE

The ultimate challenge, then, is to come to terms with the fact that contemporary security, stability, and peace—at whatever level—is essentially a political-psychological-moral issue. This issue is too broad for a singular military-police solution. The logical conclusion is to change perspectives.

It must be remembered, however, that no regime, group, or force can legislate or decree moral legitimacy or political competence for themselves or anyone else. Legitimation, stability, and well-being derive from popular and institutional perceptions that authority is genuine and effective, and uses morally correct means for reasonable and fair purposes. These qualities are developed, sustained, and enhanced by appropriate behavior over time—and the achievement of a general sense that life is or can get better.

Nevertheless, in the short term, a failed or fragile regime will likely require outside help in developing these qualities. Probably the best an outside power or coalition of powers can do is to help establish a temporary level of security that might allow the carefully *guided*, unified, and monitored development of ethical and professional political competence underpinnings necessary for long-term success in achieving a sustainable peace. This will likely entail finding and selecting legitimate and compatible internal allies and partners.

U.S. and other Western leadership, in these terms, should be that of "facilitator" for security and development more than the traditional "policeman" or "Santa Claus."[10] The special status of the United States and the West allows the opportunity to facilitate positive change. By accepting this corollary to the basic challenge of changing perspectives, the United States and its Western allies can help replace conflict with cooperation and harvest the hope and fulfill the promise that a strategic populace-oriented paradigm for stability and well-being offers.

## WHAT IS TO BE DONE?

Success in countering the "clash of civilizations" and the "chaos" of the "new world disorder," and fulfilling the hope for a better international peace will be constructed on the same pillars that supported favorable results in the past. These pillars of success are conceptual, organizational, and operational. They are a theory of engagement, unity of effort, and holistic multidimensional and multilateral organizations and programs designed to promote and consolidate legitimation efforts.[11]

## A Legitimacy Theory of Engagement

Like George Kennan's Containment Theory of Engagement that governed the Cold War effort to deal with the hegemony of an expansionist Soviet Union,[12] this theory would be intended to help decision makers, policy makers, and the public to understand the nature of the current global security environment. It does two additional things. First, it provides a conceptual framework by which to cope successfully with the central strategic problem of governance. Second, the adroit application of this paradigm can create the quintessence of American pragmatism—a marriage of Wilsonian idealism and realpolitik. Thus, one may take a proactive approach to achieve something "better," rather than react defensively against something "bad."

Critical points about a Legitimacy Theory of Engagement must be understood at four different levels. First, regime legitimacy is the primary target of the "bad guys." Second, the "good guys" must protect and enhance their own legitimacy; it is the primary means by which governments might survive being targeted. Third, parties to conflict looking abroad for support—or to deny support—must understand that legitimacy is a double-edged moral issue that will either assist or constrain willingness and ability to be become effectively involved. Most importantly, the highest priority for a targeted government must be to strengthen and legitimize the state. Without this understanding and concomitant behavioral changes, governments find themselves in a "crisis of governance." They face growing social violence, criminal anarchy, and overthrow.

## Unity of Effort

This "pillar of success" involves overcoming parochial bureaucratic interests, fighting "turf battles," and ensuring that all efforts are focused on the ultimate common goal—survival. That is to say, there must be the necessary organization to coordinate and implement an effective and timely unity of political-diplomatic, socioeconomic, psychological-moral, and security-stability effort against those who would violently take control of a failing or failed state. And there must be the ability to accomplish these things in a manner acceptable to the peoples of the targeted state—which equates back to legitimacy. Without an organization at the highest level to establish, enforce, and continually refine a national plan, authority is fragmented and ineffective in resolving the myriad problems endemic to a violent illegal assault on the state—thus, failure.

Although an organization to plan and implement a national unity of effort is necessary, it is not sufficient. Creating a more complete unity of effort requires contributions at the international level as well. Critical points are, first, that the targeted government and its internal and external allies must be in general agreement as to what legitimate governance means. Second, these parties must be in general agreement on national goals and an associated set of programs designed to contribute directly to the achievement of the mutually agreed end state. Third, these requirements reflect a need for an organizational structure for improved coordination and cooperation between and among the targeted entity and its internal and external allies. Finally, all this requires mutual cultural awareness and sensitivity. Otherwise, efforts may be irrelevant or even counterproductive.

### Holistic and Long-Term Programs to Promote and Consolidate Legitimate Governance

Once guidelines for a mutually agreeable vision of legitimacy and unifying organizational mechanisms are in place, subordinate organizations and programs must be developed to promote and consolidate legitimate governance. These organizations and programs must address the root causes that created the instability and violence in the first place, as well as a cooperative and coordinated political stability strategy for sustainable development, the creation of a just civil society, and the establishment of a durable peace. This will probably involve the changing of a failed or failing state's predatory political culture to, in fact, provide physical and structural security; serious political, economic, social, and judicial reforms; and rational ways and means of sustaining these elusive ends.

The necessary organizations and programs would, of course, be situation and culture specific, but there are multiple critical points for the "facilitator(s)." These key points are both prescriptive and cautionary. First, the "facilitator(s)" should create a small multinational organization with a long-term mandate to do four things: provide evaluation; help institutionalize the necessary consultation, planning, and implementation processes for sustainable development; generate a rational, prioritized, and synchronized set of milestones for national programs that will preclude piecemealing and "ad hocery"; and develop strategies to get relevant programs through the facilitator's, as well as the assisted country's, legislative and bureaucratic processes, which must ultimately make the investment in effective multilateralism and staying effectively engaged.

Second, the "facilitator(s)" should promulgate programs and legislation to: (1) support politically, economically, and militarily peoples who are resisting attempted subjugation by armed and violent internal factions, and outside forces; and (2) provide and institutionalize long-term administrative, technical, and professional leader development programs to impart competence and "know-how" in addition to money. Both types of legislation should not be "giveaway," but concentrate on self-help and mutual assistance within a given community.

Third, the "facilitator(s)" should also ensure that all programs directly support the mutually agreed vision of legitimate governance and apply them at the highest levels. Grassroots programs, such as the improvement of the administration of justice as only one example, tend to make corrupt institutions more effective. Again, experience strongly demonstrates that effective reform must begin at the "top."

Implementing the extraordinary challenges of reform and regeneration is not easy. It will, however, be far less demanding and costly in political, military, and monetary terms than allowing the causes and consequences of a failed or failing state's past illegitimate governance to continue to generate crises that work to the detriment of all.

## CONCLUSION

Even though every internal conflict is situation specific, it is not completely unique. Throughout the universe of *intranational* war cases, there are analytical commonalities. Seven highly interrelated dimensions have been identified as the means by which failed or failing states and their external allies either resisted or succumbed to a violent and externally supported internal foe. That is to say, no successful strategy has been formulated over the past 50 years that has not fully incorporated the decisive factors found in the SWORD Model. The logical extension of this model to a populace-oriented paradigm for the development of a legitimate civil society is viable and pragmatic. Again, it is a marriage of Wilsonian idealism with realpolitik. Hard evidence over time clearly indicates that once security is firmly established, legitimate governance defeats a violent internal foe by removing the motives that created that foe in the first place.

## NOTES

1. For an early discussion of this issue, see Amos A. Jordan, William J. Taylor, Jr., and Lawrence J. Korb, *American National Security: Policy and Process* (Baltimore, MD: The Johns Hopkins University Press, 1973), pp. 3–4. See also The White House, *National Security Strategy of the United States* (January 1988) and The White House, *A National Security Strategy for a New Century* (October 1998).

2. This and subsequent uncited assertions are derived from statistical tests based on interviews with more than 300 civilian and military officials and scholars with direct experience in 69 *intra-state* conflicts. The initial interviews were conducted in the United States, Europe, the Middle East, and Latin America over the period 1984–1992. Since 1992, more than 80 additional interviews were conducted with government ministers, former government ministers, military officers, businessmen, journalists, and former "guerrillas" by Manwaring and Corr. The resultant paradigm, originally called SSI-1 and SSI-2, is called the SWORD Model. The *SWORD Papers*, although long out of print, are archived in their entirety by a private research organization, the National Security Archives, in Washington, DC. The first publication of the paradigm dealt specifically with "insurgencies"—in Max G. Manwaring and John T. Fishel, "Insurgency and Counterinsurgency: Towards a New Analytical Approach," *Small Wars and Insurgencies* (Winter 1992), pp. 272–305. That work and the original SWORD effort has been validated in, inter alia, Edwin G. Corr and Stephen Sloan, eds., *Low-Intensity Conflict: Old*

*Threats in a New World* (Boulder, CO: Westview Press, 1992); and John T. Fishel, ed., *The Savage Wars of Peace: Toward a Paradigm of Peace Operations* (Boulder, CO: Westview Press, 1998).

3. As an example, see Larry Diamond, Juan J. Linz, and Seymour Martin Lipset, *Politics in Developing Countries: Comparing Experiences with Democracy* (Boulder, CO: Lynne Rienner, 1990). Also see Edwin G. Corr, "Including the Excluded in El Salvador: Prospects for Democracy and Development," in *Institutions of Democracy and Development*, Peter L. Berger, ed. (San Francisco, CA: ICS Press, 1994), pp. 133–207; and Max G. Manwaring and Edwin G. Corr, "Confronting the New World Disorder: A Legitimate Governance Theory of Engagement," in *Managing Contemporary Conflict: Pillars of Success*, Max G. Manwaring and William. J. Olson, eds. (Boulder, CO: Westview Press, 1996), pp. 31–47.

4. Leslie H. Gelb, "Quelling the Teacup Wars," *Foreign Affairs* (November/December 1994), p. 5.

5. For a succinct discussion of this issue, see Jessica Mathews, "Power Shift," *Foreign Affairs* (January/February 1997), pp. 58–60.

6. Steven R. David, "Saving America from the Coming Civil Wars," *Foreign Affairs* (January/February 1999), p. 116.

7. See note 2 above.

8. The SWORD Model dimensions are (1) the strength or weakness of a country's governmental institutions (i.e., the degree of a regime's legitimacy); (2) the ability to reduce outside support for an illegal challenger; (3) the ability to reduce internal support for an illegal challenger; (4) the type and consistency of outside support for a targeted government; (5) the credibility of objectives and degree or organization for unity of effort; (6) the level of discipline and capabilities of security forces; and (7) the effectiveness of the intelligence apparatus.

9. Boutros Boutros-Ghali, "Global Leadership After the Cold War," *Foreign Affairs* (March/April 1996), pp. 86–98; and *An Agenda for Peace* (New York: United Nations, 1992), pp. 11, 32–34.

10. Joseph N. McBride, "Coping with Chaos: Democracy and Regional Stability in the Post-Counterinsurgency Era," in *Essays on Strategy XI*, John N. Petrie, ed. (Washington, DC: National Defense University Press, 1994), pp. 299–325.

11. Ambassador David C. Miller, Jr., "Back to the Future: Structuring Foreign Policy in a Post–Cold War World," in *Managing Contemporary Conflict: Pillars of Success*, Max G. Manwaring and William J. Olson, eds. (Boulder, CO: Westview Press, 1996), pp. 31–47.

12. George F. Kennan, "The Sources of Soviet Conduct," *Foreign Affairs* (July 1947), pp. 566–582.

# Index

# About the Contributors

THOMAS K. ADAMS is a retired Special Operations Lieutenant Colonel and a writer on political-military affairs. While on active duty he held various command and staff positions during a period of service that extended from Vietnam to Bosnia. As a Special Operations officer his assignments ranged from counterinsurgency through humanitarian assistance to counterdrug missions. His experience in contingency operations includes Somalia, El Salvador, Rwanda, and Haiti. He is presently employed as a consultant on political-military affairs and special operations, and at the U.S. Army War College Center for Strategic Leadership. He is the author of numerous articles and books on military-related subjects including *U.S. Special Operations Forces in Action* and *Post-Industrial Warfare*.

EDWIN G. CORR is a retired U.S. ambassador. His diplomatic career under both Republican and Democratic administrations included ambassadorships to Bolivia, El Salvador, and Peru. He also served as the Deputy Assistant Secretary of State for International Narcotics Matters, as a Peace Corps Director in Colombia, and in various posts in Thailand, Mexico, and Ecuador. Additionally, Ambassador Corr served as an infantry officer in the U.S. Marine Corps. He is currently the Director of the Energy Institute of the Americas and the Associate Director of the International Programs Center at the University of Oklahoma. Mr. Corr is the recipient of several U.S. and foreign awards and has written and edited various articles and books, including *Low-Intensity Conflict: Old Threats in a New World*.

ARTHUR E. DEWEY is a Professor in Residence at the U.S. Army Peacekeeping Institute and is helping shape policy and practice for a comprehensive

civil-military response to the post–Cold War threat environment. He has had
senior practitioner experience in the U.S. Army, the diplomatic service, a U.N.
operational agency, and in a humanitarian non-governmental organization. More
specifically, Professor Dewey's previous posts include the Office of the Secretary of Defense; Deputy Assistant Secretary, Bureau for Refugee Programs, U.S.
Department of State; Assistant Secretary-General, and U.N. Deputy High Commissioner for Refugees; and Executive Director, Congressional Hunger Center.

EVERETT C. DOLMAN is Professor of Government and International Studies
at Berry College, Mount Berry, Georgia, and a former intelligence analyst at
the National Security Agency, the U.S. Air Force Space Command, and the
North American Aerospace Defense Command (NORAD). He is the author of
several articles, including "Obligation and the Citizen-Soldier: Machiavellian
Virtu versus Hobbesian Order;" "A Spatial Model of Regime Shift;" and "War
and (the Democratic) Peace: Applications from State-Building and Civil-Military
Relations."

ROBERT H. DORFF is Professor of National Security Policy and Strategy at
the U.S. Army War College. From 1980 to 1997 he was a faculty member in
the Department of Political Science and Public Administration at North Carolina
State University. His ongoing research interests include European (especially
German) security policy as well as democratization and global ungovernability.
Dr. Dorff's research has been published in such journals as *European Security,
Parameters, Journal of Politics, Publius, Comparative Political Studies*, and the
*American Political Science Review*. His books include *A Theory of Political
Decison Modes*, and *The Persian Gulf Crisis: Power in the Post–Cold War
World*.

MICHAEL J. DZIEDZIC is presently a Senior Military Fellow at the U.S. Institute for National Strategic Studies (INSS) at the National Defense University.
His principal issue areas at INSS are peace operations and security affairs in
the Western Hemisphere. Previously, Colonel Dziedzic was a member of the
faculty at the National War College (NWC). Before arriving at the NWC, he
served as Air Attache in El Salvador during the implementation of the peace
accords. Prior to that posting, he was a political-military planner in the Western
Hemisphere Division of the Air Staff, tenured professor at the U.S. Air Force
Academy in the Department of Political Science, and Visiting Fellow at the
International Institute for Strategic Studies in London. His scholarly works include various articles on hemispheric security matters, the transnational drug
trade, and current U.S. peace and stability operations. He is coeditor (with Ambassador Robert Oakley) of *Policing the New World Disorder: Peace Operations and Public Security*.

JOHN T. FISHEL is Professor of National Security Policy at the Center for Hemispheric Defense Studies of the National Defense University. Previous to taking this position, he was Professor of National Security Affairs at the U.S. Army Command and General Staff College, Fort Leavenworth, Kansas. As a reserve officer on active duty, Lieutenant Colonel Fishel was assigned to the United States Southern Command where he was responsible for organizing civic action operations associated with exercises in Peru and Honduras, civic action seminars in Bolivia, conducting assessments in Peru, Bolivia, El Salvador, and organizing a major assessment of the El Salvadoran armed forces in combination with the Salvadorans. After Operation Just Cause, Lieutenant Colonel Fishel was responsible for developing the post-conflict civil-military operations plan for Panama and establishing and training the Panama National Police. He is author and coauthor of numerous articles and book chapters on military and security issues. His books include *The Fog of Peace: Planning and Executing the Restoration of Panama; Liberation, Occupation and Rescue: War Termination and DESERT STORM*; and *Civil Military Operations in the New World.*

ROBERT M. HERRICK is a retired U.S. Army Colonel. He served as Director of the Small Wars Operations Research Directorate (SWORD) of the United States Southern Command, as a fellow and member of the U.S. Army Warfighting and Study Groups, and is responsible for the concept and development of the army's *Absolon* counterinsurgency training simulation. Colonel Herrick is the author or coauthor of articles and monographs including "Where Is the Enemy?," "A Threat-Oriented Strategy for Conflict Control," "Stability with Justice," and "Strategy for Conflict Control: An Object Suspended Between Three Political-Military Magnets."

ANTHONY JAMES JOES is Chairman of the International Relations Program at St. Joseph's University. His numerous publications reflect his continuing interest in guerrilla insurgency. His books include *The War for South Viet Nam* (2nd revised edition), *Modern Guerrilla Insurgency, Guerrilla Conflict before the Cold War* and *Saving Democracies: U.S. Intervention in Threatened States.*

JOSEPH N. McBRIDE is the Political Economic Counselor at the U.S. Embassy in Bogota, Colombia. He began his Foreign Service career as a civilian Deputy District Senior Advisor in the CORDS Pacification Advisory Program in Vietnam. His subsequent tour of duty in the Political Section ended with the helicopter evacuation off the embassy roof the night that Saigon fell, April 30, 1975. Since then, Mr. McBride has served as the economist on the Israeli Desk at the State Department during the Camp David negotiations and the development of the Peace Treaty with Egypt; a Pearson Fellow in the U.S. Congress; and assignments in Thailand, Italy, Nicaragua, and Peru. His essay, "Coping with

Chaos: Democracy and Regional Stability in the Post-Counterinsurgency Era,''
was selected as a Distinguished Essay in the 1993 Chairman, Joint Chiefs of
Staff, Strategy Essay Competition. It is found in *Essays on Strategy XI*, John
N. Petrie, ed. (Washington, DC: National Defense University Press, 1994).

MAX G. MANWARING is a retired U.S. Army colonel and Adjunct Professor
of Political Science at Dickinson College. He has served in various civilian and
military positions, including the U.S. Army War College, the United States
Southern Command, and the Defense Intelligence Agency. Dr. Manwaring is
the author and coauthor of several articles and reports dealing with political-
military affairs. He is also the editor or coeditor of *El Salvador at War*, *Gray
Area Phenomena*, *Managing Contemporary Conflict: Pillars of Success*, and
*Toward Responsibility in the New World Disorder: Challenges and Lessons of
Peace Operations.*

DAYTON L. MAXWELL is a retired senior Foreign Service Officer, U.S.
Agency for International Development (USAID), where he served in Asia, Africa, and Eastern Europe. He served as Deputy Director of the Office of Foreign
Disaster Assistance (OFDA), led Disaster Assistance Response Teams (DART)
to the Philippines (Baguio Earthquake), Northern Iraq (Operation Provide Comfort), the former Soviet Union (post-Gorbachev coup assessment, Operation Restore Hope), The Republic of Georgia (Abkhazia), and Laos (drought/flood
assessment). Mr. Maxwell is currently a Senior Adviser for Complex Emergencies, World Vision International—a large, multinational non-governmental organization (NGO). He is also the author of several articles and book chapters
dealing with problems of disaster relief and peace and stability operations, including "Facing the Choice Among Bad Options in Complex Humanitarian
Emergencies.''

RICHARD L. MILLETT is Professor Emeritus of History at Southern Illinois
University at Edwardsville and a member of the Executive Council of the American Committees on Foreign Relations. He has taught at the University of Miami,
St. Louis University, The Air Force War College, the Marine Corps University,
and four universities in Colombia. Additionally, Dr. Millett is Senior Advisor
for Latin America to Political Risk Services, has appeared on every major national TV network, has testified before Congress on 19 occasions, and has participated in election supervision in four nations. Dr. Millett has published over
100 items in *Foreign Policy*, *The Wilson Quarterly*, *Current History*, *The New
Republic*, and numerous other professional journals. He is also the author of
*Beyond Praetorianism: The Latin American Military in Transition.*

ISBN 0-275-96768-9

HARDCOVER BAR CODE